THE RENEWAL OF CHURCH

The Panel Reports

W. B. Blakemore, *General Editor*

The Panel of Scholars Reports

VOLUME I

The Reformation of Tradition

R. E. OSBORN, Editor

VOLUME II

The Reconstruction of Theology

R. G. WILBURN, Editor

VOLUME III

The Revival of the Churches

W. B. BLAKEMORE, Editor

VOLUME I

THE REFORMATION OF TRADITION

THE
Reformation of Tradition

Edited by

Ronald E. Osborn

The Renewal of Church
The Panel Reports
W. B. Blakemore, Editor

I

THE BETHANY PRESS
St. Louis, Missouri
1963

 Library of Congress Catalog Card No. 62-21959. Distributed in Australasia by the Austral Printing and Publishing Company, Melbourne, and in Canada by The G. R. Welch Company, Toronto.

Manufactured in the United States of America.

Typography and design by David Homeier

Chapters 4 and 11 first appeared in *Encounter,* copyright by Christian Theological Seminary, Indianapolis 8, Indiana.

A Statement Concerning the Panel of Scholars

THE "founding fathers" of Disciples of Christ were profound scholars and practical theologians. By "practical theologians" we mean that their theology was not developed in a cloistered cell or in the academic atmosphere of a university campus, but on the debate platform, in the pulpit, and through widespread discussion. They searched the Scriptures diligently and among them developed a system of Christian thought and doctrine that became widely accepted. They all labored, however, in a day that antedated the historical method of biblical interpretation and since their time much scholarly progress has been made in the field of textual criticism. Additional ancient manuscripts have been discovered and the Bible text has been greatly enriched.

In more recent times Disciples of Christ have not been too greatly concerned with theology, interest running more in the direction of practical churchmanship and the application of Christian truth to everyday living. In a very real sense Disciples of Christ have become shallow, unable to give a reason for the faith that is within them. Many of the convictions originally held by our founding fathers are being challenged today and on every hand the question is being raised, "Just what do Disciples of Christ believe?"

After extended consideration The United Christian Missionary Society and the Board of Higher Education of Disciples of Christ came to the conviction that the time was ripe for Disciples of Christ to re-examine their beliefs and doctrines in a scholarly way. The tenets held by our fathers in the faith needed to be restudied and validated or modified in the light of modern scholarship. New light and understanding should be sought. A new and firmer base of Christian doctrine should be laid. A new certainty concerning what we believe and why we believe it should be achieved.

As one step in the direction of bringing a new certainty and clarity of thought to Disciples of Christ the two agencies decided to join in the creation of a Panel of Scholars that would be asked to restudy the doctrines of Disciples of Christ, justifying their conclusions on the basis of the best available scholarship. It was agreed that the Panel would have complete freedom, deciding for themselves the areas they would consider and how they would proceed with their studies, but it was hoped that the Panel would see fit to consider theologically some of the more practical issues and problems confronting Disciples of Christ.

In the spring of 1956 the creation of such a Panel of Scholars was authorized and in January of 1957 the first meeting of the Panel was held. Originally it was thought that the Panel would work for three years but its life was extended for an additional two and a half years. The Panel has met twice a year and its members have shown both dedication and zeal.

In order that the thinking and work of the Panel of Scholars might involve more than the fifteen Panel members some sixty discussion groups were organized throughout the country. These groups varied from five to thirty members in size. Papers emanating from the Panel of Scholars were made available to these groups and they were invited to give their reactions to the Panel of Scholars. The reactions of these groups across the country proved very helpful to the Panel.

A Statement Concerning the Panel of Scholars

As the Panel of Scholars comes to an end it is publishing part of its work in three volumes which the sponsoring agencies hope will be widely read and studied. The United Christian Missionary Society and the Board of Higher Education also hope that the work the Panel of Scholars has done will stimulate additional scholarly thought and study among Disciples of Christ.

W. M. Wickizer
for the sponsors of the Panel

Indianapolis, Indiana
June 18, 1962

Foreword

WHEN the Panel of Scholars was proposed in 1956, the men invited to comprise the Panel took a long and serious look at the assignment. Would this venture be understood by the Christian Churches, or would it be misunderstood as an attempt to write an official theology?

Traditionally, the Christian Churches have declared the Scriptures to be the sufficient guide in matters of doctrine and worship. Our people have never appointed official commissions in the areas of faith and order. But the time had come for the initiation of new ways of thinking together about the fundamentals of the Christian faith. The Panel of Scholars was never conceived by its sponsors as an official committee to authorize beliefs and worship. It was conceived as a group to study and advise regarding the issues involved in major concerns of brotherhood life.

Each member of the Panel was at once honored, excited, and awed by his appointment.

The responsibility involved was awesome for the task was urgent. The Panel was not asked to do the brotherhood's thinking for it and to come up with the answers. It was asked to discover for our people the issues worth talking about so that there might be amongst us less talking in circles and more talking to the point. The Panel was never commissioned to write a new theology for our churches. What it did contract to do was to search out and clarify the theological, biblical, sociological, and historical issues involved in our practical life. The identification of truly relevant issues would enable our agency leaders and our pastors to ignore obsolete matters and save untold man hours in the extensive discussions necessary to properly reasoned discussions in a body which values democratic procedures. With a due sense of responsibility the Panel accepted this task.

Equally, the members of the Panel experienced excitement. To be frank about it, the members of the Panel are all men who love to talk about religion. Typically we met twice a year for long week ends during which we read papers to each other and then discussed them. We reviewed also the reactions of that wider circle who participated with us through study groups across the nation. Members of the Panel were faithful to their assignments; they prepared well, ardently defended their propositions in discussion, and, mindful of the criticisms which had been made, went home to rework their statements. The end of each meeting found us physically tired, but spiritually and intellectually refreshed. The experience of working on the Panel had recompense which would far outweigh any honorarium we might have received—and we received none. We came to the end of the experience with gratitude to the sponsors who made our sessions possible and often had their representatives meeting with us. I wish to add my special word of thanks to the members of the Panel for the resolution and congeniality which they all brought to our enterprise.

Finally, we are appreciative of the honor of membership on the Panel. Several weeks ago I sat in a committee in which one member said, "My communion makes no distinction between clergy and laity, and therefore there is no one who can speak for us officially." I have heard those words in the lips of Disciples of Christ many times. In this instance, however, they were spoken by a Quaker, and as I heard the familiar words, my amazement grew because the speaker was "typically Quaker" in everything he said and did. He could not have been a more representative Quaker had he been officially sent to our meeting with signed and sealed credentials asserting that he had been properly elected, installed, and invested with robes and symbols of office. So it was with the members of the Panel. We were mostly "Campbellite born and bred" and we represented various lines and branches of that ecclesiastical family. We even included converts—who always provided the added ardor of those who have found their spiritual home only after lonely search.

As I listened to my Quaker friend that day, I had another insight. We say, "We make no distinction between clergy and laity, and therefore no one can speak officially for us." Then I realized that the clergy amongst those bodies which do make the distinction never claim to be speaking for their laity. They always claim to be speaking for God. Surely, that is what our churches want their scholars and ministers to do—to speak on behalf of God. And that is exactly what each of the members of the Panel of Scholars, be he ever so typical a Disciple, sought to do—to witness for God as God has given light to him, a member of the brotherhood of Christian Churches (Disciples of Christ).

W. B. BLAKEMORE.

July 22, 1962.
Chicago, Illinois.

PANEL OF SCHOLARS MEMBERSHIP

July 1956 to March 1962

CHAIRMEN

Howard E. Short: June 1956 to September 1958

W. B. Blakemore: October 1958 to March 1962

MEMBERS

WILLIAM R. BAIRD: November 1959 to March 1962
Professor of New Testament
The College of the Bible
Lexington, Kentucky

PAUL HUNTER BECKELHYMER: January 1957 to March 1962
Minister of Hiram Christian Church
Hiram, Ohio

W. B. BLAKEMORE: July 1956 to March 1962
Dean of Disciples Divinity House and
Associate Dean of Rockefeller Memorial Chapel
University of Chicago
Chicago, Illinois

JAMES A. CLAGUE: August 1956 to March 1962
Associate Professor of Systematic Theology
Christian Theological Seminary
Indianapolis, Indiana

STEPHEN J. ENGLAND: July 1956 to March 1962
Dean of The Graduate Seminary
Phillips University
Enid, Oklahoma

FRANK N. GARDNER: July 1956 to March 1962
Professor of Christian Thought
Drake University
Des Moines, Iowa

VIRGIL V. HINDS: October 1956 to March 1962
Associate Professor of Religion
Lynchburg College
Lynchburg, Virginia

J. PHILLIP HYATT: July 1956 to March 1962
Professor of Old Testament of the Divinity School and Chairman of the Department of Religion of the Graduate School
Vanderbilt University
Nashville, Tennessee

CLARENCE E. LEMMON: July 1956 to March 1962
Minister of First Christian Church
Columbia, Missouri

D. RAY LINDLEY: July 1956 to March 1962
President of Texas Christian University
Fort Worth, Texas

RONALD E. OSBORN: July 1956 to March 1962
Dean and Professor of Church History
Christian Theological Seminary
Indianapolis, Indiana

EUGENE H. PETERS: December 1959 to March 1962
Associate Professor of Theology
The Graduate Seminary
Phillips University
Enid, Oklahoma

GLENN C. ROUTT: July 1956 to March 1962
Associate Professor of Theology
Brite College of the Bible
Texas Christian University
Fort Worth, Texas

HOWARD E. SHORT: June 1956 to September 1958
Professor of Church History
The College of the Bible
Lexington, Kentucky (until September 1958)
Editor of *The Christian*

DWIGHT E. STEVENSON: June 1956 to October 1959
Professor of Homiletics
The College of the Bible
Lexington, Kentucky

WILLIAM G. WEST: July 1956 to March 1962
Minister of First Christian Church
Chattanooga, Tennessee

RALPH G. WILBURN: July 1956 to March 1962
Dean and Professor of Historical Theology
The College of the Bible
Lexington, Kentucky

THE EDITORIAL AND PUBLICATION COMMITTEE

W. B. Blakemore, Chairman, General Editor and Editor of Volume III

R. E. Osborn, Editor of Volume I

R. G. Wilburn, Editor of Volume II

W. M. Wickizer for the sponsoring agencies

Contents

BY WAY OF INTRODUCTION

Crisis and Reformation 23
A Preface to Volume I
RONALD E. OSBORN

PART I
THE HISTORIC FAITH OF DISCIPLES OF CHRIST

Faith versus Theology 33
In the Thought of the Disciple Fathers
DWIGHT E. STEVENSON

The Nature and Work of Christ 61
In the Thought of Barton W. Stone
WILLIAM G. WEST

Representative Preaching about Jesus 78
Two Generations of the Middle Period
HUNTER BECKELHYMER

The Revelation of God in Jesus Christ 98
With Reference to the Phrase, "No Creed but Christ"
FRANK N. GARDNER

The Holy Spirit 111
In the Thought and Life of Disciples of Christ
STEPHEN J. ENGLAND

Man and Salvation 135
Characteristic Ideas Among Disciples of Christ
FRANK N. GARDNER

PART II
THE HISTORIC CHURCHMANSHIP OF DISCIPLES OF CHRIST

Reasonable, Empirical, Pragmatic 161
The Mind of Disciples of Christ
W. B. BLAKEMORE

The Structure of the Church 184
Freedom and Authority in Matters of Polity
D. Ray Lindley

An Evaluation of Our Ministry 199
In the Light of our History
Clarence E. Lemmon

A Critique of the Restoration Principle 215
Its Place in Contemporary Life and Thought
Ralph G. Wilburn

PART III

HISTORICAL INFLUENCES UPON DISCIPLES OF CHRIST

The Sociology of Disciple Intellectual Life 257
Historical Forms of Organization for Thinking
W. B. Blakemore

Dogmatically Absolute, Historically Relative 265
Conditioned Emphases in the History of Disciples
Ronald E. Osborn

The Influence of Population Mobility 291
On the Present Life and Thought of Disciples
Hunter Beckelhymer

A CONCLUDING ESSAY

"One Holy Catholic and Apostolic Church" 305
The Continuing Witness of Disciples of Christ
Ronald E. Osborn

INDEX 353

BY WAY OF INTRODUCTION

1

Crisis and Reformation

A Preface to Volume I

RONALD E. OSBORN

THIS volume, with the two which follow, represents the formal recognition of a crisis in the corporate career of Disciples of Christ. The books also constitute an intellectual harvest garnered during a decisive era. How did this crisis come about in the history of a major American religious movement? And what is likely to be its outcome?

For the first three generations of their history (till the 1890's), Disciples of Christ carried out their mission with a high sense of self-confidence. The plea was sweeping the country, and every evidence of progress within church and society seemed a sign of divine favor, an earnest of the imminent triumph of the good cause. For most Disciples the assumption of early victory lasted for another long generation (into the 1930's), and among some it is still professed. Many in middle life still recall hearing confident, even cocksure, addresses on the plea, the plan, the purpose of Disciples,[1] and recall sharing the enthusiastic faith that the movement was soon to prevail.

However, for the past two generations an uneasiness about our position and our destiny has affected an increasing number among us. It began with the impact of science on conventional nineteenth-century biblicism and gained force with the emergence of the historical criticism of the Bible. The social maturing of the American West, where Disciples enjoyed their greatest strength, the shift of population to the cities, and the increasing significance of religious institutions led to a softening of the early hostility toward "the denominations" and a gradual but drastic redefinition of our own self-image. The debates over federation, the growing practice of open membership, the consolidation of our agencies, and participation in the ecumenical movement (especially membership in councils of churches at every geographical level) gave expression to and hastened the process of redefinition.

For a while it appeared to some that the Disciple heritage was made to order for the new day. Seizing on the fathers' emphases on freedom, rationality, forthright biblical interpretation, pragmatic disinterest in speculation, repudiation of creeds, and rebellion against ecclesiastical authority, some of the ablest minds in Disciple history hammered out a liberal reformulation of our position.[2]

While this obvious recasting of the plea offended conservatives, it commended itself to many in positions of influence: college and seminary teachers, journalists, agency officials, and ministers of prominent churches. The liberal recasting of the Disciple position, which involved an open repudiation of certain earlier emphases, predominates in most books and articles on Disciples published up to this moment,[3] except those written in traditional quarters to deny the liberal reformulation.[4]

During the heyday of liberalism, Disciples who had accepted that reformulation assumed a position of prominence in American Christian life generally. Such names as C. C. Morrison, W. E. Garrison, E. S. Ames, Herbert L. Willett, William Clayton Bower, Walter Scott Athearn, Errett Gates, Peter Ainslie, Roy G. Ross, Clark Walker Cummings, Cynthia Pearl Maus, Harry C. Munro, Samuel Guy Inman, E. K. Higdon, Emory Ross, M. Searle Bates, Edgar DeWitt Jones, Glenn McRae, gained a wide hearing and won high regard for Disciples as a vigorous, intelligent, and co-operative communion.

Then another day dawned in American religious life. Neo-orthodoxy set the dominant mood in Christian thought. The ecumenical movement, which Disciples had so romantically espoused, shifted its center of gravity from goodwill and common endeavor in practical concerns to official ecclesiastical relationships and a preoccupation with theology. Theology as a discipline and the particular theological emphases of the "ecumenical line" proved foreign to Disciple idiom, whether traditional or reformulated in terms of liberalism. With a strange sense of discomfiture Disciples found themselves neither taking the country nor moving in the center of the ecumenical stream. Suddenly the familiar formulations of our position—traditional or amended—seemed no longer very pertinent to our own situation as a denomination or to the preoccupations of the Christian world at large.

A Tradition in Crisis

Many well-informed and thoughtful Disciples feel that the movement is caught in an acute intellectual crisis. This may be illustrated by briefly characterizing the classic plea for unity in outline form. It originally emphasized the following elements:

1. The restoration of the ancient order—acceptance of the New Testament as the constitution of the church.

2. Conception of unity as manifested locally in the life and practice of the congregation and by the dissolution of denominational loyalties.

3. Anticlericalism—conception of the ministry as composed of local officers appointed by the congregation.

4. Repudiation of ecclesiasticism (church courts) and of denominationalism.

5. Repudiation of creeds and devaluation of theology in favor of "the simple gospel."

6. Commitment to the baptism of believers by immersion.

A review of dominant Christian thought today indicates real crisis for every one of these emphases. Again the briefest outline must suffice.

1. Restorationism has been rejected or redefined beyond recognition by Disciple scholarship (*e.g.*, as found in the faculties of accredited seminaries), and the notion that the New Testament is a constitution for the church is repudiated by biblical scholars generally.

2. The dramatic movements toward unity have been at the top through ecumenical conferences composed of official delegates of denominations, and denominational lines have been strengthened in our culture.

3. Disciples have developed a professional ministry on pragmatic grounds, but with no clear doctrine of the ministry; the inherited doctrine which we state is so "low" as to be unacceptable to almost any other communion involved in ecumenical discussion.

4. Ecclesiasticism is growing. The ecumenical movement is built on denominations. Union proceeds by denominational merger. Increasingly Disciples see themselves as a denomination and seek a more rational and effective ecclesiastical institution through the efforts toward "restructure."

5. Confessions are widely held to be central in the concern of the church, and increasing though presently small numbers of Disciples see desirability in affirmations of faith. Theology has become a major Christian preoccupation, whereas the "plain message" of the Bible does not universally commend itself as a "simple gospel."

6. Baptism remains an ecumenical stumbling block. Increasingly our parish ministers are inarticulate, confused, and apologetic in their witness on baptism, despite efforts to boost morale by appealing to the utterances of Karl Barth or some recent Anglican documents on the subject. In scholarly circles Disciples have made only one modest contribution to the present theological discussion of baptism.[5]

The crisis confronting Disciples is increasingly apparent. Our congregations find that their characteristic practices—weekly communion, conduct of the Lord's supper by lay elders, the role assigned to deacons, etc.—rest on a tradition less than two centuries old, the original (restoration) presuppositions of which they have largely repudiated. The psychic need for some kind of anchoring has manifested itself in the noticeable growth, especially during the last two decades, of a Disciple mythology concerning our tradition. For example, since ecumenism is now a blessed word, Barton Stone and Thomas Campbell are often portrayed as "ecumenical pioneers" in ways that shamelessly exaggerate their influence on the modern movement among the churches and distort into insignificance their emphasis on the Bible as the rulebook of the church. The founding fathers would not recognize themselves in the figures bearing their names in some recent "pageants" and addresses presented at conventions. The myth may sustain our morale, but it sometimes bears little resemblance to our actual history.

Meanwhile, when we try to draw on our tradition for more than inspiration, what shall we say? Our students in the seminaries, especially those outside the areas of Disciple strength, find themselves with no clear theological guidance. Increasingly our congregations take over practices in worship, program, organization, and especially relationship with the ministry, which have no roots either in our own history or in contemporary doctrinal understanding but are simply copied from other denominations, practices which developed within quite different theological traditions. Writers of lesson materials for our church schools face the necessity of treating theological problems. What shall they say about them? What the fathers said? What scholars of other communions now say? Administrators of brotherhood agencies find themselves confronting practical decisions which they recognize as theological in character. Should these agency officials therefore shape our doctrine for the future by the rough-and-ready decisions they make day by day? Our ministers find it hard to preach on the "plea"—or even on important doctrinal themes such as salvation, the person and work of Christ, the nature of the church—and to explain "our position" to strangers. Shall they simply keep on repeating the old watchwords? Shall they ignore our heritage? The discomfort of the crisis led to the appointment of the Panel of Scholars in 1956.

From the outset the Panel was "given its head" in a context of complete academic freedom. It is obvious that each paper is the work of an individual author and that the views expressed are his own. The Panel took no action to "adopt" any of the papers or to subscribe to any position enunciated. Yet the essays were read within a context of mutual trust and intellectual stimulation, and it is fair to say that there was a consensus concerning many of the positions stated.

A Tradition in Reformation

And what is the upshot of it all?

After a brief interchange of opinion, the Panel reached consensus that the crucial element in the heritage of Disciples had sought expression in the slogan, "No creed but Christ." The Panel agreed to begin with a series of papers on Christology. In succeeding months, other topics logically emerged. At last three major areas were visible, each related to a well-known branch of theology—historical, systematic, practical—and these resulted in the three volumes of the Panel Reports.

At an early stage in the Panel discussions there came a clear recognition, surprising to many Disciples, that we do have a tradition. Any one who takes the trouble to learn why he is a Disciple soon comes to realize the distinctive elements in our heritage which have given shape to the life of the brotherhood. And one cannot examine this tradition, even with the criticism and objectivity incumbent upon a scholar, without a deep sense of gratitude. As the various elements in the tradition are sifted to separate the true from the false, the permanent from the transient, the relevant from the inconsequential, "though much is taken, much abides." It is a tradition for which Disciples should give grateful thanks to God.

Yet there is no denying the crisis. The time has come when we must frankly disavow certain formulations of the fathers and work out new doctrinal expressions in keeping with our present understanding of the Lord's will for his church. The process is not an easy one; sometimes it is truly painful. But it is necessary. And despite the labor and occasional anguish, the task has its joy. It is the joy of discipleship and of honest thought in the service of him who is the Truth. Such thinking will be found in these papers. It is to be hoped that more of such thinking will be stimulated by them.

The crisis that has come upon Disciples, the collapse of the old formulations, is not a tragedy. To those who confess their faith in the Lord of history, it is reformation. By definition reformation is the breaking down of a former structure and the shaping of it anew in harmony with a master purpose. Disciples who read the papers in these books may well ponder the visit of Jeremiah to the potter's house (Jeremiah 18:1-6), as well as the motto of the great Protestant Reformers, *Ecclesia reformata semper reformanda est* ("the reformed church is under constant necessity of being reformed"). It is also well to remember that one of Alexander Campbell's favorite designations for the movement he led was the "New Reformation." Some members of the Panel have whimsically referred to the present reconstruction in the life and thought of Disciples of Christ as "the twentieth-century reformation of the reformation of the nineteenth century."

In any case, remembering Jeremiah's experience as we give ourselves to the hard work of thought upon the issues of the present crisis, we may stand firm in this faith: throughout the whole church and in the case of our own brotherhood, it is not just the impersonal forces of history, not the cleverness of theologians, not the planning of administrators, not the earnestness of ministers and members which is reshaping the familiar vessel we have known and loved. Jeremiah would say it is the hand of God which is bringing about the reformation of tradition.

NOTES

1. Some important formulations of the Disciple position follow: Robert Milligan, *An Exposition and Defense of the Scheme of Redemption,* Christian Publishing Co., 1888; E. V. Zollars, *The Great Salvation,* The Standard Publishing Co., Cincinnati, 1895; T. W. Phillips, *The Church of Christ, by a Layman,* Funk & Wagnalls, New York, 1905; B. A. Abbott, *The Disciples, An Interpretation,* The Bethany Press, St. Louis, 1924; P. H. Welshimer, *Concerning the Disciples,* Standard Publishing Co., Cincinnati, 1935; Stephen J. England, *We Disciples,* Christian Board of Publication, St. Louis, 1946.

2. See especially J. H. Garrison (ed.), *The Old Faith Re-stated,* The Christian Publishing House, St. Louis, 1891; Herbert L. Willett, *Our Plea for Union and the Present Crisis,* Christian Century Company, Chicago, 1901; J. H. Garrison, *Christian Union,* Christian Publishing Company, St. Louis, 1906; Peter Ainslie, *The Message of the Disciples for the Union of the Church,* Fleming H. Revell Company, New York, 1913; C. C. Morrison, *The Meaning of Baptism,* Disciples Publication Society, Chicago, 1914; A. W. Fortune, *Adventuring with Disciples Pioneers,* The Bethany Press, St. Louis, 1942; Edward Scribner Ames, *The Disciples of Chirst,* published by author, Chicago, 1943-44.

3. Errett Gates, *The Disciples of Christ,* Baker & Taylor Co., New York, 1905; and *"The Early Relation and Separation of Baptists and Disciples"* (Ph.D. thesis, University of Chicago, 1902); also the various histories by W. E. Garrison, and the same author's *Heritage and Destiny: An American Religious Movement Looks Ahead,* The Bethany Press, St. Louis, 1961; Howard Elmo Short, *Doctrine and Thought of Disciples of Christ,* Christian Board of Publication, St. Louis, 1951; Hampton Adams, *Why I Am a Disciple of Christ,* Thomas Nelson & Sons, New York, 1957. To some extent the liberal formulation dominates, though tempered here and there by neo-orthodox influences, in *Doctrines of the Christian Faith,* Six Reports by the Study Committee of the World Convention of Churches of Christ (Disciples), Christian Board of Publication, St. Louis, 1961.

4. Harold W. Ford, *A History of the Restoration Plea,* Semco Color Press, Oklahoma City, Oklahoma, c. 1952; Earl Irvin West, *The Search for the Ancient Order,* 2 vols., Gospel Advocate Co., Nashville, Tennessee, 1949; James DeForest Murch, *Christians Only,* Standard Publishing Co., Cincinnati, 1962.

5. Stephen J. England, *The One Baptism,* The Bethany Press, St. Louis, 1960.

PART ONE

THE HISTORIC FAITH OF DISCIPLES OF CHRIST

2

Faith versus Theology

In the Thought of the Disciple Fathers

DWIGHT E. STEVENSON

I propose to focus this study upon a slight volume of 88 pages published by Robert Richardson in 1853. It bore the title, *The Principles and Objects of the Religious Reformation, Urged by A. Campbell and Others, Briefly Stated and Explained.* Richardson's brief summary of the Disciple movement purported to be a statement of the whole cause, not merely Richardson's own private view, and as such it was enthusiastically acclaimed by Alexander Campbell himself, who said of it:

> The author of this essay has himself been connected with [the reformation] for almost a quarter of a century, and is well posted in its history from the beginning. This tract gives a well proportioned miniature view of it in a lucid and chaste style, and is worthy of himself and the cause. It ought to be circulated, not only among our brethren, but the religious and reflecting of all Protestant Christians.[1]

The tract was a distillation of work spread over a period of about six years. In the *Millennial Harbinger* from 1847 through 1850 Richardson published nineteen articles on "The Reformation." The substance of these was presented in a greatly condensed, systematic form in the 1853 tract. The whole of the tract, meantime, had been published in the October, November, and December issues of the *Millennial Harbinger* for 1852 under the title, "Principles and Purpose of the Reformation." These articles, four in number, were written in the form of letters addressed to "My Dear E."

Our method of study will be as follows: First, we shall make a survey of Richardson's tract with special attention to the Disciple view of faith. Next, we shall sketch such agreements with it as we may find in the writings of Thomas Campbell, Alexander Campbell, and Walter Scott. Finally, we shall subject it to criticism with special attention to the distinction between faith and theology.

A Survey of Richardson's Tract

Richardson begins by asserting that the reformation of Disciples of Christ is based upon "the two great fundamental principles of Protestantism, viz:

1. The Bible is the Book of God.
2. Private judgment is the right and duty of man.[2]

Although Protestant denominations in general accept these propositions, in practice they violate both of them, he said.

In violation of the *first,* they have exalted human systems of theology to an authority equal, if not paramount, to that of the Bible. At the same time, in violation of the *second* of these principles, they deny to the people the privilege of interpreting the Bible otherwise than in accordance with these systems.[3]

The result of these violations is sectarianism with its party strife. To cure this strife, the reformation proposes a return to the original principles. The purpose is Christian unity. This reformation

seeks to establish a *unity of faith,* instead of that *diversity of opinion* which has distracted religious society; and to restore the gospel and its institutions, in all their original simplicity, to the world. In brief, its great purpose is *to establish* CHRISTIAN UNION *upon the basis of a* SIMPLE EVANGELICAL CHRISTIANITY.[4]

Richardson then submits his outline. First there are three principles: "1st. The distinction between FAITH and OPINION. 2d. The distinction between what may be emphatically termed THE CHRISTIAN FAITH and doctrinal KNOWLEDGE. 3rd. The true BASIS OF CHRISTIAN UNION." Then follow six "important subjects which have been brought into view during the progress of the Reformation." These include baptism and church order. We shall look at each of the nine topics in turn. We begin with the three basic principles.

Basic Principles

I. Distinction Between Faith and Opinion

When it at first appears, this distinction seems to be largely a matter of *what* is believed: faith is the belief of the Bible. Opinion is the belief of speculations, conjectures, and metaphysical subtleties which, though they may be inferred from the Bible, are nonetheless outside it. In other words, faith has to do with Scripture; opinion has to do with theology, especially as seen in the creeds and confessions of faith. Strip away the opinions—that is, the creeds and theologies—and "the mind is left alone with the word of God."[5] The reason given for this confident division is that faith deals with revealed truth, whereas opinion is nothing but man-made "truth."

We should not expect men to give up their theological opinions. On the contrary, "each individual must have a perfect right to entertain what opinions he pleases, but he must not attempt to enforce them upon others, or make them a term of communion or religious fellowship."[6] Clearly, then, revealed truth—the Bible—is supposed to have a coercive right that theology may not have.

> It is, accordingly, one of the primary objects of the present Reformation, to put an end to all such controversies, by reducing human opinions to their proper level, and elevating the word of God, as the only true standard of religious faith.[7]

Here is a very clear statement of the distinction we have been following:

> Every proposition or doctrine, then, for which there is not clear scriptural evidence, is to be regarded as a matter of opinion; and every thing for which such evidence can be adduced, is a matter of faith—a fact or truth to be believed.[8]

Some one will object, however, that the paring away of theology and leaving the Bible alone as a guide of faith and fellowship will still leave us with diversity; men will still disagree and we will continue to have serious differences. The Reformers will not concede this. If men will come to the Bible with an open mind instead of preconceived opinions to be proved by it, and if they will apply common sense and hard study to the task, they will find the Bible speaking unequivocally and in a single voice. It must be admitted, of course, that there are "some subjects too mysterious in their nature to be clearly explained in human language; some too great to be completely grasped by a finite mind; many too remote from the ordinary range of human thought, to be distinctly apprehended by the discerning intellect."[9] Regarding such mysterious matters in the Bible, Richardson says:

> These are subjects to be reverently pondered and contemplated only so far as, upon the heavenly scroll, we may discover their outline, or discern their more salient points. These are not things about which men may dogmatize; into which they may vainly and presumptuously intrude; or in regard to which they may insolently excommunicate and anathematize each other.[10]

It must be admitted too that not all Scripture is equally clear to all men, or to one man all at one time. "There will be always babes, young men, and fathers in scriptural learning." So pastors and teachers are needed.

Hence, also the necessity of speaking of scriptural matters in scriptural language.

> It is true, that Bible terms themselves may be misunderstood or misapplied, if the context be not carefully examined; and especially,

if a religious theory or favorite practice be in question. But when an individual is *unable* to express his religious sentiments, without using unscriptural expressions, it is *prima facie* evident that his religious views are not in the Bible.[11]

This seems to lead us, unfortunately, to the view that the faith required of a Christian is a complete, or all but complete, knowledge of the Bible and assent to its truths. Such is not the case, however. There is a vital core of faith, in which all biblical truth is implicit. To that we turn next.

II. THE CHRISTIAN FAITH

Christian faith is a growing experience. Since it is simply the confidence we have in divine testimony, as our knowledge of the testimony increases, our faith will increase. But the knowledge and faith necessary for salvation and membership in the church do not need to grow to their maximum in order to be effective. There is a distinction between "general belief and reception of the Divine testimony, contained in the canonical books of the Old and New Testaments" on the one hand and "the faith" on the other hand. All Protestantism makes some such distinctions, but

we differ from all the parties here in one important particular, to which I wish to call your special attention. It is this: that while they suppose this Christian faith to be *doctrinal,* we regard it as *personal.* In other words, they suppose doctrines, or religious tenets, to be the subject matter of this faith, we on the contrary, conceive it to terminate on a person—the Lord Jesus Christ himself. While they, accordingly, require an elaborate confession from each convert—a confession of a purely doctrinal and intellectual character, studiously elaborated into an extended formula—we demand only a simple confession of Christ—an heartfelt acknowledgment that he is the Messiah, the Son of God.

The Christian faith, then, in our view, consists not in any theory or system of doctrine, but in a sincere belief in the person and mission of our Lord Jesus Christ. It is personal in its subject, as well as in its object; in regard to him who believes, as well as in regard to that which is believed. It consists of simple facts, directly connected with the personal history and character of Jesus Christ as the Messiah and the promised Lamb of God who takes away the sins of the world. It is personal in its object, leading to personal regard and love for Christ, and a personal interest in his salvation. It consists not in definitions; neither does it embrace the litigated questions of sectarianism.[12]

Such a personal belief in and trust of Christ is not to be confused with merely intellectual assent to a set or system of tenets. On the other hand, it is "not simply to believe what Christ says" or that "there lived a person bearing that name." For Jesus Christ is not a proper name; it is a name joined to a title, which title makes a claim upon our faith.

To believe sincerely with the mind that Jesus is the Christ will lead to the surrender of the heart "in humility, penitence and love." That is, faith as *belief* when it is centered on Jesus as the Christ will lead to faith as *trust* and *commitment.*

To believe in Christ, is to receive him in all the glory of his character, personal and official; to trust in him in all the relations which he sustains to us, as our Prophet, our Priest, and our King; to behold in him our only hope and refuge; and renouncing ourselves, our own self-confidence, our righteousness, and every vain device, to lean on him only as our stay, and to look to him only as the "Lord our Righteousness," as our salvation and our life. It is not merely to believe what is said of him as the Son of God; as the Son of Man; as living, dying, rising, reigning, returning; but believing this, to trust in him as *our* Savior, to walk with him as *our* teacher, *our* friend; to realize his gracious presence with us, and to discern his footsteps in the path we tread. It is to be brought into direct relation and fellowship with him; to think of him as of a person whom we know, and to whom we are known; to speak to him as to one who hears, and to listen to him as one who speaks. Such, in our view, is the Christian faith; not a trust in definitions; in doctrines; in church order; in apostolic succession or official grace; in opinions or dogmas, true or false; but a sincere belief of the testimony concerning the facts in the personal history of the Lord Messiah, accompanied by a cordial reception of him in his true character as thus revealed to us, and an entire personal reliance upon him for our salvation.[13]

Richardson then quotes the scriptures at some length to support the view just presented, after which he says:

> . . . a sincere belief in Jesus as the Christ, the Son of God, is emphatically and truly the Christian faith, and the only faith which can lawfully be demanded in order to admission to Christian privileges and church fellowship. This is the CHRISTIAN'S CREED, and the only creed to which any one may be justly called upon to subscribe . . . Hence, even upon the hypothesis that the religious formularies of doctrine, now in vogue, contain nothing but truth, we deny the right of any one to complicate the simplicity of the Christian faith in this manner, and to demand, in advance, a degree of knowledge and experience in the child, which, in the very nature of things, can be expected only in one who has attained to the stature of a man in Christ Jesus.[14]

Faith in the fact of Christ—or the saving deed of God in Christ—may come from reading the Bible or from listening to preaching. In either case it must have a historical rootage, plus a fruitage in personal trust and commitment.

> It is the cordial belief of this love of God, thus manifested in the life, death, resurrection and glorification of Christ, which reconciles man to God, which overwhelms the soul in penitence and contrition for its offences, and, through the influences of the Holy Spirit, produces an entire renovation of heart and reformation of character.[15]

III. THE BASIS OF CHRISTIAN UNION

While Richardson develops this point at some length, his position can be summarized briefly: The true basis of Christian union is the Christian faith, as described in the previous principle. Christ himself becomes the basis of Christian union.

It may be objected that such a latitudinarian basis of church membership will open the door to all sorts of heresies—to Unitarianism and the like. Richardson's answer is that these heresies did not come from the scripture in the first place but were the result of unbridled speculation. Once the believer returns to the Bible, he will find himself guided to the true faith.

Again, it may be objected that a person could give intellectual assent to the Christian creed, that Jesus is the Christ, without going on to repentance and a change of heart. To this answer is given that belief of the gospel, if it is real, will always produce its appropriate results; if belief does not go beyond intellectual assent to repentance and change of heart it is not genuine. It is not really belief.

We have reviewed the three basic principles. Now we are ready to look at "the six important subjects" which Reformers regarded as springing from them.

1. Patriarchal, Jewish and Christian Institutions

This was simply the view that the Bible contains not one but three dispensations, the patriarchal and Jewish (national) dispensations having been abrogated by the dispensation of the Christian church, which alone applies to us. The main result of this recognition of successive dispensations is to free the "simple gospel of Christ" from "the corrupted admixture of Judaism, with which it is still contaminated in the minds of so many of the religious public!"[16] This is, of course, essentially the position that Alexander Campbell maintained in his "Sermon on the Law" as well as in his later sermon "On the Progress of Revealed Light."[17]

2. Commencement of the Christian Church

The Christian church began, not in Old Testament times, but *de novo* on the day of Pentecost. This point is really nothing more than a special elaboration of the previous one regarding dispensations.

3. The Action and Design of Baptism

Baptism is by immersion. All sects recognize that immersion is baptism. The differences arise from adding or substituting other forms. Therefore, "the position which the Reformation has assumed upon this subject is eminently anti-sectarian and conciliatory." The position is simplicity itself: Keep the one form on which all parties agree; discard the forms over which there is disagreement. Immersion remains, and we all practice it.

As to design, baptism is for the remission of sins. The creeds all say this, but the sects in practice have come to substitute something else as the assurance that sins have been forgiven.

You may ask, then, on what do they rely for this assurance? I answer, upon what they consider a gift of the Holy Spirit. The plain state of the case is, that a certain doctrine of special spiritual operations has gradually taken possession of the mind of the religious public, and has so enlarged and extended itself that it has become, emphatically, *the great religious doctrine* of the present age of Protestantism, and has overshadowed every feature of Christianity.[18]

Richardson was here hitting at preconversion experiences and at the requirement of these for church membership.

. . . the Scriptures do, in various forms of speech, assert the connection between baptism and remission, but they no where teach that any mental impressions, visions, or extraordinary visitations, are to be regarded as evidences of pardon; nor is it any where said, that men are to receive the Holy Spirit for the remission of sins.[19]

4. The agency of the Holy Spirit in Conversion and Sanctification

The Spirit works differently in conversion and in sanctification. In the former the spirit is outside the sinner, as a witness to truth; in the latter he is an inner presence, "an indwelling and cherished guest." "To the sinner, he is as the rain which falls upon the surface of the earth; to the believer, he is as a fountain *from within,* springing up unto everlasting life."[20] What the sinner receives is the *gospel.* This comes to him through the apostles who were in turn inspired by the Holy Spirit; but the sinner does not receive the Spirit before belief and baptism.

5. Weekly Communion

The weekly observance of the Lord's supper is advocated not only upon the basis of the assured practice of the early church but upon the approval of "pious and learned men of all parties" who have "often deplored the departure of the modern churches from this ancient order of things."[21]

6. Church Government

Elders or bishops are plural in number and have authority extending only to the particular congregation by which they are chosen. The terms pastor and elder and bishop appear to be synonymous. There is also a plurality of deacons," whose duty it is to take charge of the temporal affairs of the church and minister to the sick, the poor, and the destitute."

Almost as an afterthought, Richardson goes on to say, "*Evangelists* are also sustained by the churches, in the work of preaching the gospel to the world."[22]

Such is a quick review of the main ideas in Richardson's tract. We are, for the purposes of this study, especially interested in the first two principles—the distinction between faith and opinion, and the nature of the Christian faith. But in order to see these clearly, we have reviewed them in relation to the whole complex of ideas lying at the basis of the Disciple movement. Regarding these relationships we must have something to say shortly, but next let us see how far the Campbells and Walter Scott agree with Richardson.

Did the Campbells and Scott Agree With Richardson?

Thomas Campbell

My survey of Thomas Campbell's views has been somewhat cursory, limited as it is to a rereading of the *Declaration and Address* and to Lester McAllister's biography, *Thomas Campbell: Man of the Book*. Perhaps the most accurate thing to say is that, by the time of the *Declaration and Address*, the distinction between faith and opinion was clearly present in the elder Campbell's thinking and that the view of the Christian faith as personal in its object and personal in its nature was present in a somewhat shadowy and embryonic form.

The distinction between faith and opinion, although not so labeled, is clearly made in proposition number six:

> That although inferences and deductions from Scripture premises, when fairly inferred, may be truly called the doctrine of God's holy word, yet are they not formally binding upon the consciences of Christians farther than they perceive the connection, and evidently see that they are so; for their faith must not stand in the wisdom of men, but in the power and veracity of God. Therefore, no such deductions can be made terms of communion, but do properly belong to the after and progressive edification of the Church. Hence, it is evident that no such deductions or inferential truths ought to have any place in the Church's confession.

The distinction becomes still more specific in the seventh proposition. Thomas Campbell, meantime, reaffirms his view that (even though belief of the Bible be faith and belief of theology be nothing but opinion) belief in the whole of the Bible or understanding all about it is certainly too much to expect of new converts. Therefore, something less complex and far more simple is the faith which can be made the basis of church membership.

> . . . doctrinal exhibitions of the great system of Divine truths, and defensive testimonies . . . inferential truths . . . ought not to be made terms of Christian communion; unless we suppose, what is contrary to fact, that none have a right to the communion of the Church, but such as possess a very clear and decisive judgment, or are come to a very high degree of doctrinal information; whereas the Church from the beginning did, and ever will, consist of little children and young men, as well as fathers.

Campbell was here attacking what he later called the "cheap and easy orthodoxy, to which we may attain by committing to memory a catechism" without any real comprehension of the doctrines assented to. He saw that such "belief" was shallow, that it tended to create religious arrogance and division, and that it had no necessary connection with Christian morality. Thus in a shadowy way, Thomas Campbell was saying that Christian faith is something other than mere belief of the Bible, and that the exclusion of man-made systems of theology and the retention of the Bible alone would not suffice.

In the eighth proposition he comes close to saying that the only faith required for entrance into the church is faith in Jesus Christ:

> That as it is not necessary that persons should have a particular knowledge or distinct apprehension of all Divinely revealed truths in order to entitle them to a place in the Church; neither should they, for this purpose, be required to make a profession more extensive than their knowledge; but that, on the contrary, their having a due measure of Scriptural self-knowledge respecting their lost and perishing condition by nature and practice, and of the way of salvation through Jesus Christ, accompanied with a profession of their faith in and obedience to him, in all things, according to his word, is all that is absolutely necessary to qualify them for admission into his Church.

Again in the same document he asserts what is surely the main feature of the principle of the Christian faith as personal trust and commitment:

> A manifest attachment to our Lord Jesus Christ in faith, holiness and charity, was the original criterion of Christian character—the distinguishing badge of our holy profession—the foundation and cement of Christianity.

This same principle was under consideration in the elder Campbell's mind late in 1811 when he wrote a letter to his son, Alexander:

> . . . But, God in Christ, or God, laying and executing all his purposes of creation, sustentation, gubernation, redemption and judgment, in and by Jesus Christ, is the adequate, comprehensive and adorable object of the Christian faith.[23]

Upon the basis of this brief survey of the thought of Thomas Campbell in the first two years of the movement, we are thus able to say with confidence that Thomas Campbell was in hearty agreement with Robert Richardson's statement of the first three principles of the Reformation. And his agreement was not a mere assent to principles later elaborated by Alexander and others; it was his own basic point of view, entertained long before his son or the other leaders began to be articulate about it. The principles were later stated with greater sharpness and their implicit viewpoint was far more fully developed, but the germ of the whole matter is to be found in the *Declaration and Address.*

Alexander Campbell

We can say without hesitation that Alexander Campbell's views were accurately expressed by Richardson's tract. Faith, he held, was belief in the *facts* of the Bible which followed upon the presentation of evidence to the mind. These *facts* were really God's *acts* in history, and they were essentially different from any opinions or speculations about them. But intellectual belief of the facts was not an end in itself; it was meant to lead to personal trust in and commitment to Christ. This means, in a way, that faith was at one and the same time two different things: It was intellectual belief of evidence—a propositional kind of belief, in reality a doctrine of theology—but it was also belief of and commitment to the person of Christ. W. E. Garrison recognized this dual character of the younger Campbell's view when he pointed out in his book, *Alexander Campbell's Theology,* that the Bethany reformer transcended his own theology. Actually, this writer feels that it would be more accurate to say that there were two aspects of Campbell's view of faith, one barrenly intellectual, the other richly personal, and that he was compelled to choose between them from time to time, now veering toward one and then toward the other as the controversy or the occasion demanded. At any rate, Garrison wrote:

> It can be said . . . that, as regards the conception of faith, his theological position was a thorough intellectualism; but the practical application of that intellectualism was to counteract a determined Protestant mysticism, and in its highest religious uses it issued in a lofty conception of faith as trust in a person.[24]

Alexander Campbell held to the distinction between faith and opinion. And his view of the two, fundamentally, was the same as his father's. He was tireless in renouncing belief of anything that was nonbiblical:

> NO MAN CAN BE SAVED BY THE BELIEF OF ANY THEORY, TRUE OR FALSE: NO MAN WILL BE DAMNED FOR THE DISBELIEF OF ANY THEORY. . . . To make *new* theories is the way to make *new divisions.* To contend for the *old* is to keep up the *old divisions.*[25]

The above quotation shows Campbell's motive in making the distinction between faith and opinion. It was to further the cause of Christian unity. Theologies were not despised because they were wrong or even because Christians did not need them, but because having been made tests of fellowship they had become sources of division. Thus the formula: Opinions have speculations as their subject matter; faith has the facts of God's revelation in the Bible as its subject matter. These facts of scripture all focus in one fact: the life, teaching, death and resurrection of Jesus as God's Son. And, whereas the speculations divide Christians from one another, the facts of the divine revelation will draw them together.

So Campbell is drawn to the view represented by Richardson as *the* Christian faith.

> Faith in Christ is the effect of belief. Belief is the *cause;* and trust, confidence, or faith *in* Christ, the effect. . . .
> . . . Now the belief of what Christ says of himself, terminates in trust or confidence in him: and as the Christian religion is a personal thing, both as respects *subject* and *object,* that faith in Christ which is essential to salvation is not the belief of any doctrine, testimony, or truth abstractly, but belief *in* Christ; trust or confidence in him as a person, not a thing. . . . Any belief, then, that does not terminate in our personal confidence in Jesus as the Christ, and to induce trustful submission to him, is not faith unfeigned; but a dead faith, and cannot save the soul.[26]

Thus, superficially, it seems that Campbell is saying that we have but to render our complete loyalty to Christ and to live a Christian life in order to belong to the church. But wait! The living of the Christian life, in Campbell's view, included obeying Christ's commandments; and these commandments are of two kinds, moral and positive. While the moral commandments were actually superior, the positive commands were essential. By positive, Campbell means commandments of a nonethical nature which have to do with the life and conduct of the Christian community—such matters as baptism, communion, church polity. Thus, it is entirely logical for Campbell to follow the statement we have just quoted with another which seems to move in a different direction:

> *The belief of this* ONE FACT, *and submission to* ONE INSTITUTION *expressive of it, is all that is required of Heaven to admission into the church. . . .* The one fact is expressed in a single proposition—*that Jesus the Nazarene is the Messiah.* The evidence upon which it is to be believed is the testimony of *twelve men,* confirmed by prophecy, miracles, and spiritual gifts. The *one institution* is baptism in the name of the Father, and of the Son, and the Holy Spirit. Every such person is a disciple in the fullest sense of the word, the moment he has believed this one fact . . . and has submitted to the above-mentioned institution; and whether he believes the five points condemned, or the five points approved, by the Synod of Dort, is not so much as to be asked of him; whether he holds any of the views of the Calvinists or Arminians, Presbyterians, Episcopalians, Methodists, Baptists or Quakers, is never once to be asked of such persons, in order for admission into the Christian community called the church.[27]

The addition of baptism by immersion to the basic requirement for church membership was quickly followed by other additions, for faith and baptism brought the new member into an institution which had a rather rigid if simple structure. In practice, the acceptance of weekly communion, of congregational government, of a plurality of elders and deacons also became the positive commands of Christ to be literally obeyed, and therefore taken as essential. Further, certain theological presuppositions were added; baptism is the only assurance of divine forgiveness that is needed, the Spirit works through the Bible alone in conversion, the Bible is a rule or law of some kind to be literally obeyed. It is clear that the admission of positive commandments to stand beside the moral commandments of Jesus led Campbell logically farther than he wanted to go temperamentally and devotionally.

For a moment in the year 1837, he drew back from the logic of his position (as he had done on other occasions, *viz.*, in advocating "cooperation" from 1832 on; in serving as president of the American Christian Missionary Convention from 1849 until his death; *et al.*). Thus in the Lunenburg Letter, Campbell asserted personal adherence to the Christian faith in personal terms, exclusive of baptism, to be the one essential of church membership:

> But who is a Christian? I answer, Every one that believes in his heart that Jesus of Nazareth is the Messiah, the Son of God; repents of his sins, and obeys him in all things according to his measure of knowledge and of his will. *A perfect man in Christ,* or a perfect Christian, is one thing; and a "babe in Christ," a stripling in the faith, or an imperfect Christian, is another. . . .
>
> . . . I cannot, therefore, make any one duty the standard of Christian state or character, not even immersion into the name of the Father, of the Son, and of the Holy Spirit, and in my heart regard all that have been sprinkled in infancy without their own knowledge and consent, as aliens from Christ and the well-grounded hope of heaven. . . .
>
> . . . But mark, I do not substitute obedience to one commandment, for universal or even for general obedience. And should I see a sectarian Baptist or a Pedobaptist more spiritually minded, more generally conformed to the requisitions of the Messiah, than one who precisely acquiesces with me in the theory or practice of immersion as I teach, doubtless the former rather than the latter, would have my cordial approbation and love as a Christian. . . .
>
> There is no occasion, then, for making immersion, on a profession of the faith, absolutely essential to a Christian.[28]

There is a complexity to Campbell's supposed simplicity, as the historical sequel has abundantly proved. That apparent simplicity but real complexity appears compactly in the following statement of Campbell's:

> *Let* THE BIBLE *be substituted for all human creeds;* FACTS, *for definitions;* THINGS, *for words;* FAITH, *for speculation;* UNITY OF FAITH *for unity of opinion;* THE POSITIVE COMMANDMENTS OF GOD,

for human legislation and tradition: PIETY, *for ceremony;* MORALITY, *for partisan zeal;* THE PRACTICE OF RELIGION, *for the mere profession of it;* and the work is done.[29]

Walter Scott

The Christian faith for Walter Scott was summed up in belief that Jesus is the Christ. He termed this "the Golden Oracle" of scripture and wrote it over the door of his Pittsburgh schoolroom, so as to remind himself and his pupils of it in their going out and their coming in. As such, Christian faith is not fundamentally propositional or doctrinal at all. This could be shown from many quotations; but one from his book, *The Union of Christians on Christian Principles,* published in 1852, will suffice. The thesis of the book is that Christian union will be achieved when men are drawn to the central element of the Christian religion, which is the divinity of Christ. That is, again he asserts the centrality of the Golden Oracle: "It is no doctrine that Christ taught, nor any action that he performed, that forms the article of faith in the gospel. It is himself—as God's son."[30]

Like Campbell, however, Scott added a great deal to this simple requirement for church membership. In addition to all that Campbell had proposed under the title of "The Ancient Order," Scott proposed a precise, six-step plan of salvation which he styled "The Ancient Gospel," and which he claims to have restored singlehanded on the Western Reserve on November 18, 1827, at New Lisbon, Ohio.

Scott was at once more poetical and more legalistic than Campbell. His legalism may be explained in part as an effort to deliver America from the excessive emotionalism and subjectivism of frontier evangelism. But however it is explained, it was there. Scott's progress from the Golden Oracle into his particular legalism was logically valid, at least for him. His reasoning was like this: Faith means accepting Jesus as the Christ. Accepting Jesus as the Christ means obeying him. Obeying him means following his explicit commandments. Jesus gave us his explicit commandments not only in his own words, but in the words and actions of the apostles. The Ancient Order and the Ancient Gospel constitute the explicit commands of Christ. *Ipse dixit,* he himself said it; if we love him as we profess, we will obey him in all things. So, as with Campbell, Scott introduced a number of specific essentials—all on the basis of the supposed positive or ritual commands of Christ.

A Summary Observation

Our survey has shown that Robert Richardson was speaking for the Campbells and for Scott as well as for himself when he wrote his *Principles and Objects* of the Reformation. And, what is important for this present study, it shows that each of the fathers under review did conceive of the Christian faith as centering upon the person of Christ rather than upon any doctrine about him. Thus, when they said, "We have no creed but Christ," they did not mean to take the body of theology and reject proposition after proposition until they had come down to a creed of one proposition. They meant to change the very nature of believing. Were we allowed to put the distinction they sought in modern terms, we would probably say that faith for them was not fundamentally a matter of metaphysics or of cognition but that it was existential. It seems not unlikely that J. H. Garrison was faithful to the mood and intention of the fathers when he wrote in his book, *A Modern Plea for Ancient Truths,* "Our plea exalts Christ above all doctrinal standards, and urges loyalty to Him as the supreme condition of union and of the triumph of His kingdom in the world."[31]

By using the word "loyalty" in place of "faith" Garrison shows more sharply the distinction that the fathers sought to make. It is belief in Christ as a person working out in trust and commitment. This creed is proved in the deed and can never be assured in anything short of the deed.

It seems to this writer that, whatever our fathers may have said that belongs to the perishing order of a past epoch, here is a living principle which even today is radiating ecumenical power. We need to consider it in its historical setting and to study how to disentangle it from its grave clothes.

A NOTE IN PASSING

While preparing this paper, the writer had occasion to read some of the sermons of Martin Luther to fulfill another assignment. By curious coincidence in a sermon on "The Method and Fruits of Justification," he found Luther speaking against his opponents in the following terms:

> They make so small and slender account of faith, because they are ignorant what faith is and what it alone doth justify. They call it faith, believing those things which they have heard of Christ; this kind of faith the devils also have, and yet they are not justified. But this ought rather to be called an opinion of men. To believe those things to be true which are preached of Christ is not sufficient to constitute thee a Christian.[32]

Thus one finds the distinction between faith and opinion at the very dawn of the Protestant Reformation. (Interestingly enough, the scriptural allusion which Luther made in this quoted excerpt is to James 2:10: "You believe that God is one; you do well. Even the demons believe . . . and shudder." Thus Luther found at least one part of the letter of James which he could not denounce as "a right strawy epistle"!)

Evaluation and Criticism

WHERE THE FATHERS WERE RIGHT

There are probably few Disciples who really know what the pioneers meant by the formula, "We have no creed but Christ." Perhaps most of our members suppose that it means nothing but quantitative simplicity; that, whereas other religious bodies have elaborate creeds of many articles, we have a streamlined creed with only one article. What a sad misrepresentation of the mind of the fathers! To their thinking, the Christian faith could not be found in *any* set of doctrines or propositions, but only in the warm surrender of a whole personality to the person of Christ himself. The Christian faith is not any belief *about* Christ; it is belief in Christ himself and full commitment of life to *him.*

When Paul sought to express what the Christian faith meant to him he said, very simply, "For me, to live is Christ"; when we try to explain it, we begin telling and debating over what we believe about Christ. The object of Paul's faith was a person; the object of intellectualized faith—or bare belief—is not a person. It is a proposition about a person; that is to say, it is a doctrine, a creed, a set of human opinions.

This point is greatly clarified by Emil Brunner in his book *The Divine–Human Encounter,* where he sees all revelation and all genuine faith in this light. "In His Word, God does not deliver to me a course of lectures in dogmatic theology, He does not submit to me or interpret for me the content of a confession of faith, but He makes Himself accessible to me. . . . He does not communicate 'something' to me but 'Himself.' "[33]

Thus, when the faith becomes a doctrine—or a creed or theology—a very subtle change takes place. It is a change which makes a profound difference so radical as to disfigure Christianity completely. We have taken faith, which is a personal surrender of the whole self to God in Christ, and we have turned it into a set of human affirmations about God and Christ. We have intellectualized it. But when we intellectualize it, we also depersonalize it. For an idea or an opinion is as impersonal as a desk or a rock, and just as much a "thing" to us. Moreover, when we intellectualize and so depersonalize the Christian faith, we reverse our relationship to it. As a set of assurances, it is *ours;* we possess it, whereas formerly God possessed us. Further, this intellectualizing of faith changes our relations to each other. It makes us solitary. Correctness of doctrine becomes the important consideration between us. We quarrel and divide because we cannot agree over doctrines, and "the faith that works in love," degenerates into the dogma that festers in intolerance.

Finally, as the crown of solitariness, this intellectualizing of the faith becomes a barrier between the believer and God. Personal communion with God, warmed by humility and love, becomes the arrogant pride and self-righteousness of cold opinion.

To recapitulate, the downgrading of faith into doctrine—making it identical with doctrine—has five malevolent effects: First, it abstracts faith from the whole of life and makes it a matter of words and ideas. Second, it turns faith into a thing—it depersonalizes the faith. Third, it makes faith a property to be cherished and defended with all the pride of ownership. Fourth, it divides the believers from one another. Fifth, by substituting a propositional dogma about God for personal communion with him, it even separates the believer from God himself. Such a "faith" does not change men, it only hardens them. Let us again quote from Emil Brunner:

> But if the Word of God meets me in faith, this is all reversed. Then I do not have something like property which is at my disposal, but I myself become property. . . . Faith is no longer that knowing which enriches, which leaves me unaltered in the very core of my person. . . . Out of a lord faith converts me into a servant, and therefore transforms the whole meaning of my existence. . . . Solitariness is now also past. . . . Into my world, in which I was alone . . . —into the solitariness of the 'Thou-less' I God has stepped as Thou. He who believes is never solitary. . . . God delivers to us no course of lectures in dogmatic theology; he submits and explains to us no confession of faith. He does not say to me, 'I am the Lord thy God.' His Word is claim and promise, gift and demand. . . . The true form of faith is hence not the so-called declaration of faith, the formulated Credo which has been learned, but prayer.[34]

What are we to say about theology, then? Is there no place in the Christian life for doctrines? On the contrary, a Christian, if he thinks at all, must be able to give a reason for the faith that is in him. The reasons he gives will be his theology. But, if his faith is a living reality, he must never identify it with the reasons which he gives for it. And, what is more, he must never require others to subscribe precisely to his own set of reasons before he accepts them in Christian fellowship. Nor should all theology be a matter of solitary thinking to be done by each man when he is alone; it should be engaged in by the whole believing community, in the spirit of free inquiry.

Where Did the Fathers Go Wrong?

Having emphasized the soundness and centrality of the pioneers' basic principle, let us turn now to the question, "Where did the fathers go wrong?" For we may assume that the difficulty is more complicated than the simple failure of succeeding generations to understand what the fathers were driving at. They themselves were not unambiguous. In fact, on examination, it appears that they gave a principle of Christian unity with one hand and took it back with the other, without letting the left hand know what the right hand was doing. Let us try to be specific:

1. Although the fathers saw the divisive effects of an enforced, uniform church theology, they failed to see that an enforced uniform church polity would be just as divisive. Thus they refused to insist upon a single Christology or to divide over theories of the Trinity, but when it came to matters like congregational autonomy, baptism by immersion, or the plurality of elders, they stood adamant. What this meant, as a matter of history, is that we did not quarrel over big questions but about secondary matters, while the primary concerns which have troubled the great councils of the church through the centuries dropped in to neglect. We divided, not over matters of faith, revelation, Christology and the like, but over secondary matters like instrumental music, missionary societies, and baptism. Thus, it would appear, differing theologies are not the only causes of division, and while uniformity of creedal opinion can never be exacted of a free community as a basis for unity, neither can matters of polity be absolutized.

2. It would appear that the fathers felt the difficulty of making the Christian Creed the sole basis of union, since the church

is not only a community of faith, but it also is a community of people who must interact through some kind of institution. Institutional questions have to be settled before people with the same faith can worship and study and work together. The fathers were right in sensing this. But they were wrong in supposing that the guidance needed to settle questions of organizations and polity were revealed in mechanical detail, that they were everywhere uniform in the New Testament, and that they were to be enforced as the basis of Christian union.

We can now see that the New Testament principle for settling questions of organization was expediency. The early church adopted the organization nearest at hand which was best suited to its task in a particular locality. This organization differed from region to region, and it kept developing and changing. The fathers did not see this. They saw it as static, as uniform and as divinely given. What they should have done was to apply their principle of liberty of opinion to organization as well as to theology. Thus, although questions of organization would have to be agreed upon by a given congregation, they could be settled as matters of expediency without all the defensiveness and anxiety that went with the doing of the supposed literal command of God. Liberty of opinion should have been applied to organization as well as to theology.

3. While the fathers were right in insisting upon the Christian faith as a personal commitment to Christ, they did not adhere consistently to this single standard but added to it a belief in the letter of the Bible, selectively interpreted. Thus, to state the anomaly as boldly as possible, the movement is at one and the same time Christocentric and Bibliocentric. This dualism appears in the statement of the first two principles of the movement. When the distinction between faith and opinion was made, opinion was identified with speculative theology, faith with the Bible. Thus faith, in this setting, is not a different kind of believing from creedal dogma but merely the same kind of believing focused upon the Bible as its object. When, however,

the reformers discussed *the* Christian faith, they changed the fundamental meaning of the term and made faith a personal encounter with God in Christ. Logically this is what is called "the fallacy of the ambiguous middle term." Practically, it meant that we as a people have gone through a century and a half trying to serve two masters—Christ and the letter of the Bible. As it is true that no man can serve two masters, so it is also true that no religious communion can serve two masters and remain unified, for parts of it will despise the one and cling to the other. This is precisely what has happened, on the whole, in the division between "Bible believing Christians" and "Disciples." To say that the Bible is not in the center is not, of course, to say that it is unimportant. It is tremendously important, for without it the Christian faith is without historical content and without a criterion.

4. While the fathers saw the speculative character of the current creeds and confessions of faith, they could not see that the supposed "facts" of Scripture which they thought they knew so clearly were inextricably mixed with speculations of their own. In other words, they saw the facts of Scripture through their own theological preconceptions. You have but to read what they said about such questions as remission of sins and the Holy Spirit to see that this is true. The clear-cut division between the believing of the "facts" of Scripture and the "opinions" of theology is not clear-cut at all; no interpretation of the Bible can break free of human opinion and error.

5. Likewise, the fathers were inconsistent in what they had to say about the simplicity and understandability of the Scriptures. On the one hand they insisted that the word of the Bible was so plain that any man could understand it if he would use common sense and take the time to read it. On the other hand, they admitted, somewhat grudgingly perhaps, that there were some mysteries in the Bible that no one understands completely.

To overcome or guard against these ambiguities, the fathers proposed two safeguards: (1) Reliance upon pastors and teachers more experienced in the interpretation of Scripture. This line cannot be followed very far until it becomes some kind of authoritarianism and confounds one of the basic principles of Protestantism, the right of private interpretation. So the fathers passed over the suggestions quickly, hoping no one would notice the logical inconsistency in this. (2) The rule that biblical things will be spoken of only in biblical language. This involves religious discussion of baffling Scriptures in a verbal circle. If you are asked to tell what *sanctification* means, for example, you cannot go outside the Bible to pick up analogies from secular experience; all you can say is that sanctification means being sanctified by the Holy Spirit. Faith using such a device is just as blind as the faith that comes from memorizing and repeating a catechism.

6. Although the fathers professed to believe that theology was privately important to each believer, they were so afraid of it in the corporate life of the church that they omitted it from both study and preaching. Thus the layman is given no guidance in constructing his own "reasons for the faith that is in him" and becomes progressively illiterate in religious reasoning. We might even add that the clergy also shares in this illiteracy.

The fathers themselves were deeply immersed in theology. They assumed that this knowledge would continue as an automatic heritage of each succeeding generation of Christians without special cultivation. For example, Alexander Campbell spoke of Martin Luther with admiration and approval in talking about Luther's central doctrine: "Luther said that the doctrine of justification, or forgiveness, was the test of a standing or falling church. If right in this, she could not be very far wrong in anything. . . . We agree with him in this as well as in many other sentiments."[35]

Again, Isaac Errett in his pamphlet *Our Position* tried to correct the distorted perspective of Disciples by listing thirteen points of agreement with the evangelical parties before he stated a single disagreement. The thirteen points are as follows:

> 1. The Divine inspiration of the Scriptures. 2. The Trinity and revelation. 3. The all-sufficiency of the Bible. 4. Jesus and the Supernatural religion of the New Testament. 5. The mission of the Holy Spirit. 6. Sin and Salvation. 7. Repentance and obedience. 8. Baptism and the Lord's Supper as perpetual ordinances. 9. The Lord's Day. 10. The Church as a Divine institution. 11. Christian morality. 12. The fullness and freeness of salvation. 13. The final punishment of the ungodly.

A rather large bundle of theological beliefs! The fact that the pioneers accepted without discussion so much from contemporary Christendom while dissenting so vociferously and voluminously from other portions of it, has passed on to us a lopsided heritage. We have spent too much time and energy emphasizing our peculiarities. We have had too little to say about the great doctrines of God, man, sin, grace, and salvation. The fault is not so much in the belief of the fathers; it is more in the fact that we are the product of controversy and that so much of our literature is the literature of controversy.

What Shall We Do Now?

What are the implications for us here and now? There seem to be at least four rather clear-cut conclusions:

1. Let us take the "Golden Oracle" of the fathers seriously, so seriously, in fact, that we do not need to complicate this center of the Christian faith by adding to it. When we say "We have no creed but Christ," let us know what we mean by this and let us adhere faithfully to it, adding nothing as an absolute requirement of Christian fellowship in the church.

To meet Christ as Lord requires, as a prerequisite, some way of meeting him. Ordinarily the invitation, "Come and see," comes from the witnessing church and then passes to the biblical record. People meet Christ through the church and the Bible; they *can* go on to genuine faith.

2. Let us extend the liberty of opinion claimed for theology to

the other topics covered by what Alexander Campbell termed "the positive commands" of the Bible. In other words, matters of church organization and polity will be restored to their biblical place and settled not on the basis of divine authority but on the basis of expediency by the life of the various fellowships of the Christian community. Differing church polities will thus stand side by side without unchurching one another, and differing ritual practices—within areas of wide agreement—will also be found in the one church.

3. Let us work to produce a lay theological revival. Let us provide the literature and the mechanisms of education by which laymen in significant numbers are inducted into the serious study of all these questions, and let the study be conducted in the earnest spirit of free inquiry. In a word, let us restore the balance disturbed so long ago by controversy with other religious bodies, and let us do what we can to create a church membership which is both biblically and theologically literate.

4. Pushing questions of ecclesiastical mechanics into the background where they belong, let us devote our greatest energy in local congregations—and in the life of the whole church—to the creation of a genuine communion of saints, placing the emphasis upon the new birth and new life from the spirit in familylike relationships. For far too long we have tried to find the true church by restoring or perfecting its institution. It is high time that we devote our energies to providing the conditions for the growth of personal community—vital and redemptive—and then let the community create the institution it needs to express its life.

Theology has a dual role in such a communion of saints: (1) to prepare people to understand the nature of faith as an anticipation, warding off the scholastic danger, and (2) to interpret and deepen the faith after it is born in the believer.

One is tempted to imagine that the pioneering fathers of our movement would propose some such program, were they living in our day and looking back over their own views and deeds in a yesterday that is past. They were too creative to go on repeating themselves endlessly. They would hardly insist that they never had made any mistakes. But, on the other hand, it is entirely possible that they would cling to their central view of the Christian faith as a valid ecumenical principle and that, rescuing it from its entanglements with many aspects of the movement which deserve to be decently buried and memorialized only as history, they would advocate it with energy and enthusiasm as the golden key to Christian unity.

NOTES

1. *Millennial Harbinger,* 1853, p. 117.
2. *Ibid.,* 1852, p. 577.
3. *Ibid.,* 1852, p. 578.
4. *Ibid.,* 1852, p. 578-79.
5. *Ibid.,* 1852, p. 580.
6. *Ibid.,* 1852, p. 581.
7. *Ibid.,* 1852, p. 581.
8. *Ibid.,* 1852, pp. 581-82.
9. *Ibid.,* 1852, p. 583.
10. *Ibid.,* 1852, p. 584.
11. *Ibid.,* p. 586.
12. *Ibid.,* 1852, p. 602.
13. *Ibid.,* 1852, p. 606.
14. *Ibid.,* 1852, pp. 608-609.
15. *Ibid.,* 1852, p. 609.
16. *Ibid.,* 1852, p. 688.
17. *Ibid.,* 1837, pp. 411-412.
18. *Ibid.,* 1852, p. 702.
19. *Ibid.,* 1852, p. 703.
20. *Ibid.,* 1852, p. 704.
21. *Ibid.,* 1852, p. 706.
22. *Ibid.,* 1852, p. 707.
23. Robert Richardson, *Memoirs of Alexander Campbell,* Vol. I, p. 416.
24. W. E. Garrison, *Alexander Campbell's Theology* (Christian Publishing Co., 1900), p. 226.
25. Richardson, *op. cit.,* Vol. II, p. 153.
26. Alexander Campbell, *The Christian System,* pp. 52-53.
27. *Ibid.,* p. 122.
28. *Millennial Harbinger,* 1837, p. 411-414.
29. *The Christian System,* p. 110.
30. For further discussion of this work, see Dwight E. Stevenson, *Walter Scott: Voice of the Golden Oracle* (Bethany, 1946), pp. 204-205.
31. J. H. Garrison, *A Modern Plea for Ancient Truths,* Christian Publishing Company, 1902, p. 13.
32. Grenville Kleiser (ed). *The World's Great Sermons* (Funk and Wagnalls, 1908), Vol. I, p. 122.
33. Emil Brunner, *The Divine-Human Encounter,* trans. by Amandus W. Loos (Philadelphia: Westminster Press, 1943), p. 85.
34. *Ibid.,* pp. 88, 89.
35. *The Christian System,* p. 179.

3

The Nature and Work of Christ
In the Thought of Barton W. Stone

WILLIAM G. WEST

THE story of the rise of the so-called "Stone movement" in Kentucky at the beginning of the nineteenth century is too familiar for repetition in this paper. We may recall, however, that following the Great Revival of August, 1801, at Cane Ridge, Stone and his colleagues withdrew from the jurisdiction of the Synod of Kentucky, gave birth to their own independent Springfield Presbytery, and then killed the infant presbytery after it had breathed only nine brief months.

The three documents resulting from this action—"The Last Will and Testament of the Springfield Presbytery," the "Witness' Address," and the "Observations on Church Government"—reveal considerable closeness in feeling and ideas to the later *Declaration and Address* of Thomas Campbell. There is a strong emphasis on unity and the spiritual basis for the unity of New Testament churches.

Of the men who severed their connections with the Presbyterians, only Stone remained to give substantial support to a new American religious drama: the unity of all Christians. For a number of years following his withdrawal from the Presbyterians, the orthodox tried to prove that Stone was a heretic.

In the years between 1803 and the early 1820's, Stone was violently attacked by the church from which he had severed himself. His principal opponents were Thomas Cleland and John Poage Campbell who regarded him as not only a rebel against Calvinism, but as a dangerous person whose influence might plunge many into deism and atheism. Thomas Cleland believed that Stone was on the logical road to deism because he felt that he held Arian and Socinian views. Some Presbyterians regarded Stone as being more dangerous than the naturalists of Germany and Boston because Stone sustained his views with "religious enthusiasm." They were used to Unitarianism which was supported by learning and philosophy, but were more afraid of what they regarded as Stone's "Unitarian views," supported as they were by revivalism. Orthodoxy in Kentucky placed Stone in the same category with the heretical Unitarians and infidels. He was portrayed as preaching deism in a "thin Christian garb."

Stone, however, believed that orthodox Presbyterian preaching at the turn of the century itself contained so much fatalism and irrationalism that, along with infidel French philosophy, it cut the nerve of moral action in numerous communities. By 1835 he noted that a big change had taken place in Presbyterian preaching so that many hard doctrines had been considerably softened.

Stone's critics concentrated most of their opposition to his doctrine on the nature and work of Christ. Long after Cleland and J. P. Campbell attacked Stone, the charge of Arianism, Deism, and Unitarianism haunted him. While engaged in his most notable work, the attempt to unite the "Stoneites" with the "Campbellites" and later the Christian connection with these two groups, he was called a Unitarian and an Arian. The Baptists warned Alexander Campbell to beware of uniting with Stone and his followers because they were "the Arians of the West."

Stone rejected the use of the names, Unitarian and Arian. The fact that a few of his brethren at Hopkinsville, Kentucky, called themselves Unitarians "grieved" him. In a letter to Dr. James Blythe he wrote: "We have again and again proved that we are neither Socinians or Arians. We have as often shown that we do not deny the divinity of Christ nor the atonement."

I. Stone on the Nature of Christ

Stone was dissatisfied with both the Arian viewpoint and the orthodox interpretation of the nature of Christ. He rejected Arius because it seemed to him that Arius denied the divinity of Christ. "If we are Arians," he wrote,

> so were the Fathers of the first three centuries. This we have proved in our letters to Doctor Blythe; and if further proof be necessary we are prepared to give it. We can prove, if proof be required, that Arius and his followers apostasized from the apostolic faith, as believed and taught by the most influential Fathers of the first centuries. The Fathers believed that the Son of God, or Logos, derived his being immediately from the Father, and is therefore of the same specific divine nature. Arius believed that the Son was created out of nothing, and therefore, is not the only begotten Son of God.[1]

Here it seems Stone is on the side of the orthodox. He rejects the Arian view that the Son was created out of nothing and accepts the one orthodox view that the Son of God derived his being immediately from the Father.

However, eight years before he took this position, Stone, in his *Address to the Christian Churches,* rejected the terms "eternal Son" and "eternally begotten" as applied to the Son because he could not find them in the Bible. Since they were "human inventions," he felt justified in judging them in the light of human reason. Actually, Stone was tortured by what seemed to him to be the problem of logical contradiction in all the popular presentations of Calvinistic doctrines. He alternated between using reason and the Scriptures against hardened Calvinistic beliefs.

For example, the Westminster Confession of Faith stated that the Father and Son are "one eternal substance." Stone argued that the voice of reason asserts that "the same individual substance cannot beget itself, nor be begotten by itself." Therefore, he declared, the substance of the Son was "never begotten nor born." Stone bluntly argued:

If the Son be very and eternal God, and as there is but one only true God; then it will follow that the Son begat himself and was his own Father!—that he was active in begeting [sic] and passive in being begotten. I would humbly ask the advocates for generation, did the Son of God exist before he was begotten? If he did, he never was begotten at all—if he did not, he was begotten from eternity; therefore, not the very and eternal God.[2]

Stone's rejection of the orthodox doctrine of Christology came at two points: in the use of terms to explain the incarnation which were at once nonbiblical and self-contradictory.

Stone could not believe that there were two eternal Gods nor that the same one God could at the same instant be active in sending and passive in being sent. In order to escape this dilemma Stone apparently sided with the Arians in the crucial issues between them and the Nicene defenders. Stone believed in the pre-existence of Christ as Son, but he believed that the Son had a beginning. The Father alone was eternal; the Son had the status of a creature, yet, like the Arians, Stone believed that the Son was not a mere man. Since his creation was prior to that of other creatures and was the work of the Father alone, he was not a creature like other creatures. Christ was exalted high above other creatures.

Stone placed himself close to the subordinationist strain in Arianism which taught the absolute unity of the Father and declared that all other beings have the status of creatures. Christ stands in a mediating position between God and the created world. He is above all creatures, yet he is not deity in the full and true sense. He is not fully God because the godhead in him is derived from God and he is not fully man because the godhead at the moment of the incarnation united with the human body having no human mind or spirit. The human mind or spirit, let it be observed according to Stone who followed Isaac Watts at this point, had already been united with the godhead.

Stone's treatment of such scriptural texts as Colossians 2:9, "In him dwelleth all the fulness of the godhead," indicates that he took seriously the doctrine which he apparently learned from Isaac Watts, that the human nature of Jesus was united to the full godhead long before the incarnation. Despite all of Stone's distinction between Jesus as God and the Son of God, he believed that the fulness of God dwelt in Christ. He stated that he believed that "God was in Christ reconciling the world unto himself." Stone admitted that the doctrine that God dwelt in his Son is mysterious. However, this doctrine cleared up the interpretations of such scriptures as those attributing miracles to Christ. According to Stone it was not Christ as God, but rather God in Christ who worked miracles. He asked, "If the Son, as Son, was God independent, why did he attribute the works to the Father in him, and not to his own Almighty independent power?" Stone thus made a distinction between the Son of God and the godhead which dwelt in the Son of God.

Stone seemed to stress both the subordinationist strain of the Arians and the emphasis of the orthodox on the godhead in Christ. What he attempted to do was to maintain many of the positions of Isaac Watts on the nature of Christ with which he had become familiar as a young student of divinity. This doctrine of the pre-existence of the human-divine soul of Christ was also publicly taught by Henry Pattillo who conducted Stone's examination for ordination in the Orange Presbytery.

We must understand Watts to understand Stone's Christology. Watts believed that the Lord Jesus Christ had an existence and was personally united with the divine nature long before the incarnation and managed the affairs of God's ancient church in Old Testament history[3] and then was sent by him, divested of primitive joys, to dwell in a human body, to grow gradually, to suffer intense agony, and to submit to death. He denied that his view was Arian, because Arians attributed divine characters or attributes to the man Christ Jesus, whereas Watts believed in his personal union to the godhead.

Isaac Watts taught that Christ's human soul in some "unknown moment of God's own eternity" was united with the godhead to form a God-man. This human soul was derived from God and thus was a creature. But the "Godhead was coessential and coeternal with the godhead of the Father, for it was the same divine essence." Watts thus rejected the ancient Arian point of view which pictured Christ as being a glorious person, but "inferior to the true and eternal God." He also veered away from the orthodox position in his doctrine of the pre-existence of "the human soul of Christ" in holding that a human mind and will were not united to the godhead at the moment of the incarnation. According to Watts, the human soul of Christ which was united with the divine nature before the "world began," was united at the incarnation with a human body only.

It seems to me that Watts, who influenced Stone greatly on the nature of Christ, believed not only in the pre-existence of Christ, but also in a kind of "preincarnation"[4] of Christ.

The primary object of this interpretation seems to have been to reconcile the ascriptions of divine titles and prerogatives both to God the Father and to Jesus Christ without destroying the doctrine of the unity of God. (See John 10:30: "I and the Father are one." John 14:9: "He that hath seen me hath seen the Father." Col. 2:9: "In him dwelleth all the fulness of the godhead bodily.")

Watts pointed out that there was such a close and intimate union between God and Christ the creature that the actions and characters of either of them may be attributed to the whole compound being. He held that the divine essence or nature was communicated to the Son by the "Father's uniting the human nature of Christ to his own Godhead, or by God's actually assuming the man Christ Jesus, his Son, into a personal union with himself, which act of uniting the Godhead to the man Christ Jesus may be called a communication of the divine nature to the Son."

Watts admits that the common sense use of the word "person" signified one single, intelligent, voluntary agent. But in a theological sense, it signifies one complex, intelligent, voluntary agent having two natures, human and divine. Two distinct substances, such as a body and spirit, may be so intimately united, as that one may act in subordination to the other, and "they may both be esteemed, by virtue of this union, as one common subject of action or passion." For example, if the body sleeps or walks, do we not say that the man sleeps or walks? Moreover, in this complex person, the actions or characters, of either part of the composition, are sometimes attributed to the other in common language. Thus we say: an honest heart; a warm spirit; a heavy soul.

When God united himself with the Son, he did so in such a way that two beings became one complex principle of action. So, two trees may be planted close to each other and if barbed on one side, and bound to each other, by this union they will, as it were, grow into one and with propriety may be called one tree.

Stone adopted most of the views of Isaac Watts on the nature of Christ and for the same reason; to bring about peace among divergent schools of thought, namely, the Arian and the orthodox. Both Stone and Watts maintained that their views of the nature of Christ exalted him more than did the orthodox doctrine. By holding that the Father and Son are two distinct beings, he did not "fritter" Christ down to a "mere mode or abstraction." Stone felt that both Trinitarians and Unitarians were agreed on the object of their worship, the only true God, and on "refusing to worship the Son of God, as a being, not the true God." He implied that there was too much speculation on the subject which prevented men from worshiping Christ as the Son of God. He failed to see that much of the concerted opposition against him and his movement arose from his own speculation and failure to follow all the intricacies of the Christology of Watts.

II. Stone on the Atonement

Controversy between Stone and the Presbyterians likewise developed over the doctrine of the work of Christ. Stone rejected the doctrine of substitutionary atonement. One of his opponents, Thomas Cleland, felt that this was the logical outcome of Stone's position on the deity of Christ. Stone was accused of following the new German School, headed by Semler, Henke, Herder, Eckerman, and others. His views on the atonement were compared to those of the deists. Stone was accused of borrowing the "language of infidels" when he wrote on the atoning sacrifice.

When we consider Stone's position on the work of Christ, we must understand it against the background of contemporary backwoods preaching which tended to stress God's wrath rather than his love. James McGready and other frontier preachers preached fire and brimstone. They believed that the torment of the sinner in hell would be a "growing torment." The misery of the sinner will increase as he receives the "unmilled wrath of a sin-avenging God."

In one of his sermons, for example, McGready declared,

> While the one hand of enraged Omnipotence supports the sinner in being and enlarges his capacity for suffering, with the other, he tortures him with all the miseries and pains which infinite wisdom can invent, or Almighty Power inflict. Oh, how dreadful must be the torments of hell![5]

Barton W. Stone rebelled against such portrayals of God's wrath. He would in our day receive support from such a scholar as D. M. Baillie, late professor of systematic theology in the University of St. Andrews, who in his influential book on Christology asserts:

> Throughout the whole of this New Testament material there is no trace of any contrast between the wrath of God and the love of Christ, or the idea that God's attitude to sinners had to be changed by the sacrifice of Christ from wrath and justice to love and mercy. There is ample use of the terminology of the Jewish sacrificial system, but it is highly doubtful whether even in the Old Testament

period the purpose of the sin-offerings was to change God's attitude in that sense. A great deal of confusion has been caused by the fact that the English word 'atonement' has moved away from the sense it had when the Bible was translated, viz., reconciliation. The Hebrew word which lies behind it originally meant 'covering' or 'wiping out,' and it may have included the idea of an 'expiation' that had to be made before the sinner could be acquitted, but it certainly did not imply anything like propitiation of an angry God. For, as scholars have pointed out, it is always God Himself, who is regarded, in the Old Testament, as having appointed the ritual of sin-offering, in His desire for reconciliation.[6]

The crux of the argument over the atonement came over its design. The orthodox held to a substitutionary theory of the atonement while Stone generally accepted the moral influence theory. The conviction is inescapable that Stone's opposition to the orthodox theory resulted from hearing presentations of the substitutionary doctrine by emotional frontier preachers who heightened the effect of their sermons by the use of extreme metaphors. Until 1804 Stone believed that Christ died as a substitute or surety in man's stead and "to justify man by making satisfaction to law and justice for man's sins." He rejected this doctrine that Christ's sacrifice purchased reconciliation because it seemed to him not to be in the Bible and also to contradict biblical teaching on grace, forgiveness, and the love and character of God. Stone's opponents held that he reduced the death of Christ to a natural event, which robbed it of its efficacy, and moreover stressed love in God's nature without any consideration of his exercise of judgment on man. The most potent argument made against Stone's movement was directed against his doctrine of the atonement since the average frontiersman entertained more precise ideas on this subject than on the more abstruse subject of the nature of Christ.

Stone had accepted Watts' doctrine of the pre-existence of Christ, but he rejected Watts' doctrine of the atonement, which was presented in an orthodox substitutionary pattern. Having little time for either reading or writing, Stone carried materials to the cornfield to write his first pamphlet, which was on the atonement. He discussed the subject more fully at a later date in the *Address to the Christian Churches.*

Stone rejected the doctrine that the blood of Christ satisfied God's law or justice. He argued that the orthodox doctrine militated against the Christian idea of grace and forgiveness. If a surety or substitute paid a debt for man, it would "not argue grace in the creditor" to forgive him.[7] The doctrine also seemed to contradict the teaching that God was no respecter of persons. If Christ served as a "surety" of the "elect" only, then these blessings would be for a part of mankind only. This struck at the heart of Stone's belief that Christ died for every man, and that God's grace must be freely offered to all. The doctrine also represented God as being full of wrath toward the sinner who was "appeased" by the blood of Christ. If wrath were in God, Stone observed, it would argue two infinite and unchangeable principles in him, namely, love and wrath. When God's wrath fell on any creature, he could not be saved unless God changed. God's nature must be unchangeable. Therefore, the "wrath of God" mentioned in the Scriptures is not really in God, but is a "relative term only" which Stone understood to be "nothing else but his holy nature standing in opposition to sin."[8]

Stone's opponents felt that he failed to stress the judgment of God on the sinner. For example, John Poage Campbell believed that God's nature included the principle of wrath and vindictive justice. When Stone spoke of forgiveness of sin, he meant no more than that "the sinner has made himself free from his own wrath." Thomas Cleland, a more able opponent of Stone than Campbell, accused Stone of using the "language of infidels" against the orthodox doctrine of the atonement. He warned Stone of the "awful consequences" of "philosophizing" the doctrine of the vicarious atonement of Christ into "Naturalistic Christianity."

This criticism probably kept Stone from going too far in his theory of the atonement. Though he rejected all substitutionary theories of the atonement, he had to face up to the criticism of

J. P. Campbell and Cleland relative to his tendency to reduce the death of Christ to the level of a martyrdom. Salvation then would be man-centered. While opposing the orthodox doctrine of the atonement, Stone nevertheless used many scriptural phrases regarding the death of Christ which seemed to be satisfactory to a man like Thomas Cleland, who specifically stated that Stone's affirmative views were satisfactory as far as they went.

Stone insisted that the word "atonement" meant reconciliation in the scriptures. In Old Testament history sin separated man from God. The sacrifice was made to rid the transgressor of his pollution. The consequence of this act was that atonement or reconciliation took place between God and the now purified offender.

The main point of difference between Stone and the orthodox was over the influence of the death of Christ on God. The orthodox Presbyterians were afraid that Stone's doctrine tended to deism by reducing the death of Jesus to the level of the death of other men. Stone feared that the substitutionary theory of the atonement was so contrary to the true nature of Christianity as to be itself a cause of infidelity. He believed that the alternative was the moral influence theory of the atonement. The moral influence is exerted not on God, but on man. The death of Jesus has a "moral tendency" to lead man to repentance, obedience, and love. His enemies attacked him more strongly at this point than at any other to stop the defections from the orthodox ranks. They attempted to expose him as a deist and an infidel on this question. They were unable to see any merit in any substitutionary theory. The battle was hard fought here and Stone's movement was in danger of being submerged in the frontal attack of the Presbyterians on the Unitarians and other liberals, who for a time threatened to penetrate Kentucky.

Stone was unalterably opposed to the orthodox doctrine, but did not hold that man must have an intellectual understanding of the death of Christ before he could enter into the Christian community. If a sinning individual discovered the love of God in the face of Jesus, he could trust the Father before he fully comprehended the atonement. Stone drew the analogy of a father who provides for a large family of children.

Some of them may know the means by which the father got the provisions—others may not so well know, and the youngest may scarcely know anything more than that the father's love provided these things. Yet, they all eat and thrive, without quarreling about the means by which the provisions were obtained. O that Christians would do likewise![9]

This was written in 1815. A little later Stone wanted to forget this theological controversy completely. He was interested in laying a practical basis for Christians to be united and he was likewise conscious of the softening of the harsher presentations which had characterized earlier popular Calvinism in Kentucky. Good biblicist that he was, Stone proposed that the controversy be ended by using "scriptural expressions" on the doctrine and nothing more.

In order to remove this unprofitable and injurious controversy, I would propose, that we all teach this doctrine, and speak of it in the language of scripture, none affirming that God was influenced by Christ's death to forgive and save the sinner, and none denying it. To affirm it we cannot be clearly supported by scripture; to deny it we cannot be positive.

Till this course be pursued by us all, the controversy can never cease.[10]

This is a different mood from that of the man who had vigorously replied to opponents who had accused him of using the language of Thomas Paine on the atonement. Stone had previously written that he did not wonder that infidels opposed a doctrine so absurd.

It is rather a wonder that there are not a thousand infidels for one, when such doctrines has [sic] been held up to the world as the doctrine of revelation, and supported and defended by the whole weight of talents, learning, and religion of the christian world, as the foundation stone, and the distinguishing trait of the Christian religion.[11]

However, Stone entered very reluctantly into controversy with Alexander Campbell on the question of the atonement in 1839 and 1840. Stone defended the moral influence theory of the atonement and Campbell, while rejecting the orthodox terminology of Christ's propitiatory death, still retained enough of the idea to disturb Stone. For example, Stone rejected Campbell's description of Christ's sacrifice as "a sweet smelling savor pleasing, propitiating, reconciling God to man." "I know that he [Stone] repudiates the idea," wrote Campbell "of effecting a change in God—of changing him from an enemy to a friend. So do I. But I still say God repents, is propitiated, and purified, and even reconciled to us."[12]

The fact that Campbell did not hold to some of the cruder presentations of the substitutionary atonement had brought the two men fairly close together at this point. In the end, Campbell apparently concurred with Stone in most of his views, though not with all his "explanations." He felt that Stone did not go far enough, for he omitted the greatest design of the death of Christ, namely, "to expiate sin." The controversy terminated with the two men in substantial agreement except on this point. The agreement between the two movements at Lexington, Kentucky, in 1832, to use biblical language and to abandon speculation, was adhered to so closely that the christological question has never been too serious a problem among Disciples of Christ or Christian Churches.

Stone described what in effect has become the general practice of the majority of Disciples of Christ when he stated that his group was willing to acknowledge all to be Christians "who acknowledge the gospel facts and obey Jesus Christ." They were willing to accept both Unitarians and Trinitarians, if each would agree to use "Bible words" to express their faith concerning Christ. They would reject Unitarians if they contended that Jesus Christ "is not the Son of God," but would accept the Unitarians who acknowledged that Jesus Christ "is the Son of God in a sense of their own." If the Unitarian will ascribe to Jesus all Bible attributes, names, works, and worship, we will not fight with him about scholastic words: but if he will not ascribe to him every thing which the first christians ascribed, and worship and adore him as the first christians did, we will reject him, not because of his private opinions, but because he refuses to honor Jesus as the first converts did, and withholds from him the titles and honors which God and his apostles have bestowed upon him.

In like manner, Stone was willing to receive the Trinitarian.

If he will ascribe to the Father, Son, and Holy Spirit, all that the first believers ascribed, and nothing more, we will receive him—but we will not allow him to apply scholastic and barbarous epithets to the Father, the Son, or the Holy Spirit. If he will dogmatize and become a factionist, we reject him, not because of his opinions, but because of his attempting to make a faction, or to lord it over God's heritage.[13]

III. The Nature of Christ and Christian Unity[14]

Stone asserted that the kind of unity existing between the Father and the Son is a prototype of the kind of unity which should exist in the churches. Christ prayed that his followers might be one "even" as he and the "Father were one."

The Father and Son are not one in substance; even if they were, our Lord did not pray "that believers should be one in this sense." The kind of unity existing between the Father and Son is threefold and suggests the kind of unity which should exist among his followers on earth:

(a) The Father and Son "are one in character." God is manifest in the flesh, so that when believers see this glory in Jesus, they are changed into the same image. The character of God is manifested in all the love, mercy, grace, goodness, and truth seen in the activity of Jesus. "This same character is formed in all believers by their being in the Father and the Son and the Father and Son in them."

(b) The Father and the Son are one in the spirit of love. Believers share this spirit of love. When they love the Father and the Son, they manifest that love in unreserved obedience to his commandments, they love one another "fervently" and they also love all mankind.

(c) The Father and the Son are one in operation—"one in the work of creation, providence and redemption." By becoming co-workers with the Father and Son in the work of redemption, believers become one with one another.

If believers were to analyze the unity of the Father and the Son and see clearly the character of God reflected in Jesus, they would themselves become partakers of the divine nature. They would manifest the divine spirit of love to one another as they cooperated in the divine work of redemption (by which I think Stone means interdenominational evangelism and missionary work). Such unity would help the world to see and believe in God.

One of Stone's most ardent convictions was that there would never be unity among professed Christians unless they possessed the spirit of Christ. A formal union on the Bible was impossible until a spirit of humility and forbearance existed in Christians. The spirit of Jesus was the test of religion in apostolic times, he felt, and when men have his spirit, they manifest love, joy, peace, and long-suffering. Faith, prayer, and baptism are only means of salvation and not until the test of love alone is "received and acted out" shall we see Christian union.

Summary[15]

I shall sum up Barton Stone's Christology simply but will have to forego my original plan to relate it to some modern Christologies.

1. Stone was neither orthodox in an ancient or modern sense nor was he a humanist. He had a high Christology. He believed in the pre-existent Christ and in what I should call a pre-existent

incarnation. In order to harmonize the Scriptures and common sense, he, with Isaac Watts, projected the "incarnation" back in heaven rather than on earth. This is unorthodox for it asserts that Christ's humanity does not belong to our order of created things. From a modern viewpoint, one of the biggest objections to Stone is not that his Christology is not high, but that it is so high that it undercuts the essential identification of Christ's humanity with our own. The real difficulty with Stone's doctrine of the nature of Christ is the same defect Athanasius pointed out with reference to the Arians: namely, that man's salvation came from a created being and not directly from God.

2. Jesus Christ is central to the Christian faith and is the primary source of authority in the Christian religion.

3. The death of Jesus did not change the character of God from wrath to love, but exerts a moral influence to change man.

4. Christ died not for the elect but for every man.

5. The acceptance of "Christ as the Son of God" rather than any metaphysical terms about him is alone essential for salvation.

6. No speculations concerning either the nature of Christ or his death ought to divide the Christian fellowship. The plain biblical statements regarding him, free from theological terms, are a sufficient test of Christian fellowship for men who throughout the ages have differed in their theories of Christology.

7. In my judgment, the experience of Stone with the Presbyterians in Kentucky over the doctrine of Christology illustrates the disadvantage of using creedal formulae to express what has been experienced by some Christians, but can never be adequately expressed in words. Blind conformity to creeds as a primary condition of membership in the church betrays their true purpose and often repels honest minds within and without the church. While each generation must express its faith in new ways, to freeze an expression of faith so that new interpretations are objectionable is to make impossible the knowledge of salvation through Christ which was the experience of the early Christians.

Note: Obviously, Stone's stress on accepting only Bible names on the nature and work of Christ is an oversimplification of the problems involved in finding a meaningful Christology. Men cannot be circumscribed to such poverty so long as they have questing minds. Dr. Robert L. Calhoun suggested in one of his classroom lectures a few years ago that modern theories of man's nature may help us find a significant modern Christology. Nevertheless, if the ecumenical ideal is to grow, our fathers have a contribution to be made here in the use of biblical terms as the basis for enough agreement to make ecumenical communication and activity possible. However, the stress on biblical terms must, in my judgment, be nonrigid and creative rather than dogmatic and legalistic.

NOTES

1. *Christian Messenger,* III (1829), p. 275.
2. Stone, *An Address,* p. 14.
3. See *The Works of Isaac Watts* (London: 1821), VI, pp. 586-587.
4. This is an expression I have coined to express the viewpoint of Watts.
5. McGready's Works, II, p. 241.
6. Baillie, D. M., *God Was in Christ* (New York: Charles Scribner's Sons, 1948), pp. 186-187.
7. Stone, *An Address,* p. 65.
8. Stone, *Atonement,* pp. 5-6.
9. Stone, *An Address,* p. 62.
10. *Christian Messenger,* IX (1835), p. 233.
11. *Christian Messenger,* VI (1832), p. 234.
12. *Millennial Harbinger,* IV (New Series; 1840), p. 296.
13. *Christian Messenger,* IV (1830), p. 166.
14. I am indebted to Dean Blakemore for helping me to see more validity in this concept of Stone than I have heretofore sensed.
15. For an extensive and authoritative treatment of Stone's thought on this and other issues as well as for an extensive bibliography, the reader is referred to Dr. West's *Barton Warren Stone, Early American Advocate of Christian Unity* (Nashville, Tennessee: The Disciples of Christ Historical Society, 1954).

4

Representative Preaching about Jesus

Two Generations of the Middle Period

HUNTER BECKELHYMER

THE selection of representative ministers in any generation is somewhat risky, and of necessity arbitrary. The selection of a representative sermon from among the works of each man chosen is even more arbitrary. The choice of the men is probably best made by a competent contemporary, and the selection of the sermon is best made by each man chosen. For Disciples of Christ, in the middle period of their history, such a collection of sermons is to be found in two volumes, edited by the same man, William T. Moore of Cincinnati, and published just a half-century apart: *The Living Pulpit of the Christian Church* in 1867, and *The New Living Pulpit of the Christian Church* in 1918. Together these two volumes present 56 sermons by as many distinguished ministers of an American communion from the younger contemporaries of its founders to the older contemporaries of ourselves. The substance of this paper is taken mostly from those sermons by those men. Not all of the sermons were on the subject of Jesus' person and place, but most of them included enough on that subject to indicate, at least, the writer's general views on it. At least, we may assume so.

There is a remarkable thread of accord binding together the ministers of the early and the latter days of this movement when they spoke of the deepest matters of the faith. That accord can be conveniently and accurately stated in the familiar slogan of Disciples of Christ: "No creed but Christ." None of these men used that slogan in these sermons, but many of them restated it with emphasis and fervor. The editor, W. T. Moore himself, in his contribution in the first volume, wrote,

> The Christian's Faith is not *doctrinal,* but *personal*; not belief in a *theory,* but in a Divine and glorious *character;* not the reception of a cold, lifeless *dogma,* but a hearty, earnest trust in one whose love is *stronger than a brother's:* who is "touched with a feeling of our infirmities"; who "knows our frame, and remembers that we are dust."[1]

"Instead of doctrines," agreed L. L. Pinkerton of Lexington, Kentucky, "He [God] offers to us a mysterious person, who draws the hearts of men to him because he is their brother, and who, at the same time commands their devotion, because he is "the only begotten Son of God."[2] The same sentiments are echoed by Charles Louis Loos of Bethany College:

> Doctrines do not save us; we are saved by Christ. Doctrines do not cleanse us from our sins; it is the efficacious blood of Christ. We are not converted to doctrines, but to God. We do not believe in doctrines, but in Christ. We are not baptized into them, but into Christ. We do not hope in them, trust in them, but in Christ Jesus the Lord.[3]

David Staats Burnet of Baltimore asserted that the apostles themselves had nothing to do with doctrines. "They preached a person, Jesus, made of a woman, as human as his mother, and having been declared to be the Son of God with power, as divine as his Father."[4]

One of the most thorough developments of this theme was that of Ely Vaughn Zollars in his address "The Creed that Needs No Revision." He laid down ten conditions that a creed must meet if it is to stand above the flux of theological thought and the erosion of time. It must possess universality; it must be simple; it must be profound; it must have vitality; it must be life-giving and practical; it must serve as a sufficient bond of fellowship between all Christian hearts; it must furnish a model for imitation; it must be an incarnation of God; it must be translatable into each man's own language without loss; and it must be a full and complete revelation of the glory of God. The one such creed, he concludes, "is not the Bible, but it is revealed in the Bible. It is not a philosophy, but a Divine personality. It is not a human conception, but a Divinely perfect revelation as embodied in a Divinely perfect life."[5] This creed, of course, is Jesus Christ.

It is remarkable that this almost vascular antipathy to formal theology continues among Disciples unto the third and fourth generation. William E. Crabtree of San Diego, in his sermon in Moore's second volume, fifty years after the above excerpts, said: "Jesus in his Kingship and Lordship is the universal and unrivaled creed, the one object of faith, and is accepted into the life more like to the silent rising of the tree sap, than by the compelling process of inflexible logic."[6]

Burris Jenkins of Kansas City asserted that "wherever one stands before the door of the church of Jesus Christ with analytical creed tests he is doing violence to the kingdom of God."[7] And Harry D. Smith of Phillips University finds in Jesus himself the attitude toward doctrine in general, which recurs so continually in the Disciples' tradition:

> He puts himself in the place of truth. . . . He exhibits himself as his own best credential. . . . No argument is necessary to prove to the eye that light is light nor to the human system that bread and water are what they are. Thus Jesus exhibits himself to the mind. He does not argue much in support of doctrines. He does not appeal to authority. He himself is the center of authority and he himself, and not a system of doctrines, is to be received and trusted.[8]

In all fairness one must concede to these gentlemen that they were honest in their low estimate of theological speculation and their lower estimate of normative doctrine. They were not being deliberately evasive, intellectually lazy, or religiously irresponsible. They held these things to be the source of quarrelsome sectarianism, which they were eager to transcend. "The Church will never be united in 'doctrines' of any kind," insisted L. L. Pinkerton. "She must be one in Christ Jesus, or divide still more, and remain divided till the Lord shall come."[9]

However, theology is easier to disavow than it is to avoid. If our esteemed and respected forebears did not discover this fact, at least they demonstrated it. We will have noticed that some of the quoted statements disparaging doctrine are in themselves profoundly doctrinal. The theology involved is, to be sure, biblical theology in that it is suggested or supported by holy scripture. But it is theology nonetheless. And we would not be unjust in labeling their presentation dogmatic. "Jesus the Nazarene, the son of the virgin, is the Christ, the Son of the living God," asserted Henry T. Anderson of Harrodsburg, Kentucky. "Whatever has been written of him must be received as true."[10] And D. S. Burnet, immediately after exonerating the apostles of any involvement in doctrine, makes this statement:

> "Other foundation can no man lay than that is laid, which is Jesus Christ"; that is, *Jesus Christ doctrinal*—Jesus Christ in this *formula* [the good confession], with its accompanying proofs, illustrations, and enforcements.[11]

And Charles Louis Loos, also quoted above in eloquent disavowal of doctrine, says later in the same sermon:

> It is Christ the crucified, as the God-man, the Savior of men, "the Lamb slain from the beginning," who shed his *atoning, expiating, sacrificial* blood for the sins of the world, *as the only price that purchased our redemption,* and thus to man the only hope in life and death. With the proud, Christ-degrading negations of Unitarianism, in every possible shape and form, from that highest type of ancient Arianism to that lowest of modern Socinianism, the words of Paul, in our text [Gal. 6:14] . . . are forever utterly irreconcilable.[12]

If this be not doctrine, what shall we call it?

If we are right in observing that these ministers were—albeit unwilling and unwitting—theologians, it is in order to examine their theology and doctrine for what it is. Their statements were indeed, for the most part, biblical. All, or almost all, of the titles they applied to Jesus were applied to him in the Bible. And all that the Bible said of him they said. King, Immanuel, Lord, Christ, Savior, Daysman, Mediator, Logos—all these they said of him synonymously and in apposition. And the implications of these several names were elaborated with feeling and eloquence. The title of Henry T. Anderson's sermon was "Jesus of Nazareth Is the Theanthropos," a postapostolic term, but his elaboration of two other titles is apostolic both in content and in devotion.

> That being, who is here called the Logos, was with God, and active in creation. . . . He did exist, then, before the world existed. He began the creation. He was before all things. He is not, then, as the Nicene Creed says, "God of God," but he was God. In the simplest, broadest, only sense, he is God: for to him is creation attributed. No one can create but God.
>
> . . . .
>
> He is Immanuel, God with us. In him God comes near us. . . . The incomprehensible grandeur and unsearchable greatness of God, now clad in flesh, are not such as to overawe our souls, and make us shrink within ourselves, terrified, alarmed, and awe-struck. No; through Jesus we draw nearer to God, for he has come very near to us.[13]

There are, however, three New Testament concepts of Christ's person and work which stand above the others in the usage of these men, and to them we now turn.

Son of God, Lamb of God, High Priest

By far the most frequently used title applied to Jesus was, of course, "the Son of God." This term appeared so universally in the sermons of these ministers of both the earlier and later generation, that it represents the most characteristic single confessional statement among them. And although they considered this "good confession" to be a sufficient doctrinal statement for church membership, the older generation of preachers at least did not understand the term "Son of God" in any vague or latitudinarian sense. It implied no minimal faith. "Jesus is not *a* son of God by creation, but *the* Son of God by birth—the only begotten of the Father," insisted D. S. Burnet.[14] This confession of faith, concurs Robert Graham of Fayetteville, Arkansas, is the whole gospel in epitome.[15] No unprejudiced mind can avoid the conclusion, he said,

> that the Gospel is the good news concerning the death, burial, and resurrection of the Lord Jesus; that these prove him to be the Christ, the Son of God; that this is the great central truth—the germ of spiritual life—which received into a good and honest heart, by faith, becomes the incorruptible seed of which we are begotten of God.[16]

In his sermon on the subject of "Reconciliation" between God and men, James Challen of Davenport, Iowa, said,

> The One Great Minister sent of God on this embassy of reconciliation is Jesus Christ, the Son of the living God. He is his special servant in accomplishing this work. He came from heaven with full powers to treat with men on this subject. He represents all the dignity, authority, and glory of the Father who sent him; and all the weakness, poverty and suffering of those he came to reconcile. In his person, we see all that is divine in his Father, and all that is human in his mother.[17]

A second term applied to Jesus almost as frequently as the one discussed above, is "the Lamb of God." The confession of John the Baptist is used almost as often as the confession of Peter in the sermons which these older brethren chose to represent them. Here the meaning is in no sense honorific. These men are explicit that they mean a victim sacrificed on an altar to appease God. "He is the antitype of every bleeding victim slain as a sin offering from the very morning of time," said George W. Longan of Sedalia, Missouri.[18] "Without the shedding of blood, there could be no remission" (Heb. 9:22), quoted William Baxter of New Lisbon, Ohio. "Man must die, or the Son of the Highest must bleed. God gives the just for the unjust, and the spotless Lamb of God is slain for us."[19] The compelling grip of this concept is demonstrated by a statement from O. A. Burgess of Indianapolis:

"Behold the Lamb of God that taketh away the sin of the world." Toward this the whole life of Christ tended, and for the consummation of this even his life was offered up. Not an offering burnt upon Jewish altar, not a lamb bled by the hand of Jewish priest, that did not look toward the offering of an acceptable sacrifice for the forgiveness of sin. Whatever details of doctrine may hereafter appear here, at the very threshold of every religious inquiry, stands the unalterable truth, that without the shedding of blood, there is no remission of sin.[20]

In one statement, T. P. Haley of Louisville suggested this concept as an alternate "good confession." "He who accepts Jesus as the Lamb of God, slain for sinners, and yields to his authority expressed in the commandments given to the Gospel, is a Christian.[21] References to the blood of Christ as being cleansing were too numerous to catalog.

Another concept of the role of Christ which was developed by preachers of both generations is that of his priesthood. The texts, of course, were from Hebrews. John Shackelford of Cincinnati made just this the subject of his contribution: the qualifications of a priest are that he have power and ability to save; that he have purity; and that he have sympathy. Christ, having all of these qualities to the utmost degree, is "the only perfect Priest." For example,

Men sympathize with their class. Our sympathies are contracted. The rich often can not sympathize with the poor, the learned with the ignorant, men with children. But Christ can sympathize with all. . . . Christ can sympathize with women in their trials and temptations.[22]

Then he concludes, "Christ reveals the mercy and compassion of the Father of all. It is not more true that there is one God than that there is one Mediator between God and men, the man Christ Jesus."[23] Commenting on an Old Testament passage (Zech. 6:13) A. S. Hayden of Hiram, Ohio, said,

The oracle which reveals Jesus Christ as a *priest on a throne* unfolds more fully than any other the counsels which originated man's recovery. It sets him forth in the highest possible glory, combining the royalty with the priesthood—a kingly priest, a sacerdotal monarch, ruling the universe in reference to the salvation of the human race.[24]

Governmental Analogies

In discussing the place of Christ in God's scheme of things, and in elaborating upon the terms of salvation to men, these older ministers made frequent use also of analogies and metaphors from the area of government. Indeed, the term "government" appeared frequently in their sermons, along with the words "authority," "obedience," and "judgment."

In his sermon entitled "Atonement," Thomas Munnell of Mt. Sterling, Kentucky, combined in an interesting and unusual way the theories of Anselm and of Grotius in explaining the work of Christ. God wants to be merciful, but must be just. This is the problem posed for God by human sin. "If justice be exacted, every sinner will feel the bottom of perdition; if mercy prevail at the expense of justice and the law, it would ruin the universe."[25] Then Munnell drew this illuminating analogy. It is as though there were a rebellion in a realm, in which the 10,000 rebels deserved and drew the sentence of exile. But the government wants to be merciful. So the prince of the realm, who is both innocent and "governmentally worthy," voluntarily assumes and serves the sentence imposed upon the rebels, and in their stead. This makes possible mercy to the rebels, while still upholding the dignity and authority of the law. In due time the prince becomes king. The rebels are pardoned if they accept what their sovereign has done for them, and respond with gratitude and obedience. If not, they deserve and will receive their punishment.[26]

W. H. Hopson of Richmond, Virginia, using governmental analogy to the fullest, called the great commission "The Savior's Amnesty Proclamation."

Now the Crucified One is crowned King, clothed with supreme power, and the scepter of authority is passed over into his hand.

Now, he makes laws in his own right as Soverign of the heaven and the earth. The first exercise of authority under his reign as absolute monarch was to enact the conditional amnesty above mentioned.[27]

Then he adds, "The great commission contains the New Testament statutory law with reference to the pardon of rebel sinners."[28]

Joseph King of Alleghany City, Pennsylvania, agrees.

The proof of Christ's having all judgment committed to him is his resurrection from the dead. . . . Now, Christ is governing the universe, administering the affairs of his vast empire, and interceding for his people; but . . . he will come . . . and, laying aside other things, will devote the necessary length of time to one thing—judging "the world in righteousness."[29]

All judicial authority has been given to Christ; and the Father's purpose, in giving him such authority, is that his Son may be honored equally with himself. Christ is to receive equal adoration with God; and, wearing *our* nature as well as the Divine, he is thus an "impartial Judge."[30]

In discussing Christ's authority, Henry T. Anderson said that we can conceive of only three kinds of authority and no more: legislative, judicial, and executive. In Christ's person is centered all of this.[31] The corollary of this type of analogy is that man's part in the whole process is acknowledging the authority of Christ, and obeying his commands, baptism in particular.

Although the foregoing are the predominant patterns in the preaching of the older generation of ministers concerning the person and work of Jesus, two other themes should be mentioned. David Walk of Paris, Kentucky, elaborated the theme of the Second Adam.

. . . Independent of our own volitions, and irrespective of moral considerations, we die because Adam died, and on precisely the same terms we shall all be made alive in Christ.

. . . In short, whatever man lost in Adam, independent of his own volitions, he will, in like manner, find in Christ[32] [i.e., both physical and spiritual life].

> . . . [Jesus] kept that law [the moral law of God] perfectly, that he might become the Savior of man, who could not keep it. . . .
>
> . . . God has accepted the obedience of Christ, has accepted the offering which he made of himself, that man, through the obedience of faith, may be made righteous *in* Christ Jesus.[33]

Of all the ministers whose works appeared in these volumes, William K. Pendleton, Alexander Campbell's son-in-law, came the nearest to developing a full-orbed trinitarian theology. He called the period of the universe before the fall of man, the dispensation of the Father. All time from Adam's fall through the crucifixion is the dispensation of the Son. This dispensation ends when "Upon the altar of his divinity, he [the Son] offers the sacrifice of a perfect humanity." With the glorification of the Son a new era is opened up, the dispensation or economy of the Holy Spirit.[34]

These excerpts from characteristic sermons of characteristic ministers among Disciples of Christ in the midnineteenth century should serve to dispel the notion that they were not theologians. Whatever they thought themselves to be, they reasoned from and elaborated the biblical material concerning the deep things of God and men, and particularly the person and place of Jesus of Nazareth. A modern reader is somewhat amazed and amused by the supreme confidence with which they spelled out the workings of the divine mind, and the details of the divine plan. Although there were occasional hymns of devotion to Christ, and an occasional recognition that "great is the mystery of godliness, God manifest in the flesh,"[35] there were many more assertions of his authority, and much wider use of such definitive words as formula, proposition, plan, ordinance, law. Faith was defined primarily as belief and obedience, only occasionally as trust and loving response. These men were singularly untroubled by such problems of biblical study as whether a concept was from Isaiah, Zechariah, the synoptics, the Fourth Gospel, Paul's epistles, the pastorals, Hebrews, or Revelation. But then, who was troubled about these things in those days?

A Transition in Emphasis

One man, however, stood so far from his contemporaries among Disciples of this period in spirit and faith that he is in a class by himself. Belonging with these men in time, he belongs with the later group in thought. He was literally a half-century ahead of his time. That man is Alexander Procter, of Independence, Missouri. In his sermon, "Following Jesus," he took this position:

> The whole of what is meant by the great fact of the incarnation is in this: God wanted men to follow him; to live like He lived; to think like He thought; to follow the activities that are divine. But how could men do that unless He became a man; unless He showed Himself to us in human form; unless He came to us in our way of living; unless He thought, lived, felt, rejoiced, and wept as we do? Before this could be said to the human race the incarnation was an absolute necessity. And this is what we have in . . . these gospels.[36]

Procter died in 1900, and a memorial address in his honor was given before the Missouri State Convention at Moberly by his friend T. P. Haley, who differed from Procter in theology. It included this summary:

> . . . While he did not use the stock phrases of the day, such as "very God and very man," "God the Son" and the "Triune God," no man, living or dead, in his preaching, ever exalted Christ more as Immanuel—God with us—than did he.
>
> . . . .
>
> . . . He taught that under every dispensation the sinner was saved from his sins only when he repented and because he repented, and not because of faith in any theology or *any governmental provision.* As an *enabling act* Christ revealed the wonderful love and goodness of God, and the goodness of God "leadeth to repentance." Ordinances were therefore of value chiefly because they *exhibited the presence of that faith* in the soul that brings the physical conditions that enable God to be Just and the Justifier of him that believes. He did believe that Christ was the Daysman through whom was brought the atonement. . . . He taught and felt that a man saved from sin by the power of the *life* of Jesus Christ was safe in all worlds in time and in eternity.[37]

This comment on Procter's theology serves very well as our introduction to the thought of the men represented in Moore's second volume, *The New Living Pulpit of the Christian Church.*

If the thought of Alexander Procter belongs with his brethren of the following generation, the thought of P. H. Welshimer seems more akin to that of the men who had gone before him. "Christ has given his [God's] law for men," he said. "God went to the trouble of sending his Only Begotten Son down to this world to be the Great Law-Giver. He has given a plain, Gospel statement and he has said to the whole round world, 'This is my law; do certain things and you will be a Christian; you will be in Christ.' "[38] This statement is noteworthy because it was the only one of its kind in the second volume of sermons. In the fifty years between the two collections of sermons, a sea-change had taken place in the Christology of the Disciple ministry. The term Lamb of God almost disappeared. The term Son of God was still the predominant designation for Jesus. It was still used for the most part in a singular sense, but not altogether in the singular by all the men, as had been true of the earlier group. Not many of the later preachers went so far as did Herbert L. Willett, and J. J. Haley. Dr. Willett affirmed that "Jesus knew more of God than any other who has passed this way." Still, he maintained,

> That timeless and blessed relation of sonship which Jesus first experienced has become the haunting dream of the noblest spirits of the ages. And not in vain has been the quest. Into that intimacy there is open way for any who are smitten by the great desire. The discovery of the secret is hidden only from those who will not see.[39]

In his discussion of the Lord's Prayer, J. J. Haley of Cynthiana, Kentucky, said that "[God] reveals himself to me, not only in words, but in and through the incarnate personality of his Son, who became the equivalent of God to my soul in ways and words that I can understand."[40] He then pointed out that there are seven spirits displayed in the Lord's Prayer: the filial spirit, the reverential spirit, the missionary spirit, the obedient spirit, the trustful spirit, the forgiving spirit, the spirit of holiness—realized in their absolute completeness only in Christ.[41] Then he added this rather startling statement:

> Embody these seven spirits in a human personality and you have Jesus Christ—as he was in the days of his incarnate life. . . . If a man have all this, if he possesses all these characteristics, what is he? A Christian? Yes, he is more than a Christian; he is a Christ.[42]

But if these represent a high watermark, or a low watermark, the bearing of this generation of Disciple ministers was in this as direction. F. W. Burnham, president of the American Christian Missionary Society, asked, "May it not be that one of the chief differences between the life of Jesus and that of the average man with respect to the accomplishment of purpose—the attainment of true success—lies in the hold which the sense of moral obligation takes upon his life? . . . The force which moved Him was the sense of the Father's will and of a weak world's need.[43]

In general the explanations of Christ's role in God's plan and man's affairs were given less precisely and more pragmatically by the later generation of preachers. There is none of the old-time precision in the statement of Frank Dowling of California when he said:

> Whatever may be our view as to the necessity and meaning of Christ's death, . . . we cannot escape the feeling . . . that Christ's death has a meaning that attaches to no other death, and somehow is related to our peace and pardon and everlasting life.[44]

But none of the old-time preachers ever felt the need to defend Christ's authority so pragmatically as did Dowling when he said:

> The life he lived, the teaching he gave, the signs he wrought, the resurrection he attained, the influence he exerted and still exerts, establish the divine claims he made and justify our reason when we make his word the end of controversy.[45]

Edgar DeWitt Jones of Detroit was not precise when he said:

> . . . God's reaching out to man, and man's reaching out after God —these two endeavors meet in Jesus Christ. A mediation Godward and manward, satisfactory, sustaining, imcomparable. whatever theology one may have of the work and office of Jesus Christ, every sincere student of his life must concede this mediatorial ministry of the Nazarene.[46]

But his argument was thoroughly pragmatic when he concluded: "The world has never been the same since Jesus came; life has never been precisely as it was before; death has lost somewhat its darkness and its tragedy."

B. A. Abbott of St. Louis lacked the precision of the earlier Christologies when he said:

> By his life and by his revelation he interprets those undefined longings of man's heart that have made him struggle toward the light and toward the heights. He satisfies earth's hunger for love by the sufferings of the cross. Over against the change and decay of time he sets the fact of the resurrection.[47]

But his proof of the resurrection is pragmatic:

> His perpetual presence in the world is proved daily by exalted experiences and the noble deeds done in his name. He is the living Christ and he is with his people all the days even unto the end of the world. . . . Our attitude to Him determines our destiny.[48]

Less Legalistic, More Lyrical

Of a piece with the change in emphasis and argument here noted are other trends. In their statements about Jesus the later generation were less legalistic and more lyrical, less dogmatic and more devotional. There was less speculation about what the death of Christ had effected, and more testimony to the appeal his life exerted and exerts. The old governmental analogies all but disappeared from the preaching of these ministers. When they referred to Christ's supreme authority, as all of them did, they referred not to the authority of status, but the authority of influence. "He is the embodiment of truth," wrote I. N. McCash of Phillips University. "Christ, the incarnation of that essential truth which must be appropriated by men, is perfect satisfaction to the human mind and heart. . . . Christ has gone like the sun at evening beyond our vision, but like the unhidden presence of the sun reflected in the moon, he is imaged in the life of his followers."[49]

In the same vein J. H. Garrison of *The Christian-Evangelist* wrote of Christ,

> *He lived a life of such wonderful beauty and perfection, of such marvelous love and self-sacrifice, and sealed it with a death so sacrificial, and a resurrection so victorious, as to have revealed God, and man, and human duty, and human destiny.*[50]

There is no trace of legal mechanisms in Dr. Garrison's comment upon the atonement. It was by Christ's own triumphant life and death and resurrection "and rising to heights of supreme power and influence on the life of the world, [that] men came to realize the essential dignity of human nature and its mighty possibilities when brought into union with God."

> Never did the world know the exceeding sinfulness of sin until it nailed Christ to the cross. Never did the world know the height and depth and breadth of the love of God for mankind until he gave his only begotten Son to die, the just for the unjust, that he might bring us to himself. . . . It took the sacrificial life and death of the sinless Son of God, and Son of Man, to *bring this truth home to the hearts of men.*[51]

To all of which F. W. Burnham's comment is a natural conclusion:

> So God commands us to accept his Son, not as an arbitrary enactment of Supreme Legislation, but as the essential condition of spiritual soul-building. We must accept Him, and embody His spirit or salvation from sin is impossible.[52]

What Burnham said of acceptance of Christ, Hugh McLellan of San Antonio said of the other "steps" in the traditional "scheme of salvation," which McLellan felt had become degraded into mechanical, arbitrary, and legalistic forms. They are indeed, "conditions of salvation," he said, but not "cogs in the wheel of redemption." We are saved "not by a system or a plan, but by a person."[53]

Impact of Modern Scholarship

There can be no doubt that all these men had felt the impact of the biblical criticism of their day, and were profoundly influenced by it. Their sermons reflect their sense of necessity to reground their central confession of Jesus' lordship from its earlier basis in the verbal absolutism of scripture to the more difficult and complicated, but more convincing, basis of human history and Christian experience. In general, they made this transition with cogency and power. Although Z. T. Sweeney of Columbus, Indiana, met this issue head on, his attempt to resolve it was something less than satisfying.

> . . . The arguments against the divinity of Christ all run at last into the one great objection, that he had a supernatural origin [miraculous conception]. This is true. But was there ever any other kind of origin? Did ever anything originate naturally? . . . Everything began supernaturally. Man began supernaturally, and Christ began like everything else.[54]

Sweeney then attempted to refute the contention of Strauss that Jesus was built into a divinity by his disciples. It is historical fact that Jesus died around A.D. 34, and that he was worshiped by Christian churches as divine by A.D. 60. This is *not enough time,* declared Sweeney, to build a deity. "They [the disciples] lived nearer to him than we do to President Garfield, and there certainly has not been time enough for President Garfield to grow from humanity into an accepted divinity."[55]

George Hamilton Combs of Kansas City may have been premature in detecting "a return to the Supernatural Christ . . . a return not to a saintly teacher but to a divine Lord . . . a return not only to a king but to a Savior . . . a return not only to the preacher on the green mountain sides but to him who could say, 'Thy sins be forgiven thee,' and 'if any man believeth in me, he shall never die.' " But none can escape Combs' searching question:

. . . Accept if you will, the easy explanation that Jesus was of purely human birth, lived a purely human life, died a purely human death, and then answer the tremendous question, how could such a life have so profoundly influenced the age in which he lived and all the ages that have followed? How did this scepterless teacher come to the lordship over all?[56]

On this matter, most of this group of distinguished and thoughtful ministers would do well and be pleased to let George A. Campbell of St. Louis be their spokesman:

. . . We must restore to ourselves faith, vital, compelling faith in the absolute leadership and redemption of Jesus Christ. . . .

. . . .

Criticism cannot rob history of his personality and power, nor of our own consciousness of him.

Christ is the New Testament. And he is the message for the Church. He is the gospel.

In the New Testament we find this sublime personality conscious of God, conscious of his own holiness and of his Godlikeness, and his redeeming power for all men. Here is no personality that depends upon the technicalities of historical or textual criticism. . . . We have done them too much honor.

. . . .

Christ is a living Spirit. The human soul experiences him. The writers of the New Testament defined the gospel as Power. It has ever been that. Through emotion, mediation, prayer, the soul finds its way to the living Christ. He speaks to it great sustaining words of conviction. "Once I was blind but now I can see," is the testimony of countless souls. The power of Christ redeeming and keeping and holding to the eternal things is evidence that no science can destroy.[57]

Peter Ainslie of Baltimore affirmed the efforts of the new scholarship, with complete confidence that his faith would endure it.

Nothing is too sacred in the life of Jesus to be investigated. He invited it, saying: "Come and see." Lift every curtain from the manger to the ascension. Crowd in upon every scene with a thousand questions and be prepared to follow your conclusion. Be free—free in the atmosphere of a genuine companionship with Christ, which is satisfied with nothing less than oneness of life with Him. The issue is too great to be influenced by the superstition of the Middle Ages. My peace here, my life yonder, hangs upon my knowledge of Jesus Christ and the hope that He gives me of immortality and eternal life.[60]

Jesus Christ, the Abiding Center of Faith

Whatever be our feelings about the faith of our fathers, and the way they expressed it, they demonstrated that a minimal confession does not mean a minimal faith. Though all would have stoutly resisted making any more than the good confession a requirement for church membership, it was not the extent of their Christology. Behind that simple confessional tie, there were Christologies as complicated and as simple, as high and as low, as orthodox and as unorthodox as any in all Christendom. The economy of words carried a wealth of meaning.

Another observation which deserves to be made is that in the transition from the days of biblical literalism to the days of biblical criticism, the place of Christ in the thinking of the ministers did not decline. If anything, it was elevated. The older brethren lavished upon Jesus both biblical and nonbiblical titles, rank, and offices. The later generation lavished upon him testimony of personal devotion and love. This is not to say that devotion was lacking in the older generation, or that titles were not used by the younger. But the shift in emphasis is unmistakable. The older brethren used the Bible to defend the Christ. The younger generation called upon Christ as the defense of the Bible. There is no downgrading of the person and place of Jesus, in such a transition. Quite the contrary is true. He becomes truly the pioneer and perfecter of our faith.

As William E. Crabtree testified,

> . . . To gather up in himself the light of God for us, sufficient to lead us out of night into the light of life; to bring it down to the

plane where we live, make it intelligible, make it warm, make it compelling, this was the mission of Jesus Christ. . . . Because it is easy and natural to understand and love Jesus Christ, it becomes easy and natural to understand and love the Almighty God and to possess toward him the spirit of sons and daughters by which we cry, Abba, Father.[59]

And as L. L. Pinkerton warned,

. . . Let these questions be discussed, then, by those who may have taste and talent for such discussion; discussed in books and periodicals, by the fireside and in the lyceums; but let us not *evaluate our reasonings into Divine oracles,* and make them causes of strifes and divisions among the people of God.[60]

NOTES

1. William T. Moore, "Faith and Sight," in Wiliam T. Moore, *The Living Pulpit of the Christian Church* (St. Louis: Christian Publishing Co., 1867), p. 551.
2. Lewis L. Pinkerton, "Jesus the First and the Last," in Moore, *op. cit.,* p. 128.
3. Charles L. Loos, "Glorying in the Cross Only,' in Moore, *op. cit.,* p. 462.
4. David Staats Burnet, "The Good Confession," in Moore, *op. cit.,* p. 50.
5. E. V. Zollars, "The Creed that Needs No Revision," in *World's Congress Addresses* (Chicago: S. J. Clarke, 1893), p. 144.
6. William Edgar Crabtree, "True Apostolic Succession," in Moore, *The New Living Pulpit of the Christian Church* (St. Louis: Christian Board of Publication, 1918), p. 242.
7. Burris Jenkins, "Violence to the Kingdom of God," in Moore, *New Pulpit, op. cit.,* p. 311.
8. Harry D. Smith, "Rest," in Moore, *New Pulpit, op. cit.,* p. 381.
9. L. L. Pinkerton, *op. cit.,* p. 127.
10. Henry T. Anderson, "Jesus of Nazareth Is the Theanthropos," in Moore, *Pulpit,* p. 73.
11. David Staats Burnet, "The Good Confession," in Moore, *Pulpit,* p. 52.
12. Charles Louis Loos, *op. cit.,* p. 467.
13. Henry T. Anderson, *op. cit.,* pp. 80, 76.
14. David Staats Burnet, *op. cit.,* p. 64.
15. Robert Graham, "Regeneration," in Moore, *Pulpit,* p. 224.
16. *Ibid.,* p. 217.
17. James Challen, "Reconciliation," in Moore, *Pulpit,* p. 133.
18. George W. Longan, "The Conditions of the Gospel Reasonable," in Moore, *Pulpit,* p. 192.
19. William Baxter, "The Love of God," in Moore, *Pulpit,* p. 439.
20. Otis Asa Burgess, "What Must I Do to Be Saved?" in Moore, *Pulpit,* p. 170.
21. Thomas Preston Haley, "Building on the One Foundation," in Moore, *Pulpit,* p. 367.
22. John Shackelford, "The Priesthood of Christ," in Moore, *Pulpit,* pp. 393f., 396.
23. *Ibid.,* p. 398.

24. Amos Sutton Hayden, "Conscience and Christianity," in Moore, *Pulpit,* p. 499.
25. Thomas Munnell, "Atonement," in Moore, *Pulpit,* p. 95.
26. *Ibid.,* pp. 95f.
27. Winthrop Hartly Hopson, "Baptism Essential to Salvation," in Moore, *Pulpit,* p. 285.
28. *Ibid.,* p. 287.
29. Joseph King, "The Judgment to Come," in Moore, *Pulpit,* pp. 583f.
30. *Ibid.,* p. 585.
31. Henry T. Anderson, *op. cit.,* p. 75.
32. David Walk, "Death and Life," in Moore, *Pulpit,* p. 417.
33. *Ibid.,* pp. 423, 424.
34. William Kimbrough Pendleton, "The Ministry of the Holy Spirit," in Moore, *Pulpit,* pp. 311f.
35. Lewis L. Pinkerton, *op. cit.,* in Moore, *Pulpit,* pp. 111f.
36. Alexander Procter, *The Witness of Jesus and Other Sermons* (St. Louis: Christian Publishing Co., 1901), p. 167.
37. *Ibid.,* pp. 393, 397f. T. P. Haley's memorial address for Alexander Procter at Missouri Convention in Moberly, October, 1900. (Italics mine.)
38. P. H. Welshimer, "A Sermon to the Moral Man," *New Pulpit,* pp. 364f.
39. Herbert L. Willett, "What Does God Do?" in Moore, *New Pulpit,* p. 76 .
40. J. J. Haley, "Ideals of the Lord's Prayer," in Moore, *New Pulpit,* p. 291.
41. *Ibid.,* pp. 293f.
42. *Ibid.,* pp. 294f.
43. Frederick W. Burnham, "The Compulsion of Responsibility," in Moore, *New Pulpit,* p. 266.
44. Frank M. Dowling, "The Appeal of the Cross," in Moore, *New Pulpit,* p. 219.
45. *Ibid.,* p. 221.
46. Edgar DeWitt Jones, "The Ministry of Mediation," in Moore, *New Pulpit,* pp. 135f.
47. Byrdine Akers Abbott, "The Call of the Divine," in Moore, *New Pulpit,* p. 336.
48. *Ibid.*
49. Isaac Newton McCash, "Established in Present Truth," in Moore, *New Pulpit,* p. 215.
50. James Harvey Garrison, "The Light of Life; or God's Method of Revelation," in Moore, *New Pulpit,* p. 85.
51. *Ibid.,* pp. 83f. See also Allen Moore, "The House Beautiful," in Moore, *New Pulpit,* p. 399.
52. Frederick W. Burnham, *op. cit.,* in Moore, *New Pulpit,* p. 275.
53. Hugh McLellan, "The Philosophy of the Conditions of Salvatian," in Moore, *New Pulpit,* p. 143.
54. Zachary T. Sweeney, "First Principles," in Moore, *New Pulpit,* p. 57.
55. *Ibid.,* p. 58.
56. George Hamilton Combs, "The Return to Faith," in Moore, *New Pulpit,* pp. 160f.
57. George Alexander Campbell, "Conviction," in Moore, *New Pulpit,* pp. 342f.
58. Peter Ainslie, "The Pain of Thinking," in Moore, *New Pulpit,* pp. 342f.
59. William Edgar Crabtree, "True Apostolic Succession," in Moore, *New Pulpit,* p. 243.
60. Lewis L. Pinkerton, *op. cit.,* in Moore, *Pulpit,* p. 107.

5

The Revelation of God in Jesus Christ

With Reference to the Phrase "No Creed but Christ"

Frank N. Gardner

TOGETHER with other Christians, members of the Christian Churches believe that God revealed himself in Jesus Christ. In contrast with most churches, Christian Churches have rejected specific formulations of this belief as a necessary condition for Christian fellowship. It is pertinent to examine the reasons why they have done so, and whether such a position is relatively adequate for today.

The Problem of Definition

Historically and presently when we use the term "revelation," we run into difficulties. What do Christians mean by the term "revelation"? While Christians universally are agreed that God revealed himself in Jesus Christ, historically they have disagreed as to whether or not God has revealed himself in other religions. Those who have held that he has, have disagreed as to the extent to which God has revealed himself to the faithful in other religions.

Christians have disagreed as to whether God has revealed himself in nature. Those who hold that he has, disagree among themselves as to the degree and extent to which God has so revealed himself. Christians have disagreed as to whether or not God has revealed himself in cosmic history, earth history, or whether his revelation is confined to human history. Those who confine the revelation in history to human history, differ as to the degree and extent to which God has revealed himself in human history. Some, for instance, hold that God reveals himself in all human history. Others hold that God revealed himself in certain great and mighty acts. Still others hold that God's revelation in human history is limited to the revelation in Jesus Christ, or one great and mighty act in human history, rather than several.

Again, although Christians have agreed that God revealed himself in Jesus Christ, they have disagreed as to whether the revelation in Jesus Christ is final and ultimate. Is there more and/or better to come? The answers are by no means in agreement.

Further, Christians have disagreed as to whether God continues to reveal himself. Some believe that "the building has been completed and the roof put on," to use Berdaiev's expression. Others hold that God's revelation continues. As to precisely how it continues, those holding to this viewpoint are not in agreement.

Our historical situation in regard to the doctrine of revelation is immediately seen to be considerably muddied. When we turn to the other signs involved in such a propositional statement as "God revealed himself in Jesus Christ," analysis reveals that all other signs in this statement have likewise been interpreted in a multitude of ways. For instance, when we say, "God revealed himself in Jesus Christ," we assert something to be the case. It is a proposition and can be checked for truth or falsity. In addition to the sign "revealed," the sign "God" in the proposition has meant for Christians all kinds of things. Among the meanings which this one term has been given are the meanings involved in varieties of classical theism, deism, pantheism, panentheism, empirical theism, and shades of meaning within each. If only one sign such as this sign "God" has had historically and, in our contemporary world, so many different meanings, there is a real question which can be raised as to whether the sign has any *denotatum* at all, or whether the sign carries simply emotional feeling on the part of the person who uses it. In a similar way, historically and at present, the signs "Jesus" and "Christ" are given multiple meanings. Quite frequently the proposition "God revealed himself in Jesus Christ" is given a reverse twist. That is, since many Christians believe that they already know what God is like, that is, God is omnipotent, omniscient, infinite, perfect in all respects, etc., then "Jesus" is a term which must be understood with such meanings. Similarly the term "Christ" may for some persons mean simply "Messiah," while for others the term "Christ" is used as a synonym for "God."

We must conclude that simply to enunciate that one believes that "God revealed himself in Jesus Christ" says nothing—unless one understands the meaning of the various signs which are involved in the proposition. We must further conclude that since up to the present time there is considerable lack of unanimity on the precise meaning of any one of these signs considering Christianity as a whole, the question of the truth of the proposition *per se* is one which would yield a field day for our philosophical analysts. It might be that since each sign has no *denotatum* capable of being pointed out by Christians which is commonly accepted by Christians as being the *denotatum* of a particular sign, the group of signs form nothing but a "collection of nonsense syllables" as such philosophical analysts would say.

By no means is it to be understood that particular Christians do not have very definite meanings which they give to the signs in the proposition. Many have an abundance of emotional certainty that their own interpretations of the signs are correct. The statement is in the overwhelming majority of cases an expressional statement—not a propositional statement at all. Moreover, most theologians confuse the expression of a feeling with a matter of truth and knowledge. We must face the fact that emotional certainty or an expression of feeling is not a guarantee of either truth or adequacy.

In addition, considerable bodies of Christians have arrived at "official" interpretations of these signs which are supposedly binding on members of such bodies. However, it is a notorious fact that thousands of adherents of such bodies pay only lip service to the interpretations which are supposed to be binding. It is even more notorious that the various bodies find it more than difficult to agree with one another. As a result there is a search for the "minimal" ideas on which all can seemingly agree. To the extent that this can be done there is the naïve belief that some kind of "unity" has been achieved.

Historically, because individual Christians or bodies of Christians were confident that they and they alone had the "correct" and "true" interpretation of this proposition, they sought to impose their formulation upon all those who claimed to be Christian and to insist that their formulation be normative for the church.

As a result those who refused to assent, if they were in the minority, became "heretics." Those in the majority became "orthodox." The history of post-Nicea is a humorous and yet tragic illustration of the way in which different parties became "orthodox" or "heretical" depending upon who could muster the most votes or get the backing of the temporary political sovereign.

Churches and sects developed until by the dawn of the nineteenth century on the American frontier they could be numbered by the dozens. Since that time they have multiplied and I doubt if a really accurate listing of all the Christian bodies has been made. Some such "bodies" are composed of single congregations. Why throughout Christian history has such diversity risen? For one thing, Christians have never developed a commonly agreed upon method of inquiry. Although there has been a rapid agreement by scholars in many fields other than religion upon a common method of inquiry, Christians have not done so. Truth is variously determined by "authority," by "immediate intuition," by the "scientific method," by "emotional grasping," by rational processes of "deductive logic," or, as in some instances, by "signs and wonders."

Until Christians can develop *a commonly agreed-upon method of inquiry* for determining the truth or falsity of beliefs, opinions, and propositions, we face the fact that this diversity will continue and will increase. Christian theologians need to work at the problem of distinguishing between mere awareness and what is called truth and knowledge. Until a critical method of inquiry can be developed which will (and can) be used with precision, this diversity will continue. Whether continuing diversity is "bad" or "good" is another question and is not relevant to our present discussion.

For another thing, Christians have never solved the problem of the relation of "reason" to "faith." As Toynbee has correctly seen, Christianity arose out of the conflict between Syriac and Hellenistic cultures. As it took form, it contained vestigial remainders of both Hellenism and Semitism. The Greeks contributed to the world a love for logical thinking and an eagerness for truth and clarity of thinking. The Near East, particularly Judaism, contributed a zest for righteousness and for religious devotion. The wedding of these two in the dawn of Christianity did not result in a harmonious marriage. Paul was usually hostile to Hellenism: "The Jews demand signs and the Greeks seek wisdom; but we preach Christ crucified, a stumbling block to Jews and folly to Gentiles" (1 Cor. 1:22), and it would seem that he almost gloated over the idea that God has "made foolish the wisdom of this world." In return, non-Christian intellectuals such as Tacitus thought Christianity was actually foolish. Tacitus referred to it as a "pernicious superstition," notable, said he, for its "hatred of the human race." To Suetonius, Christianity was a "mischievous superstition," and Pliny regarded it as a "depraved and extravagant superstition." These three intellectuals so judged Christianity because of its aversion to logical clarity and consistency. Tertullian replied passionately "Away with all projects for a 'Stoic,' a 'Platonic,' or a 'dialectic' Christianity. After Jesus Christ we desire no subtle theories, no acute inquiries after the gospels." Then he summed up his own attitude in the famous phrase, "I believe *because* it is absurd" (a notion which later fascinated certain medievalists and Kierkegaard).

Following Tertullian's path which had been earlier blazed by Paul, many Christians have tended to be suspect of reason, scorning it as useless or even dangerous. (Luther called reason "that filthy whore, covered with scabs and diseased.") In our time Continental theology has played variations upon this theme—so much that an American writer, L. H. De Wolf, has written a book entitled *The Religious Revolt Against Reason.* Yet, again glancing backwards at early Christian history we find fully as many great "Fathers" who placed the utmost faith in reason. Justin, called Martyr, waxed eloquent at this point and declared that "those who live according to reason are Christians, even though they are accounted atheists." In logical sequence he thus concluded that Socrates and other eminent Greeks and Romans were among the "saved." Clement of Alexandria asserted that the truth of the matter was that "philosophy was a preparation, paving the way towards perfection in Christ." Eventually the synthesis of the Hellenistic and Syriac strains resulted in the doctrine that reason is necessary for elucidating the basic truths revealed in the Bible. As is well known, this is the official stand of the Roman Catholic Church.

It is intriguing to note during the Middle Ages the emphasis upon reason made by Peter Abelard at a time when many theologians were insisting that the more absurd a doctrine is, the greater is the faith of the Christian who believes it.

In our time the emphasis upon reason is being made by various English and American philosophers and the theologians, most of whom are liberals or neo-liberals—among whom we include the "naturalists." The unresolved relation of reason to faith has been complicated by the fact that Christian doctrine could not acutally be subjected to critical intelligence to determine its validity. The ultimate criterion for the truth of its propositions was the authority of the apostolic tradition as it has been incorporated in the closed Canon. As early as the time of Ignatius we find this expressed in his letter to the Philadelphians, "Of some who say: 'Unless I find it in the originals in the gospel, I do not believe,' and when I said to them, 'It is written,' they answered me, 'That settles it.' " (*Phila.* 82 and cf. *Smyrnans* 7:2) The Canon was something reason could not question. Yet the Canon itself did not contain a clear and consistent body of theological ideas and frequently contradicted itself.

Given a body of doctrine which could not be tested by reason, the appeal to reason made by the scholastics (including St. Thomas) was a fiction. They already knew what they believed and reason was simply a device to bolster beliefs they were going to hold in any event. Beliefs which went contrary to reason were relegated to the supernatural—a convenient harbor for many a distressed thinker. The dogmas in regard to God's revelation in Jesus Christ which eventually emerged were held to be "divinely true." Those who disagreed or who found difficulty in comprehending the incomprehensible were branded as heretics and consigned to eternal damnation in hell. Before long, the fervent Christian orthodox believers could not wait for the fires of hell to punish the wicked heretics, so they made a hell for them on earth.

The Witness of Disciples of Christ

In the face of this situation in the early 1800's a number of men in various parts of the New World came to the conclusion that although it was incumbent upon every Christian to believe that God revealed himself in Jesus Christ, and to formulate his own interpretation as precisely and as adequately as possible,

Christian fellowship was not dependent upon agreement. Further, some of them insisted that to seek to impose particular normative dogmas upon others as a requirement for Christian fellowship in the church was actually un-Christian. It is characteristic of the Christian Churches that they have rejected all attempts to determine "orthodoxy" by adherence to a particular intellectual formulation of the Christian faith. I have often reflected upon my own experience at the time I made a public confession of my own faith in Jesus Christ. As a young boy I went down the aisle and was greeted by the minister, my father. He took me by the hand and asked me if I believed that Jesus was the Son of God and if I took him as my Savior. I replied that I did. Then we and the church prayed together. Not a word was asked me as to what I meant when I used the terms "Jesus Christ." I was not asked to give my interpretation of the phrase "Son of God" or of the word "Savior."

As a minister, I myself have never asked those questions of any person who desired to make his confession of faith. This is typical of our procedure.

This is pertinent to an understanding of the historical use of the phrase "No Creed but Christ." For the Christian Churches, one's faith is a personal faith in the living Christ himself found operating in one's own life—not a particular doctrine regarding the person and work of Christ. The articulation will vary. As individuals, we may be full of conviction that our own ideas of God, of Jesus Christ, and of revelation are more adequate than alternatives to be found among the rest of us. The conclusions we have reached are the result of long years of study and life as Christians. Yet none of us would dare to insist that his own formulation *must* be normative not only for the rest of us but for the religious body we represent. Our mutual acceptance is not based upon dogmatic agreement.

The roots of this approach are to be found in the early leaders among the Christian Churches. Illustrative is this extract from one of the writings of Barton W. Stone:

How differently did the Christians think on many subjects, even in Apostolic times! Yet how far were the Apostles from making this diversity of opinions a term of fellowship among these humble Christians! On the contrary, they exhort them *to forbear one another, endeavoring to keep the unity of the Spirit in the bond of peace, till we all come in the unity of the faith.* . . . In those days there were but a few terms of communion among Christians. All were admitted to fellowship, who believed in the Lord Jesus Christ, and obeyed him; and their obedience was considered the best evidence of their faith. This was the lesson taught them by their Lord, who said, *By their fruits ye shall know them;* and *Whoso doeth the will of my Father, the same is my brother, my sister, and my mother.* If opinions of truth were to be made terms of fellowship, it is much questioned whether any two men on earth could so perfectly agree in all points, as ever to unite; there would be no end of terms—there could be no union or fellowship on earth.

The fact that Jesus is the Christ the Son of God is believed by all Christians of every name; and if they prove their faith by their good works, their peculiar notions of his person should not be made terms of fellowship and union.[1]

Alexander Campbell seemingly wavered between this position and a more rigid requirement. An exchange between the two, Stone and Campbell, is of interest at this point. In *The Christian Baptist* Campbell began a letter to Stone with these words:

Brother Stone,

I will call you *brother* because you once told me that you could conscientiously and devoutly pray to the Lord Jesus Christ as though there was no other God in the universe than he.[2]

To this Stone replied,

Brother Campbell,

I will call you *brother,* but for a different reason than you have assigned why you call me *brother.* . . . I am heartily sorry to say any thing that may prevent you from fraternizing with me; yet that honesty, by which I wish to regulate my life, compels me to state some things in order that you may not be deceived in me, and that your brotherly affection may not be displaced. If you call those only *brethren,* who can conscientiously pray to the Lord Jesus as though there were no other God in the universe than he, and who *supremely* venerate him, then, my dear Sir, I am excluded from the number. . . . From all your public exhibitions from the press and from the pulpit, as well as from your private communications, we have been induced to believe that you fraternized with all who believe that Jesus Christ was the Son of God, and who were willingly obedient to his commands. This we have thought was the only term of fellowship on which you insisted with so much zeal and sound argument. Have we misunderstood you?—Or have you changed your mind?[3]

Fortunately, Alexander Campbell never finally adopted the more rigid alternative and when he wrote *The Christian System,* a statement of the Christian truth as he saw it, he never insisted that his own interpretation of God's revelation in Jesus Christ ought to be normative for the body of which he was such a powerful leader.

The Present Situation

Since the Christian Churches have spurned dogmatic requirements regarding the revelation of God in Jesus Christ and have made no creedal formula in this regard, the question for our time is, "Is the position which we have taken historically relatively adequate for today?"

The predicament of Christians in interpreting God and his revelation in Jesus Christ is to be seen in that, on the one hand, merely to use the words as signs without giving the terms content is to make them more or less meaningless. The formula in the proposition "God revealed himself in Jesus Christ" is no more meaningful than the use of the abstract symbols in a mathematical formula such as $a - b = xy^2$, unless each linguistic sign has specifiable content of meaning. And yet, when we do so, and accept such structures of truth as that which the human mind can know, we tend to limit our appreciation of God to the stated structure of meaning. Ideas thus tend to become idols before which we bow in worship. Among others Karl Barth has sensed this temptation keenly and has constantly reminded his readers that God is always other than and more than we can think. By the device of unspecific symbols Barth and others seek to avoid the evil which comes when man impoverishes himself by his arbitrary limitation of the richness of life which is possible to human experience. Consequently, for Barth the symbols tend to remain abstract and void of specifiable content. It is impossible to say something about that about which nothing can really be said. For every structure of ideas is limited by the finiteness of man, but man tends to imagine that he is God and commits idolatry by falling in love with himself. What he worships is not the living God but something which is the figment of his imagination, corrupted by his sin, and limited by his finiteness.

Another possible way of avoiding this danger has been suggested by H. N. Wieman. This is to treat every idea of God or any other religious idea as we treat other ideas when we think scientifically, that is, to treat them as operational ideas, capable of being modified and transformed as man's experience demands it. By a rigorous method of inquiry it is his conviction that over a long period of years of community effort a growing body of fairly reliable knowledge can be accumulated as has been the case in other modern disciplines using such a method of inquiry. Yet, Wieman would hold that such a structure of ideas, held to be true, must always be considered as "operational" rather than "absolute," capable of being revised in the light of new knowledge. Thus the symbols do not remain abstract, but are given content. Yet the content is not fixed and is open to "amendment."

It would seem that, in either case, the position of our churches has been essentially more adequate than that taken by the creedal bodies. God and his revelation in Jesus Christ cannot be confined within the narrow restrictions of any human language. To insist that a particular formulation of language about the revelation must be accepted as a condition of Christian fellowship is actually to engage in idolatry. Christian history is replete with examples of men who served the language and the ideas involved in the creed with zeal far in excess of that with which they served the living God.

Quite obviously, there are two basic presuppositions which lie at the foundation of the position of the Christian Churches and which are implied in the phrase "No Creed but Christ." First, there is the implication that creeds are useless because God is not static but dynamic. Anything which could be said about him today, even if it could be said completely (which is impossible about anything, let alone God), would be partial tomorrow because of this dynamism of God. His creative activity will make any specific formulation out of date, so far as exactness of meaning is concerned. Second, there is the implication that the world changes also; men change and their knowledge of the world changes as time goes on. Even translators of the Scriptures are frustrated by this fact when they confront the changes in meaning of particular words. And words and their meanings are only a minute portion of the total change in which man himself is involved. Given both a dynamic God and a dynamic world which includes man, static words and ideas will have rough going.

Since I am convinced that these basic ideas of God and the world are more tenable than alternative possibilities, I believe that the historic position of the Christian Churches evinced in the expression "No Creed but Christ" is more relatively adequate for religious living and growth, more adequate for Christian fellowship, and more adequate for the unity of the church than specific Christological formulas, be they "elaborate" or "simple," which are made tests of fellowship for all who love our Lord and seek to do his will. The problem for the Christian Churches in mid-century is not to seek to abolish dogma or intellectual formulations of the faith which never become dogma. No human life, no group, can live without intellectual formulations of the faith which never become dogma. Rather it is to interpret the interaction of God and man, particularly that action occurring in the church so that it is a profound expression of the actual life of man under God. Such interpretation will remain plastic, capable of modification, renewal, and possibly rejection.

Only so can we prevent eventual dishonesty from occurring, or flight from doctrine altogether.

Such an undertaking can take place only where there are both freedom and responsibility, both individuality and community. Our forefathers were convinced that unity containing diversity was not only possible but that it was the only kind of unity possible in Christ, where the hand cannot say to the eye "I have no need of you." These and other basic considerations are caught up in the total complex of meanings in the phrase "No Creed but Christ"; and in taking another look at it after some years of being busy with other intellectual problems, I must confess that I prefer this alternative to others available to the church at this time.

Thus it would seem that all members of the Christian Churches must be careful sailors—able to steer between Scylla and Charybdis. On the one hand, as Christians dealing with the question of Jesus Christ in the life and thought of the church, it is imperative that we interpret the central doctrine of Christianity so as to make clear that operative and dynamic reality present in the event "Jesus Christ" in order that other men may be led to "the good life." Yet, in so doing we must in our humility recognize the transitoriness of all specific interpretations and our own finiteness. Above all, we must refuse to impose these specific interpretations of our own upon others as a necessary condition of fellowship.

Only by so doing can we sail forward with the living God who advances into the future, and not founder.

NOTES

1. *Christian Messenger,* Dec., 1827, pp. 27, 38.
2. *Christian Baptist,* October, 1827.
3. *The Christian Messenger,* November, 1827, p. 10.

6

The Holy Spirit

In the Thought and Life of Disciples of Christ

STEPHEN J. ENGLAND

A few months ago the weekly paper from one of our important metropolitan churches gave a digest of the sermon of its minister the previous Sunday. In the course of the sermon, the minister asserted that Disciples have never believed in the trinity. Instead, they have held that the Holy Spirit is the influence of God in the world, but certainly not a third entity, or person of the godhead. He was promptly taken to task by the minister of a church in another metropolitan area who asserted that this was nothing more than the wishful thinking of a few "liberals" trying to impose their theology on the whole brotherhood. In support of his view, he cited the writings of Alexander Campbell, to prove that the trinitarian position is the only authentic view of this brotherhood.

I mention this slight controversy, not to stimulate debates over the orthodoxy of trinitarianism among Disciples, but to point out that both the "liberal" preacher and his opponent are guilty of the same error: citing their choice of ancient authorities and assuming that those cited prove the "orthodoxy" of their respective positions. Neither seems aware that from the start of this movement in America, both views of the Holy Spirit have been evident, and both are authentically in the theological bloodstream of present-day descendants.

The fact is that Disciples of Christ have been even more reluctant to frame a consistent doctrine of the Holy Spirit than they have to speculate on other Christian doctrines. As a result, they have been accused by their more reflective neighbors of various types of "heresy." Some modern thinkers, even those among Disciples, have used the terms "binitarian" or "unitarian" to describe their theology. Difficulties have arisen in ecumenical conversation when leaders of Disciples have attempted to state the position of our people in regard to the Holy Spirit. Ministers have been troubled by religious problems in the lives of members of churches who have fallen victim to certain fads and extravagances in prayer or who find no deep peace and joy in their lives as Christians. Recognition of these problems has led the writer to attempt to trace the development of thought about the Holy Spirit from the start of the movement to the recent past and to point out the present dimensions of the problem.

In the Career of Alexander Campbell

Campbell's thinking about the Holy Spirit grew out of his own developing religious life. In 1809, according to his biographer he mentioned in his diary as a youth of 21 years that the reading of the scriptures must be under the influence of the Holy Spirit if it is to render one wise, humble, and holy. He held that God gives the Holy Spirit in response to prayer, along with gracious pardon of offenses. Such trust in God, he held is "true Christianity; anything . . . less or more than this is delusion."[1]

This was before Alexander joined his father in America. Committing himself to Thomas Campbell's proposed reformation and plan for union and unity, he changed from his Presbyterian view, that trust in God was the result of special, divine, regenerating grace; so that by 1812 he came to hold that faith, brought about by the preaching of the Word, must precede regeneration; hence that the Holy Spirit is given only after faith, not in order to impart faith. This marked the great change in his views. His biographer remarks,

> . . . His view of converting faith came to be . . . that entertained by J. A. Haldane and John Campbell. . . . It taught him to look off to Jesus rather than to trust to the varying moods and emotions of the mind, and to rest his hope upon the merits and faithfulness of Him . . . rather than upon any inward impressions or transient feelings. . . . It became the labor of his future life to dethrone these theories from the power they had usurped over man's minds, and to restore the Word of God to its proper authority.[2]

The most casual look at Campbell's writings shows that his teaching about the Holy Spirit was largely concerned with the activity of the Spirit in connection with conversion. He was also affected by other considerations. One was the radical biblical character of his reforming proposals, relying on a literalistic reading of passages that refer to the Holy Spirit. This was inevitable for one who held that a principal, if not the exclusive, action of the Holy Spirit was the production of the scriptures. As a result, Disciples, both "liberal" and "conservative," have generally paid little attention to theological speculation concerning the Holy Spirit. The strongly biblical bias in Campbell's thought allied itself with his opposition to creedal statements, including those about the Holy Spirit, and down to the present time Disciples have been reluctant to attempt the formulation of any logically coherent and theologically responsible theories. The tendency was furthered by the low standards of education for the ministry for many generations; a difficulty which, of course, did not affect Campbell personally. To these factors we may add that Campbell's writings were largely polemic and issued in periodicals, which tended to make them occasional rather than calmly reflective.

It is impossible to give a comprehensive survey of Campbell's writings on the Holy Spirit within the limited compass of this paper. He began writing on the subject in the *Christian Baptist,* while he was disputing with the Baptists on various theological issues, and continued in the *Millennial Harbinger*. In the latter periodical, from 1830 to 1864, there are over 75 articles that can be identified as Campbell's and that discuss the topic either directly or incidentally. Many of these were replies to letters or articles by others, or were reviews of books. At the risk of doing Campbell's thought an injustice, we select a few items that seem characteristic. In April, 1825, in the *Baptist,* while holding that the Spirit exerted influence through the printed page of the Bible, Campbell admitted certain other special influences, which he did not describe; and held that prayer is irrational unless one believes in the Holy Spirit. In a series of four "Dialogues on the Holy Spirit," in the *Harbinger* for 1830, he took the position that all of God's dealings with man must include the reason as well as the emotions; that the action of the Spirit must therefore be intelligible; and that the Spirit must move men in the same way that one person moves another: by words and ideas rather than by mysterious direct influences. He was probably affected at this point by the Lockean epistemology with its theory of the *tabula rasa,* and seemed to hold that the presenting of the gospel in preaching of itself generated faith. The difficulties in this view were remarked on by Richardson:

> . . . Why, if faith comes by the word of God, is it not produced in *all* who hear that word? Why is it that, when the gospel is preached, a few particular individuals *only* believe and obey it? . . . Why is it that it is proper to *pray* for the conversion of individuals or the world at large, unless it be agreed that some special influence or interposition is to be expected in answer to prayer?[3]

Richardson's statements express difficulties not resolved in the thinking and practice of Christian Churches in our time.

It is notable that Campbell, holding to the theory of the place of preaching and of the Word in conversion, did not himself eliminate other influences of the Spirit in his own religious life. That he was a man of prayer is part of the record. He engaged in family worship and private devotions. On a tour about 1825, he met "Raccoon John" Smith, who, while frankly entranced by Campbell as a thinker, suspected him of being a rationalist in religion. At Smith's request, Campbell told him of his own "experience,"[4] probably including the story of his own religious struggles while in Ireland, that led him into religious peace and certainty.[5]

When pressed for a statement about his views on the Holy Spirit, Campbell affirmed his agreement with the statements of Walter Scott, to which we shall refer below. In his *Christian System,* Campbell stated briefly what may be regarded as his deliberate thoughts on the subject. He held that

> The Spirit of God inspired all the spiritual ideas in the New Testament, and confirmed them by miracles; and he is ever present with the word that he inspired. He descended from heaven on the day of Pentecost, and has not formally ascended since . . . for he is to animate and inspire with new life the church or temple of the Lord.[6]

Campbell goes on to say that, while obedience to the commands to believe, repent, and be baptized is within the power of man, the formation of Christian character is more difficult and requires aid from the Spirit of God.

> Christians are . . . quickened, animated, encouraged, and sanctified by the power and influence of the Spirit of God, working in them through the truth . . . ; and without this gift no one could be saved. . . . He knows but little of the deceitfulness of sin, or of the combating of temptation, who thinks himself competent to wrestle against the allied forces of the world, the flesh, and the devil.[7]

The attributes of Christian character, Campbell held, are each of them a communication of the Holy Spirit. Thus we are sons of God in fact as well as in title, and the Holy Spirit works all that is needful to our present, spiritual, and eternal salvation.

Campbell's debate with Rice involved as one item discussion of the work of the Holy Spirit in conversion and sanctification. Campbell affirmed that while conversion is to be attributed to the Holy Spirit, it is *only through the Word that the Holy Spirit works.* It has not been sufficiently observed that Campbell and Rice differed basically in their soteriology; that is, their doctrine of conversion and of salvation; and also in their view of man. Rice held a thoroughly Calvinistic view of the total depravity of man which rendered him spiritually incapable of exercising faith. Any activity of a seeker after salvation is actually sinful. Man must be "regenerated" or "re-created" by the direct action of the Holy Spirit before he can exercise "faith." Campbell, on the other hand, held (in opposition to both Arminian and Calvinist) that conversion is the *moral change* of the individual, to be brought about through the Word, when it is voluntarily accepted. Man, in his freedom of will, is capable of accepting and obeying; the moral change is then brought about by the Holy Spirit.

Since neither Campbell nor Rice seemed aware of their basic differences, they hardly met the issues. It is this kind of divergence that Neville Clark comments on in his *Approach to a Theology of the Sacraments.* He observes that the traditionally "Catholic" position thinks more highly of man, hence focuses on redemption; while the traditionally "Protestant" view holds that only a new act of creation can avail, and man is helpless until the act occurs.[8] Campbell's soteriology, and his view of man, have been held by most Disciples since his time.

In the Rice debate, Campbell affirmed a trinitarian position, while repudiating "the scholastic jargon of the Arian, the Unitarian and the Trinitarian hypotheses." Campbell affirmed that the Holy Spirit was given "by the Father and the Son," thus in words avoiding the subordinationism characteristic of the Eastern Church bodies. But on the other hand, nowhere in his extant writings is there any identification of the Holy Spirit, as the possession of the Christian, with the ever-living and ever-present Christ. In practice, Campbell did not invoke or address the Spirit in worship, and he tended to the position that the Spirit, speaking in the words of the inspired record, cannot be expected to communicate in any other way. To Campbell, the Christ and the Holy Spirit were separated perhaps too clearly, with results that have survived in present-day thought.

The Holy Spirit in Stone and in Scott

Two of Campbell's contemporaries were closely involved in the controversies about the Holy Spirit. Barton W. Stone, originator of the earliest stream of the movement, was from the beginning far more intensely evangelistic than was Campbell. His relation with the Cane Ridge revival introduced him to ecstatic phenomena which were attributed to the presence of the Spirit; and Stone did not reject them as such. His separation from his Presbyterian connections was due directly, as is well known, to his belief that the scriptures were not being followed closely as the supreme authority in the church. The resulting Christian Churches were in the main stream of the frontier revival movement, winning large numbers of additions before the Campbell movement was launched separately, and continuing in the revival trend while Campbell was engrossed in the details of restoring the ancient order. While we have little direct information as to the way in which Stone conducted revivals, it is likely that he encouraged "spiritual exercises" as a part of the procedures. At the same time, he turned directly to the New Testament as the sole authority for the Christian. Eventually, he came to the same theory of conversion held by Campbell: that man, in his free will, is capable of response to the preaching of the gospel, hence needs no direct influence of the Spirit to enable him to exercise faith. Stone seems thus to have been caught between two positions. He valued "spiritual influences" because he understood clearly that unless the emotions are stirred, men will not act. But he also valued the clear and specific statements which he found in the New Testament as to how the gospel is to be accepted. In the end, he affirmed that the assurance of pardon is to be found in conscious obedience to the gospel rather than in "experiences," although he was able to relate experiences and struggles of his own. It was this fundamental agreement in the matter of conversion that made possible the so-called union of 1832 between "Christians" and "Disciples."

It was, however, in the realm of theological speculation, in particular regarding Christ and the Holy Spirit, that Stone found himself in difficulties. The doctrine of the trinity always seemed to baffle him. He held, for example, that the Christ, while divine, was not eternally the Son. This lead to the accusation of Arianism. He also held that the Spirit was "an energy of God" but not a person in the trinity—an interesting anticipation of some twentieth-century views. The Eastern "Christian Churches," with whom Stone was friendly, were frankly Unitarian, although they called themselves "Evangelical Unitarian." In the end they could not stomach Campbell's "trinitarian" position, and Stone eventually threw in with the western group and with Campbell.

Walter Scott, eminent evangelist, developed highly logical and profoundly influential views of the Holy Spirit. In his *Gospel Restored,* Section VII is devoted to his views, stated in as nearly a systematic and theological fashion as anything surviving from that generation. His statement, which received the approval of Campbell and of Richardson, was based on an extension of Campbell's ideas of "dispensations." He held that Christianity is sustained by three separate and distinct missions. The first was that of Jesus, which was to the Jewish nation; the second, that of the apostles, to the world, with the purpose of preaching the gospel and announcing the terms of pardon; and the third, that of the Holy Spirit, which was and is solely to the church. Scott held that the Holy Spirit is given only to those who obey the gospel, hence is given only in the church; and that the Spirit can do nothing now but by the members of the body of Christ, in which he is resident. It is in this way that the Spirit works for conversion, for it is only through the activity of the members that preaching can occur. Scott did not extend his discussions of the activity of the Spirit into the area of special providences and guidance of individuals, where his theory would seem to involve him in difficulties. Neither did he discuss the theological question of relations among the persons of the godhead.

Scott is better known, perhaps, for his famous "five-finger exercise," in which (as the last "finger") he logically developed "the gift of the Holy Spirit" as the final step (an act of God, not of man) in human salvation. He thus linked his doctrine of the Spirit with evangelistic fervor and forged a tool of tremendous effectiveness in winning numbers. He also stated a doctrine that was susceptible of perversion into legalism: the evidence that one has received the Holy Spirit is the provable fact that he has been baptized.

In the beginning generation of the movement, attention was focused almost exclusively upon two related questions: (1) in conversion, does the Spirit work directly, or only through the medium of the word, as preached and read? and (2) does the Christian's assurance of his standing with God depend upon some "experience," emotional in character and attributed to the Spirit, or upon the testimony of the scripture? Focus upon these issues served to divert attention from the question of the providential guidance of the Christian's life, the answer to prayer, and the relation between the Holy Spirit, as the promised indweller of the Christian, and the ever-living Christ. From the start, there was strong reliance on overt statements of the New Testament as definitive; the conviction that the Holy Spirit is given after faith and obedience, not as the "regenerator" that brings faith; and emphasis on the function of the human reason in conversion. The succeeding generation dealt with exactly these issues, and its thought was conditioned by the same factors.

The Successors to the Fathers

In the decades after the disability of Alexander Campbell, leaders of thought continued to struggle with the doctrine of the Holy Spirit. In part, discussions dealt with matters of interpretation of New Testament passages. Holding (as nearly all of them did) that the New Testament was the product of inspiration by the Holy Spirit, certain difficulties arose. Was the ability to perform miracles by the power of the Holy Spirit promised (as in Acts 2:38) to all believers? If so, how account for the cessation of miracles? And how account for the inability of moderns to perform them? Answers varied. In some instances (as in McGarvey's *Commentary on Acts*) a theory of transmission of the power to work miracles was advanced. Based on Acts 8:17, this said, in effect, that the power of the Holy Spirit was granted to those upon whom apostles laid their hands, and to those in turn upon whom these laid hands; thereafter the endowment ceased. Others made a distinction between the "baptism" of the Holy Spirit (which conferred the power to work miracles) and the "ordinary gift" of the Spirit, which did not. This led naturally to a debate over the definition of "baptism of the Holy Spirit."

Other questions were more theological. We may take two of the more characteristic as examples. One dealt with the part played by the Spirit in conversion and with the consequent interpretation of such a passage as Mark 3:28, 29 (the "unpardonable sin," or blasphemy against the Holy Spirit). Some of the more rigid argued logically that the New Testament, containing the gospel plan of salvation, was given by the Holy Spirit. Hence, if one rejects this "plan," he has blasphemed against its author. Interpretation of Romans 8:16, dealing with the ground of Christian assurance, caused some difficulties. In what way does "the Spirit bear witness with our Spirit?" Frequently, the tendency was to equate "the Spirit" with "the New Testament." On this basis, it was readily possible to say (with M. M. Davis, in his *First Principles*) that the Holy Spirit gave the "gospel plan of salvation," with its promise of sonship to those who obey. The Spirit tells us to do certain things (believe, repent, be baptized); the man's spirit testified that he has done so; therefore, he may know certainly that he is a son. In a slightly different direction, Moses Lard (in his *Commentary on Romans*) suggests that the verse means that, in the New Testament, the Spirit has given direction for Christian living. If the man's spirit testified that he is actually living in this way, he may be assured of his status. This is obviously a drift in the direction of rationalism and a Pelagian soteriology. In the end, it means that the Holy Spirit tells man what he must do to be saved, and he saves himself by doing it. When his mind assures him he has done what is required, he may be secure. In practice, this view too easily falls into a legalism that would earn salvation by the doing of deeds. A similar legalism tended to hold that the best (and in fact the only scriptural) proof that one has the Holy Spirit is the fact that he has been scripturally baptized; for in the New Testament the promise (as in Acts 2:38) is quite clear.

The tendency to equate the Holy Spirit with the words of the New Testament, which it was believed was given by a highly mechanical process of inspiration, is illustrated by an ancedote of the late Dean Frank H. Marshall, of Phillips University. He recalled an evangelist of the theological persuasion of Benjamin Franklin, whom he had heard in a revival meeting. The evangelist, preaching on the Holy Spirit, held up a pocket New Testament and said, "I can buy all the Holy Spirit there is in the world for ten cents." The dean used to add, with his dry and incisive humor, that, if the evangelist had paid as much as a dime for the Holy Spirit he actually possessed, he had been overcharged.

One of the more systematic statements of this period came from the pen of Isaac Errett, whose *Our Position* describes the doctrinal atmosphere of Disciples about 1880. He lists, among those things held in common with all "evangelicals," the belief in "the tri-personality of Father, Son and Holy Spirit" and "the personal and perpetual mission of the Holy Spirit, to convict the world . . . and to dwell in believers." As an item in which "Our Plea" differed from all others, he mentioned the view of the operation of the Holy Spirit. "We repudiate all theories . . . which logically rule out the Word of God as the instrument of regeneration and conversion, or which make the sinner passive and helpless. . . ."[9]

Errett did not discuss the interesting and important questions of Christian asurance and of providence and guidance in the life of the Christian.

One of the most interesting of the treatments came from the pen of Robert Richardson, biographer of Campbell. In his *Memoirs,* written after Campbell's death, he looked back on the earlier scene and made this sharp criticism:

> . . . Some of those who were professed advocates of the Reformation were led to construct a word-alone theory which virtually dispensed with the great promise of the gospel—the gift of the Holy Spirit to believers. . . . They were disposed to resolve religion entirely into a system of moral motivity; to disbelieve the actual indwelling of the Holy Spirit in believers; to deny special providences and guidings, and, by consequence, the efficacy of prayer. Taking Locke's philosophy as the basis of their system, and carrying his "Essay on the Human Understanding" along with the Bible in their saddlebags, they denied even to its Creator any access to the human soul except by "words and arguments," while they conceded to the Author of evil a direct approach, and had more to say in their discourses about "the laws of human nature" than about the gospel of Christ.[10]

He elaborated on the same theme in *The Office of the Holy Spirit,* a book which, in its view of the scriptures, its generosity of spirit, and its clear perception of the basic theological and religious issues, was far ahead of its time, and has not even yet been superseded in the treatment of its subject. Like Stone, Richardson regarded the Spirit as the "energy" of God. He desired to help Christians avoid two errors: that of the rationalist, and that of the sensualist; or, phrased differently, religion of the head alone, and religion of the heart alone. Differing from most of his contemporaries, he held that there was no single "pattern" in the New Testament for the receiving of the Spirit, and therefore no single pattern for today. "A want of faith . . . is the only insuperable obstacle" to receiving the Spirit.

The work of the Spirit in conversion is that of moral transformation, which could not be accomplished by the moral example of the life of Jesus, during his ministry, and much less by what Richardson calls "the partial records of his life which remain in the New Testament." Some influence of the Spirit is needed beyond the account of the life of Jesus to make a person a believer, and some action of the Spirit to make a believer actually a member of the body of Christ.

In the believer, Richardson held, the Spirit works to give him an inner witness (Rom. 8:16) which goes beyond the rational; to give him the "earnest" of the future life as a steadfast hope; and to assist him in the development of personal character and the life of devotion.

In keeping with the tradition of Disciples, Richardson resolutely held to the necessity of faith, evidenced by obedience, as requisite to the receiving of the Holy Spirit. He was willing to interpret certain ecstatic phenomena as "psychological" rather than of necessity a manifestation of the Spirit.

Coming at the end of the century was J. H. Garrison's book, *The Holy Spirit*. Like all good Disciples, he held that faith and obedience are required before the Spirit is given. His book is chiefly the interpretation of New Testament passages rather than theological speculation. He asserted the definite trinitarian position. In conversion, he held that the influence of the Spirit, in addition to the inspired word, the Bible, is seen in the personality of the preacher, the lives of Christians, the events of God's providence, and the experiences of people.

In the Twentieth Century

In the present century, Disciples (in common with other religious groups) have felt the impact of three developments that have profoundly, though often unperceived, affected their thinking about the Holy Spirit. One of these was the new biblical criticism which made it impossible to hold to any "mechanical" theory of inspiration of the Bible. If the Holy Spirit spoke only in a "dictated" Bible, we have none of his words. A second was the rise of that humanistic liberalism which elevated men and tended to eliminate the sense of the numinous presence of God. A third was the development of depth studies in psychology, which offered many explanations other than the interposition of the Holy Spirit, for apparently mysterious phenomena in human experiences of conversion and religious activity. Under this impact, the writings on the topic, which had decreased noticeably from the high point in Campbell's time, declined almost to nothing.

It is a procedure of doubtful validity to draw conclusions as to the theology of any group on the basis of a standard hymnal; hence, the listing of only nine hymns under the topic "The Holy Spirit" in *Christian Worship—a Hymnal,* may indicate nothing more than the preference of the editors. At the same time, the meagerness of listings suggests that Disciples have at least not been preoccupied with the subject; and other available evidence comes to the same conclusion.

Apparently the organ of the more conservative wing, the *Christian Standard,* has printed more articles than its more liberal contemporary, *The Christian-Evangelist.* In 1935 the *Standard* published two companion articles, one by the late P. H. Welshimer, the other by the late George Knepper, of Akron, Ohio. Welshimer wrote on the way in which the Holy Spirit inspired the scriptures. He affirmed a mechanical theory of inspiration for the Bible, and held that there is no influence of the Spirit upon persons save through the words and ideas expressed in the New Testament. Knepper wrote on the influence of the Holy Spirit on persons. He held that the Spirit leads men *to* the truth; that is, to places where they may hear it; and *into* all truth, that is, an understanding of the scriptures that makes Christ real to the believer. The Spirit also leads the Christian into right choices, and confers inward peace and comfort. This advocacy of the direct action of the Spirit led the editor to warn that Knepper's articles were dangerous, although they offered opportunity for growth.

Also in the *Standard,* in 1937, an outline of views on the Holy

Spirit was presented by James DeForest Murch. He went far beyond the mechanical theory of inspiration of the scriptures, and beyond the idea that the Spirit speaks to men only by the scriptures. He held that the Word of God is the standard by which we are to determine the validity of any experience of the Holy Spirit, and that the Bible can become the Word of God only if it is read under the guidance of the Spirit.

The theologically conservative British brethren may be represented in an article by E. Woolrich, in *The Christian Advocate* for February, 1959. Woolrich wrote that "the motivating power of . . . lives [of Christians] is the energy of God," a position substantially that of Stone. This energy, however, operates prior to baptism, to persuade the person to confess his faith and come to baptism.

In *The Christian-Evangelist*, in 1939, a symposium appeared under the title "The Fifth of Walter Scott's Five-Finger Exercises." The total scope was little more than a page; five authors contributed. Irvin Lunger and C. J. Armstrong rejected "a trinity of persons" quite vigorously, while E. H. Stringfellow, of Drake, upheld a more trinitarian view. The diversities of outlook were, perhaps, the most significant feature of the symposium.

Starkly revealing of the disinterest of Disciples in the doctrine, if not the activity, of the Holy Spirit was the approach to the "1900th anniversary of Pentecost" in the year 1930. A veteran minister, J. B. Hunley, was asked to produce a book which was published under the title, *Pentecost and the Holy Spirit.* Hunley pointed out that the widespread belief among Disciples that the mission of the Holy Spirit ceased with the writing of the books of the New Testament had been responsible for both the lack of interest in the subject and the deplorable lack of spirituality in the church. His book is largely devoted to interpretation of New Testament passages, with special application to religious life and the work of the church. It is warm and religiously moving, but not intellectually deep and compelling. In the organized cooperative work of the brotherhood, the actual celebration of Pentecost was focused almost exclusively upon winning large numbers of converts, while the Holy Spirit was mentioned only incidentally. That the evangelistic effort was relatively unproductive may be interpreted by some as the natural result of neglecting the doctrinal basis for the effort.

Some insight into more recent thinking may be gained by reference to certain documents prepared for consideration at the Edinburgh Assembly (1960) of The World Convention of Churches of Christ. Each of these documents is a synthesis of a number of studies, each produced by a local committee to which its topic had been assigned by the Central Study Committee. The local committees, composed of ministers and lay people, were set up in every land where there are Churches of Christ. These conditions seem to assure reasoned judgments on the subjects discussed. While no special study was assigned on the topic of the Holy Spirit, several studies incidentally touch on the doctrine, while the silence of others seems significant.

One study, on "Ethical Implications of the Christian Gospel," mentions the Holy Spirit almost casually as a theological factor in Christian ethics; but the part played by the Holy Spirit today, in both ethical insights and ethical response, is so minimal that it may be set aside as a serious factor in the thinking of those who produced the document.

Another, on "The Theology of Evangelism," is almost equally silent about the Holy Spirit. Some action of the Spirit is perhaps implied in the thought that "the Kerygma is an empowering approach so that the gospel is called the power of God unto salvation"[11]; in the convert's progressively knowing God's righteousness, and growing in it; and in the concept of a dynamic faith. But the place of the Holy Spirit in evangelism is not stated; and while baptism is included as a part of "conversion," Walter Scott would be horrified to learn that "the gift of the Holy Spirit" is left out—a hand from which the last of the fingers has been amputated!

Another document, "Who Is Jesus Christ?" speaks of the

Holy Spirit vividly and positively. "Christ in you" is equated with "the gift of the Holy Spirit" as that factor which, in New Testament times, was determinative of all human relationships within the church. "It is only as the Spirit—one with Christ himself—comes to perpetuate the spiritual presence of our Lord . . . that we are liberated from . . . lifeless doctrine, or the historically verified events of an ever-receding past." The presence of the Holy Spirit (as "Christ in you") becomes an assurance that Christ is living, not dead; and the risen Lord "continues his work as Savior by entering into the life of the convert through the Holy Spirit." The document notes that Disciples are skeptical of mystical religion and pentecostal excesses and ecstasies, but goes on to point out that Disciples have also been subject to the perils of "historicism"; that is, regarding "the event of salvation almost exclusively as an event of the past," with the result that they have tended to believe that the fulness of grace is contained in the Bible—a special danger to those who hold "restorationist" views of the church. This perversion of the meaning of personal faith can be guarded against only by belief in "the potency and intimacy of the Holy Spirit." This will also guard the church against becoming a society merely for the purpose of celebrating events that once took place, and will give meaning to the communion service as something beyond rational understanding of the scriptures. Such a belief also guards the church against identifying its real "hope" with its successful work in missions, or with its efforts to bring in the kingdom of God on earth by social action.[12] To identify the Holy Spirit with the risen Christ seems to imply the orthodox trinitarian position.

A document on "Authority and Revelation" asserts that such authority as the scriptures possess is due to their origin in the activity of the Holy Spirit. Without affirming any "mechanical" theory of inspiration, it is held that the Holy Spirit spoke within the church to produce the books by the activity of men and thereafter to collect a canon of scripture, by which the church is ever to be measured. The Holy Spirit has led the people of God in each age to understand anew and better what God would say to them through the scriptures. It is held that "to the Christian, the Holy Spirit speaks with authority beyond that of the printed word of the Bible, although not unrelated to that word." In the producing of the scriptures it was the Holy Spirit that perceived historical events as the act of God; and thereafter illuminated individuals who would understand such "acts" and record their interpretation in the inspired scriptures. The Holy Spirit carries the ultimate authority which is to be found in revelation. The document warns against the twin dangers: (1) of not making an adequate place in the life of the individual and in the church for the work of the Holy Spirit; and (2) of claiming the Holy Spirit as the author of our own desires.[13]

Two statements in the document are worthy of special note. It is observed that there is among Disciples, "a diminishing interest in the doctrine of the Holy Spirit until today there is a generation for whom this element of Christian experience is all but lost." A quotation from Otto Piper is approved:

> For ages the Holy Spirit has been the stepchild of Protestant theology. The doctrine has been left almost exclusively to Holiness movements and similar offshoots of the evangelical faith. The result has been a serious impoverishment both of the life and of the faith of the theological thinking in our churches.

Evidently Disciples of Christ are not alone in their wanderings in this particular theological wilderness.

As a means of supplementing information about present-day thinking among Disciples, the author of this paper circulated a questionnaire among a selected group of ministers of Christian Churches. The questionnaire itself was very brief, and the answers could be a simple "yes" or "no," if the respondent so desired. In the choice of respondents, the attempt was made to be theologically representative. Men were chosen from both "conservative" and "liberal" wings; some "independent" as well as the more numerous "cooperatives" were included. Graduates of various schools and men in various geographical areas were picked out. Some of the replies were so brief as to be of little help. Others took advantage of the invitation to write at some length, and quite helpfully. Following is a brief summary of what the replies disclose.

The soteriology of the respondents favors redemption rather than regeneration, although acceptance of a "new birth" and imparting of a new life was generally expressed. Similarly, it was generally held that power (that is, of the *person*) was *released* rather than *imparted* (that is, from God as an outside source). Nearly all held that the word of scripture was not the sole influence that led to conversion. The question whether the Holy Spirit acted directly on persons in response to prayer for their conversion brought an interesting variety of answers. The direct answers were almost equally divided between "yes" and "no." But these were qualified. Some held that we must believe that this type of prayer is effectual because it is mentioned in the Bible. Others had observed such an effect, or had been told by others that it worked. Some said that prayer probably brought about some direct action of the Spirit, "although it can't be proved" apart from actions of persons, who might be made more zealous in evangelism by their own prayers. Only a few commented on the theological difficulty of supposing that human prayer could change God's will to save, or "stir up the Holy Spirit" in some way.

The replies to questions as to what follows, in the life of the individual, after some "gift" is conferred were almost unanimously affirmative that ethical insights are sharpened, ethical strength for decision and action is increased, and ability to understand the Bible is improved. In some cases, strictures were put on these to indicate that this "smacks of magic" or that it seems to take the human power of decision away. The conferring of an "inner assurance," as indicated by Paul in Romans 8:16 was generally accepted, but hardly in the sense that Paul meant. One comment was "in the sense that the conscience is uneasy at wrongdoing, and easy when doing right." In a similar way, the Spirit as the guarantee of an eschatological hope (as in 2 Cor. 5:5) was generally accepted, but again hardly in Paul's meaning. For example, one said, "Yes; but not apart from the rational and historical assurance." A good many simply passed the eschatological question without reply or comment.

One question inquired whether the Spirit, in answer to prayer, gives providential guidance to persons in making decisions. In general, the replies were affirmative. Some replies reflected the influence of "the power of positive thinking" in such a statement as "Many believe in such guidance, but do not attribute it to the Holy Spirit." The question whether "prayer changes things," in the sense of affecting nature or healing disease, brought a heavy negative response. The general attitude was to say, "Yes; but more by changing the person who experiences the things." A number felt that this sort of attitude looked on religion as magic. None of them remarked upon church people going astray after vagaries of answered prayer, but this may have been due to the way in which the question was phrased.

Nearly all the replies commented upon the question whether church members identified their faith as acceptance of the verity of facts about Christ, to the exclusion of or failure to realize an "inner presence." Some reported "far too many" in this condition, with the result that Christianity becomes, to many, merely an ethical system devoid of power and joy. Others observed that church members were able to repeat Paul's words about being "in Christ," or "Christ lives in me," without any experience of their own to correspond. But others found no problem at this point; while many of those who perceived a problem made no connection with any belief about the Holy Spirit as its cause.

Respondents were given the opportunity to explain the nature of their belief in the Holy Spirit either by a choice between the trinitarian position and that of Stone; or by describing their attitudes and practices in worship and preaching. Not surprisingly, there was some inconsistency at this point. A few who asserted that the Holy Spirit should be given the same emphasis as the Father and the Son in worship and teaching affirmed Stone's position that the Spirit is an energy of God. In general, there was a practical subordination of the Spirit. Few address the Spirit in worship; in some instances the term "Eternal Spirit" is employed, reflecting the Johannine statement, "God is a spirit" (John 4:24). Few of the ministers preach regularly on the topic, because of their confused thinking or the feeling that it is irrelevant or would be confusing to their hearers, but chiefly because they focus their thought on God and on Christ, with the result that the Holy Spirit is incidentally considered. A number expressed the opinion that more preaching and teaching would be profitable, if they could come to some conclusion as to what to say.

Responses to the direct question whether the view of Campbell (in general, the trinitarian) or that of Stone (that the Holy Spirit is an energy of God) represents the position of Disciples brought an almost even division among the replies. A number rejected the *word* "trinity" while affirming that *position*. One said that Campbell's position is that of most Disciples, though he personally did not hold it; while another said that the position of Stone was that of most Disciples, though he could not accept it. One suggested that most Disciples hold the position of Stone, but would deny it; while another said that Stone's view was "tragically" that of Disciples; and yet another advanced the idea that Stone's position went with higher education for the ministry.

The replies give the writer some general impressions that may be illuminating. One is the high regard for New Testament statements about the Holy Spirit. Evidently the New Testament is still normative for the thinking of many, or most; although not in the literalistic sense of a century ago. The second is the assumption, displayed in many overt statements and underlying all of the replies, that man has the freedom of will to respond, whether in conversion or in response to some leading of the Spirit, however it might be described. Somewhat surprising was the observed lack of the typical Calvinistic or Lutheran concept that the response of the believer as well as that to which he responds is given him by some action of the Spirit. A third impression is the strong survival of reliance on the human reason.

On the other hand, there was deep dissatisfaction expressed by a number with the low tone of spiritual life among Christians, along with a concern that the worship services of the church shall become religiously meaningful, especially in their sacramental aspects. One younger minister said:

> I am appalled at the woodenness with which the church manages to use the scriptural references to the Spirit . . . in teaching about the Spirit. Even the most orthodox words in the world can be completely vitiated by the bald, mechanical, almost spatial way in which they are sometimes used.

Another commented:

> Our people are too much caught between two extremes. One is the loyal-to-the-Bible faith, that rests on the written word alone, in which there is no power to give freedom, happiness, and wholeness. The other is that of the so-called "liberals" who have rebelled against literalism, have taken the gospel to use it for social and ethical application, but who still fail to find in it that power of God which is the act of living faith and which bears the fruit of the Spirit.

Recognition of a lack in this area of spiritual development led a number of respondents to express the hope for systematic instruction on the topic, for the benefit of ministers, in order that church members might be taught. One of the younger ministers has already taken steps. Believing that we must bring the Spirit into our worship, because the doctrine is so important to Christian life, and because people learn more from worship than in any other way, he selects the hymns and plans the worship services with this in mind. In the full baptismal service of his church for new converts, he includes a formal and solemn ceremony for the imparting of the Spirit. The confession of faith is followed by immersion in the triple name. This is then followed by the laying on of hands, "usually of the local bishops," with the formula (adapted from Eph. 3):

> God Almighty, the Father of our Lord Jesus Christ, grant to you (name) to be strengthened with power in the inward man; that Christ may dwell in your heart through faith and that you may be filled unto all the fulness of God.

It is evident from the replies that Disciples, regardless of what theological view they say they hold about the Spirit, are not trinitarian in the traditional sense. The writer must disagree strongly with one of the younger theologians whose intellectual competency is high and who wrote recently to the effect that he believes he has a mission to restore the Holy Spirit to Disciples because they are unitarian in their theology. They are not unitarian, but they are hardly trinitarian; they would probably best be characterized as "Monarchian." Their Monarchianism is not that Modalism of Praxeas who, in the third century, was accused by his opponents of crucifying the Father and driving out the Holy Spirit. It is nearer that of Sabellius; one respondent suggested that he might be successfully accused of Sabellianism. A number referred to the Spirit as one of the "manifestations" of God. One said that he thought of the Holy Spirit as God in action in his creation, including people. Another emphasized the Holy Spirit as God and Christ now active as spiritual power. One suggested that theological difficulties have clustered around the capitalizing of the adjective "holy," thus giving rise to trinitarian dogma. It was evident that most respondents did not think of the Holy Spirit in the same separate personal terms they employ in their thinking about Jesus Christ. One of the younger men said clearly:

> I do not think that the focus of the Christian changes from Christ to the Holy Spirit. As it is true that the God I know is the God revealed in Christ, so the Christ I receive is the Spirit of Christ who operates in me in conversion through the kerygmatic message by which I am confronted with Christ, and operates in my life through the response in faith and love to the person of Christ.

A similar unity in emphasis of preaching was mentioned by several. Their focus is on God and Christ, but not on the Holy Spirit as a separable entity or personality. They would be aware of God in their lives, rather than that of a separate "Holy Spirit."

The diversities in beliefs about the activities of the Spirit, and about the theological explanation of matters of religious experience, are a surviving evidence of one of the basic principles of the Campbell-Stone movement: that Christian faith, and thus the union of Christians, does not depend on agreement in doctrinal detail. The widespread desire for some consensus in teaching about the Holy Spirit should not lead us into demands for creedal conformity in this, any more than any other, area. It is perhaps possible that our ecumenical neighbors, among whom the orthodox trinitarian view of the Spirit seems regnant, may be reluctant to accept us while such diversities remain. This is a problem that will have to be faced at some time in the future.

NOTES

1. Robert Richardson, *Memoirs of Alexander Campbell,* Vol. I, pp. 144ff.
2. *Ibid.,* I, 425ff.
3. *Ibid.,* I, 427.
4. *Ibid.,* II, 111.
5. *Ibid.,* I, 48ff.
6. Alexander Campbell, *The Christian System* (St. Louis: Christian Board of Publication), p. 64.
7. *Ibid.,* p. 66.
8. Neville Clark, *An Approach to a Theology of the Sacraments,* pp. 73, 74, stereotype ed.
9. Isaac Errett, *Our Position* (Louisville, Kentucky: Wm. S. Broadhurst), pp. 7-8.
10. Richardson, *op. cit.,* II, 349f.
11. World Convention Study Papers, "The Theology of Evangelism," p. 8.
12. *Ibid.,* "Who is Jesus Christ?" pp. 9-11.
13. *Ibid.,* "The Authority in Revelation," pp. 7-8.

7

Man and Salvation

Characteristic Ideas Among Disciples of Christ

FRANK N. GARDNER

DISCIPLES of Christ are a part of Western Christendom and, as is to be expected, portray historically the characteristic pattern of thought in the West in their ideas of the nature of man and of salvation. Some of the early leaders rebelled against certain aspects of Western or Latin theology and accentuated some of the ideas of the Eastern type. Yet, in the main, our early leaders were dominated by Latin expressions.

The Eastern expression of the Christian faith as it was born and developed became marked by typical Greek concerns for metaphysics and Greek views of man as possessing abilities and powers which gave man essential worth and dignity. In the West the Roman concern for law, order, and justice came to dominate the forms of Christian thought. The early theologians in the East were not only tinctured by philosophy but many of them were professional philosophers as well as theologians, such as Clement of Alexandria and Origen. The early theologians who set the characteristic pattern of theology in the West were dominated by a legal cast of mind, notably Tertullian (himself a lawyer), Irenaeus, and Cyprian. As early as the inner struggle for power in the church at Corinth, we find in the letter we know as I Clement this characteristic temper of mind. Man was seen primarily as a disobedient lawbreaker. As such he did not have the status usually assigned to him by theologians in the East. As this legalistic cast dominated the history of Christian thought in the West it is not surprising that in Protestantism it was furthered by John Calvin who, as a young man, had studied law with the intention of becoming a lawyer. Since both Alexander and Thomas Campbell were Presbyterians, as was Barton W. Stone, early Disciples of Christ (as well as those of our time) inherited the Western theological cast of mind.

Early Eastern Thought

Similarly, notions of salvation in East and West were quite different. In the East salvation was the act of God through Jesus Christ, by which the mortal and corrupt nature of man was transformed into the divine and immortal. The primary concept of salvation was through deification or incarnation. As Athanasius writes in *The Incarnation of the Word of God,* "He assumed humanity that we might become God." Man had been created by God in God's own image. That image had been corrupted by man's sin so that man was no longer immortal. But God, through his mercy, sent the Christ, his Son, who in human form died on the cross as a man dies, but rose from the dead by the power of God and broke the power of sin and death over man.

Baptism and the Lord's supper were viewed as a part of the process by which the believing Christian robed himself in the immortality made possible by Jesus Christ. Early Eastern Christians found much in the Pauline *corpus* which assisted this view of salvation. In Paul's letters to the young churches they gathered that salvation was something effected in man whereby the man is transformed from a creature conditioned by the earth or by "the flesh" to a spiritual creature on the model of Jesus Christ.

At the beginning stands the preaching of the divine proclamation and the invitation to men to be reconciled with God (Rom.

10:17; Gal. 3:2; 2 Cor. 5:20). Belief must be without condition and without limit. Action follows the decision of faith. The convert sinks beneath the water of baptism and dies (Rom. 6:2-11). He arises a "new man," he has been transfigured, he has been "baptized into Chirst," or he has "put on Christ." He is now a member of the spiritual body of Christ which is made up of the entire church (Gal. 3:27ff; 1 Cor. 12:13). The heavenly substance of the divine and immortal spirit is granted to him. The sinner dies in baptism, he rises from the water as a Christian and is a "new creation" (2 Cor. 5:17; Rom. 6:4). He is now "in Christ." As in baptism we share in the death of Jesus Christ, just so in coming up out of the water we share in his resurrection.

Similarly, the Lord's supper is no mere memorial feast like many others held in Paul's time. The fellowship bound the faithful into a unity; the one bread they ate made them one body, the body of Christ (1 Cor. 10:16-21). But in some mysterious way the bread and wine are not simply bread and wine; they are by no means common food; rather they are immortal nourishment, the blood and body of the risen Lord. These pneumatic substances enter into the bodies of those who share the sacred meal and transform them into the spiritual body of Christ. That these are not ordinary foods is seen in Paul's admonition and warning in 1 Corinthians 11:27-30 to those who would partake of these supramundane foods as if they were only normal foods. Anyone who partakes of them dishonorably will find that they become poison in his body and that they will bring illness and death to a wicked person.

Seizing upon these ideas a typical early Eastern theologian, Ignatius of Antioch, bishop of the church which was located in the city where Paul made his headquarters for a time, speaks of the bread as "the bread of God" in the eating of which we receive a pledge of resurrection. The "flesh and blood" of Christ he calls the "medicine of immortality" and says that they provide an antidote against death, guaranteeing the Christian eternal life. Already, while on earth, the Christian bears the "flesh of the Lord" in his body. His body, interpenetrated with the eternal substance of the body of Jesus Christ, is now able to withstand dissolution and so experience a resurrection like the divine Lord's (Ignatius: *Ephesians* 5:2; *Trallians* 7:2; *Magnesians* 7:2; *Philadelphians* 4).

In the early East, Christians believed that men were endowed with free will and could believe, follow Christ, and live righteously if they chose to do so. Their typical attitude is to be found in one of its instances in Justin's *Apology* (1:43).

> God did not make man like other things such as trees and quadrupeds which are unable to act freely. For man would not be worthy of reward or praise if he did right not from choice but because he was made thus; nor could he be justly punished if he did evil not of himself but because he was unable to be otherwise than he was.

Thus if a man's character is due solely to God, his character is not his own and deserves neither reward nor punishment. God, says Justin, has endowed men with both reason and freedom of choice. God declared his purpose for men and sent Jesus Christ to make his purpose clearer and more certain. Men are free to make their response.

Therefore we can say that in the early East, Christians tended to emphasize the worth and dignity of man, man's abilities to know and discern between good and evil, and his powers and freedom of choice. Man had been made in the image of God, that image had been marred and distorted by man's sin, and man was no longer immortal but mortal and corrupt. God through Jesus Christ had made possible man's return to his original and immortal state. Through faith and the sacraments this state was reached when he became a part of "the body of Christ." Salvation was both a changed life in this world and immortality in the world to come.

The Mind of the West

In the West, Irenaeus of Lyons, meeting the crisis raised by the Gnostics, laid the foundations for the whole Western or Latin ecclesiastical system. Although much of his background was Eastern, he was thoroughly Western in temper of mind. He was Eastern enough to believe that salvation was the transformation of fallen humanity into divine being through the sacraments. Repeated observance of the eucharist augmented the process of making the physical body incorruptible, which process began at baptism. Baptism he viewed as "the baptism of regeneration unto God." The repeated partaking of the "flesh and blood" of Jesus Christ made possible progressive deification. "We are not made gods at the outset, but at first men, then at length gods." Yet Irenaeus had little time for metaphysics. His teaching called primarily for obedience, not logical justification. To Irenaeus, Christ's obedience to God and man's obedience to the church constituted the whole foundation on which salvation rested. Adam's disobedience had brought man to a calamitous and hopeless state. Obedience was the way back. By making legalistic imagery the basis for his notion of salvation he showed himself to be a true exponent of the Western and Roman frame of mind. The truth of any doctrine, including the doctrines of man and salvation, no longer rested upon justified conclusions arrived at by inquiry, logic, or reasoning, but rested instead upon the postulate of universal institutional authority and regularity. Certainty of truth and salvation was established by obedience to the church, actually to the hierarchy who had "received the sure gift of truth."

Tertullian, educated as a lawyer and known as the "Father of Ecclesiastical Latin" viewed the God-man relationship in legal terms also. His notion of salvation based upon this premise later became dominant in Cyprian's thought and through Cyprian became normative for the Western church. In Tertullian's thought the gospel is "the law peculiarly ours." God is conceived as the divine "lawgiver." He is also the judge and the avenger of transgressions of the law. Thus the basic and fundamental relation to, and attitude towards, God on the part of man is that of fear. Man must be obedient. If he is obedient and repentant he earns salvation for himself in baptism. To Tertullian, the grace of God is necessarily connected with baptism. By baptism guilt and punishment are removed. We are, says he, born in the water. Baptism "brings remission of sins, abolition of death, regeneration of the man, and the obtaining of the Holy Spirit." Tertullian saw this impartation of the Holy Spirit in baptism as the infusion into the convert of a divine substance.

This notion of "baptism for remission of sins," along with the corrolary idea of obedience, was a part of an old tradition dominant in many parts of the early church. The idea is to be found in several places in the New Testament canon (Acts 2:38; Mark 16:16; Acts 22:16; with 1 Peter 3:21 asserting that baptism is *the test* which assures us of a good conscience before God), and by the time of Hermas and Justin (*Mandates* Book II 4:3; *Apology* 61) the view was general that baptism washed away all previous sins. In the early nineteenth century this doctrine was prominent in the thinking of early Disciples, particularly Alexander Campbell and Walter Scott.

The development of Christianity and Christian doctrine in the West centered, increasingly, upon conceptions derived from law and its emphasis upon authority. As the episcopate developed, the complete adoption of the episcopal constitution coincided with the introduction of the unlimited right to forgive sins. In the process of the development of the episcopacy the original conception of the relation of the church to salvation was altered by this development. The ancient tradition held that the church was the sure communion of salvation and of saints. This communion rested in the forgiveness of sins mediated by baptism, and it excluded everything unholy. In this tradition it is not the church, but God alone, that forgives sins. As a rule this is done in baptism, though, in virtue of God's unfathomable mercy he may by special proclamation pardon repentant sinners, after death, in heaven. But by the time of Cyprian a new interpretation was given to the proposition *extra ecclesiam nulla salus* ("outside the church there is no salvation"). To Cyprian the church was no longer the sure communion of the saved. She includes both the saved and unsaved; from her proceeds the communion of saints. The institutional and hierarchical church is the indispensable medium and the absolutely necessary preliminary condition for salvation. She alone guarantees the *possibility* of salvation.

So by the time of Cyprian, Western Christian thinking can be said to be marked by the following characteristics: (1) a conception of God in which the chief categories are power and authority, contrasted with the Eastern emphasis upon God as "Spirit," (2) the sinfulness of man who had broken the laws of God, primarily by an act of his will in disobedience, (3) God's authority resident in the church, basically the episcopate, to which the Christian man must be obedient, (4) a legal conception of the relation between God and man, (5) the view that God and man can come to each other only through the church, (6) salvation thought of primarily as redemption from sin, (7) redemption from sin made possible by the church, (8) a consequent development of sacramental grace, (9) a centering of God's power and authority in the clergy, *i.e.*, the hierarchy, and (10) the notion that truth, both practically and intellectually, was guaranteed by the authority of the church.

In succeeding centuries this central notion of Christianity as the "New Law" with corresponding legalisms of various kinds had variations played upon it by Augustine, Aquinas, Duns Scotus, Calvin, and others. The medieval church was semi-Augustinian, Pelagianism having had, actually, little effect upon the basic pattern. During the Reformation, the extremely harsh doctrines of rigid Calvinism were modified slightly by Arminius and the Federal theologians. Thus it was that at the beginning of the nineteenth century in the United States this characteristic legalistic pattern of thought in regard to man and salvation was the predominant pattern upon the Western frontier.

Campbell on Man and Salvation

Alexander Campbell's thinking was one more variation played upon this general theme. Although in his famous "Sermon on the Law" Campbell repudiated the attempt of Johannes Cocceius (1603-69) and of the Federal Theology to link the "old" with the "new" covenant, he nevertheless interpreted the "new" covenant in terms of an authoritative view of God and a legal concept of the process of salvation. The New Testament was the new "law book" for Campbell. Old Testament laws, ceremonies, and institutions are no longer valid and only in the New Testament does one find the requirements, the laws, the practices, and the institutions which began with the new covenant in Christ. In this respect Campbell was a nineteenth-century Marcionite.

Campbell was quite orthodox in his view of man and sin. Man's sin was the origin of evil in the world and constitutes man's original state. In Campbell's debate with Robert Owen he seems to believe that man's inferiority to all other animals in instinctive powers and his helplessness at birth support the account of the "Fall."[1] Yet, in the same debate we find Campbell holding that man is not altogether "riveted to his physical and social circumstances." Although man is both sinful and responsible he has elements in his nature which make possible his transcendence over his environment, nature and society. But this is only a possibility—he cannot do it himself—he is dependent upon a power greater than himself.[2]

Campbell's series of "Essays on Man" in the *Christian Baptist* discloses that Campbell viewed man as composed of *body, soul* or *animal life,* and *spirit*. The "body" is composed of the earth elements; the "soul" or animal life, Campbell believed, was given much as was the case with other animals, while "spirit" (which to Campbell was an intellectual principle) was infused by God.

Spirit consists of the faculties of reason, intelligence, and volition. The *soul* consists of emotions and passions while the *body* consists of physical appetites and abilities.

To Campbell, his "faculty psychology" provided for a harmonious concert of the three faculties. That is, ideally they are so designed that they act in concert.

At the beginning in Adam the spirit (intelligence, reason, will) ruled, the *soul* (passions and emotions) was subservient to the spirit, and the *body* was the servant of both. However, Adam allowed his soul (passions) to usurp the government rightfully belonging to the *spirit*. The Fall was the triumph of passion and the original harmony was destroyed. Born a son of reason, man became a slave to passion.

God had placed Adam under law, for, says Campbell, "where there is no law there can be no liberty, virtue, or happiness."[3] But Adam disobeyed the law and as a consequence all mankind is under condemnation and death.

> In Adam all have sinned; therefore "in Adam all die." Your nature, gentle reader, not your person was in Adam when he put forth his hand to break the precept of Jehovah. You did not personally sin in that act; but your nature, then in the person of your father, sinned against the Author of your existence. In the just judgment, therefore, of your heavenly Father, your nature sinned in Adam, and with him it is right that all human beings should be born *mortal,* and that death should lord it over the whole race as he has done in innumerable instances even "over them that have not sinned after the similitude of Adam's transgression," *i.e.,* by violating a positive law. Now it must be conceded that what God can righteously and mercifully inflict upon a part of mankind, he may justly and mercifully inflict upon all.[4]

This typically Western (and particularly Calvinistic) interpretation of man, man's sin, and his punishment reaches its height in Campbell's discussion of death as the wages of sin.

> Now this reward of sin is at present inflicted upon at least ONE-FOURTH of the human race who have never violated any law, or sinned personally by any act of their lives. According to the most accurate bills of mortality, from one-third to one-fourth of

the whole progeny of man die in infancy, under two years, without the consciousness of good or evil. They are thus, innocent though they be as respects actual and personal transgression, accounted as sinners by Him who inflicts upon them the peculiar and appropriate wages of sin. This alarming and most strangely pregnant of all the facts in human history proves that Adam was not only the common father, but the actual representative of all his children.[5]

This barbaric doctrine of Campbell's should be placed alongside the more familiar statement of Jonathan Edwards' that "there are in hell infants no more than a span in length" as one aspect of early American Calvinism.

We should also note that Campbell's reference to Adam as the "actual representative of all his children" shows Campbell's indebtedness to Federal Theology, a type of Calvinism showing the cultural influence of a newer political pattern of representative government which was beginning to replace some of the absolute monarchies in Europe.

Campbell relieves the stark picture somewhat when he concludes that

none are punished with everlasting destruction from the presence of the Lord but those who actually and voluntarily sin against a dispensation of mercy under which they are placed, for this is the "condemnation of the world that light has come into the world, and men *choose* darkness rather than the light, because their deeds are evil.[6]

However, Campbell does not tell us what he believes to be the process by which infants and others who would fall into this category or those who may possibly be redeemed, are redeemed. He evidently thought it of little consequence to detail the provisions of some sort of Calvinistic purgatory or limbo.

To Campbell, salvation was made possible by Christ who is our "priest," our "Leader," a "Sun of Righteousness," our "Prophet," our "Light," the "Oracle," and "Sacrifice," which God provided. The initial step in salvation is made by God, in fact *was* made by God in and through Christ. Yet all the things that God has done for us "will truly be to us as though they were not, unless they are believed."[7] Faith in Christ is the effect of belief. Campbell asserts that faith is basically belief of testimony or of the truth, but as a principle of action it terminates in trust and confidence in Jesus Christ as a person.[8] Campbell holds that we should take Paul's definition of faith, "God has from the beginning, chosen you to salvation, through the sanctification of the Spirit; through *the belief of the truth* (2 Thess. 2:13) as "perfectly simple, intelligent, and sufficient. For the term faith he [Paul] substitutes *the belief of the truth*."[9] Then turning to Johannine literature such as 1 John 5:9, Campbell argues further that faith is the receiving of testimony and belief in it.

Faith produces repentance, and repentance is followed by baptism by immersion for the remission of sins.[10] Campbell insists that "the only apostolic and divine confession which God, the Father of all, has laid for the church—and that on which Jesus himself said he would build it, is the sublime and supreme proposition: THAT JESUS OF NAZARETH IS THE MESSIAH, THE SON OF THE LIVING GOD."[11] Conversion, which is consummated by immersion, is a change consisting of four parts: (1) a change of views (being enlightened), (2) a change of affections (being reconciled), (3) a change of state (being quickened, or "born again," or "passing from death to life") and (4) a change of life (turning to the Lord, "repentance unto life," etc.).[12] This change fits Campbell's psychology of "spirit," "soul," and "body." It is interesting to note that the change of views of the "spirit" spoken of as "being enlightened" carries overtones of the Greek notion of sin as primarily ignorance, rather than as primarily rebellion. Campbell thus deserts the Western tradition temporarily although he previously had described sin in thoroughly Western terminology. He held that Christians are persons pardoned, justified, sanctified, adopted, and saved. To them is given the "gift of the Holy Spirit," God's spirit, dwelling in them. The fruits of the spirit are "love, joy, peace, long-suffering, gentleness, goodness, fidelity, meekness and temperance."[13]

We can conclude that Campbell's ideas of man and salvation

were characteristically Latin or Western, semi-Augustinian, influenced by Calvinism and especially its modification known as Federal Theology, and also influenced by "faculty psychology." Biblically, his ideas draw heavily from Pauline sources and secondly from Johannine sources. Scarcely any reference is made to Synoptic materials.

The Thinking of Stone

When we turn to the thought of Barton Warren Stone, we will do well to ponder upon the shrewd observation made by the late Elmer Ellsworth Snoddy twenty-eight years ago in the *Introduction* which he wrote to C. C. Ware's *Barton Warren Stone*. Discussing the neglect by historians of Barton Stone's contribution to Disciples of Christ and their overemphasis upon the Campbells he says,

> To Stone belongs priority in time, priority in American experience, priority in the ideal of unity, priority in evangelism, priority in the independency of his movement, priority in the complete repudiation of the Calvinistic system of theology, and, finally, priority in sacrificial devotion to his cause. . . .
>
> This theology [Calvinism] Stone repudiated radically and totally . . .
>
> In this Stone differed radically from Alexander Campbell. Although the latter repudiated Calvinism as a basis of Christian fellowship he never did repudiate it as a type of thought. In this respect he remained a Calvinist to the end. For this reason he was never able to understand and appreciate Stone without reservation.[14]

Stone's repudiation of Calvinism began when, after a long inner struggle in which he was despondent because he had received no instantaneous work of Almighty power and consequently felt he was damned, he heard young William Hodges' sermon on the text "God is love." Stone writes, "With much animation, and with many tears he spoke of the Love of God to sinners, and of what that love had done for sinners. My heart warmed with love for that lovely character described. . . . My mind was absorbed in the doctrine—to me it appeared new."[15] However, torn by doubts that he might be deceived, Stone retired to the woods with his Bible, read and prayed, torn between hope and fear. Then he continues, "But the truth I had just heard, 'God is love,' prevailed."[16]

This was only the beginning of his repudiation of Calvinism, for it was not until he was minister of the Presbyterian Churches at Concord and Cane Ridge, Kentucky, that he clearly made his choice of repudiation. As he says,

> . . . I at that time believed, and taught, that mankind were so totally depraved that they could do nothing acceptable to God till his Spirit, by some physical, almighty, and mysterious power had quickened, enlightened, and regenerated the heart, and thus prepared the sinner to believe in Jesus for salvation. I began plainly to see, that if God did not perform this regenerating work in all, it must be because he chose to do it for some, and not for others, and that this depended upon His own sovereign will and pleasure. It then required no depth of intellect to see that this doctrine is inseparably linked with unconditional election and reprobation, as taught in the Westminster Confession of Faith. . . .
>
> Scores of objections would continually roll across my mind against this system. These I imputed to the blasphemous suggestions of Satan, and labored to repel them as Satanic temptations, and not honestly to meet them with scriptural arguments. Often when I was addressing the listening multitudes on the doctrine of total depravity, their inability to believe—and of the necessity of the physical power of God to produce faith; and then persuading the helpless to repent and believe the gospel, my zeal in a moment would be chilled at the contradiction. How can they believe? How can they repent? How can they do impossibilities? How can they be guilty in not doing them? Such thoughts would almost stifle utterance, and were as mountains pressing me down to the shades of death. I tried to rest in the common salvo of that day, i.e. the distinction between natural and moral ability and inability. The pulpits were ringing continually with this doctrine; but to my mind it ceased to be a relief; for by what ever name it be called, that inability was in the sinner, and therefore he could not believe, nor repent, but must be damned.[17]

Constantly seeking the truth, Stone tells us, one evening he was engaged in prayer and the reading of the Bible. His mind was filled with comfort and peace. At the moment he felt such a love for all mankind that he greatly desired the salvation of all. He remarked to a friend a few days later that so great was his love for sinners, that if he had the power he would save them all. The "pious person" to whom these remarks was addressed was horrified and asked Stone, "Do you love them more than God does? Why, then, does he not save them? Surely he has almighty power." Stone relates that he was immediately thrown into confusion. He retired to the woods again for reflection upon this, a very old problem for theologians holding both to the absolute power of God and also to his perfect goodness. Stone felt that it was incumbent for him to hold to both these doctrines but he could not see how it could be done. He asked himself, "Does God love the world—the whole world, as the Scripture states? And does God have almighty power to save? If so, all must be saved for who can resist his power?"[18] He thought to himself, "Had I a friend or child, whom I greatly loved, and saw him at the point of drowning, and utterly unable to help himself, and if I were perfectly able to save him, would I not do it? Would I not contradict my love to him—my very nature, if I did not save him? Should I not do wrong in withholding my power? And will not God save all whom he loves?"

As Stone wrestled with this problem his ire grew and grew at the concept of a God who would condemn men to hell for not doing an impossibility, and he says that "blasphemy rose in my heart against such a God, and my tongue was tempted to utter it."

After many days of wrestling with the problem he "became convinced that God did love the whole world, and that the reason he did not save all, was because of their unbelief; and that the reason why they believed not, was not because God did not exert his physical, almighty power in them to make them believe, but because they neglected and received not his testimony, given in the Word concerning his Son. 'These are written, that ye might believe that Jesus is the Christ, the Son of God, and that believing, ye might have life through his name.' " As Stone concluded, the requirement "to believe in the Son of God was reasonable; because the testimony given [in the Scriptures] was sufficient to produce faith in the sinner; and the invitations and encouragement of the gospel were sufficient, if believed, to lead him to the Saviour, for the promised Spirit, salvation and eternal life."

Stone evidently did not see that he had not really solved the basic problem. He had only pushed it a little further back. If God is omnipotent, he could make man believe. But if man has power to go against God, then God's power is in some sense limited and he is not omnipotent.

Then Stone relates that this was the first ray of light which led him out of Calvinism which he describes as "among the heaviest clogs on Christianity in the world." He says,

> I now saw plainly that it was not against the God and Father of our Lord Jesus Christ that I had been tempted to blaspheme, but against the character of a God not revealed in the Scriptures—a character no rational creature can love or honor—a character universally detested when seen even in man; for what man, professing great love for his children, would give them impossible commands, and then severely punish them for not doing them; and all this for his mere good pleasure? What man acting thus would not be despised as a monster, or demon in human shape, and be hissed from all respectable society? Shall we dare to impute such a character to the God of the universe?[18]

The conclusion one reaches about Stone is that his theology was largely influenced by Johannine materials (much as was the case with the church in the East) while Campbell was shaped much more by the Pauline *corpus*. In his Bible study as he wrestled with this problem, Stone, quite evidently, did not spend much time on Paul's Roman letter, particularly Chapter IX, where Paul argues that Old Testament passages referring to Esau and Jacob, Moses and Pharaoh, prove that God loves some and has wrath toward others and that why this is so is none of our business.

Stone's View of Baptism

Consequent to Stone's conversion experience and subsequent decisions in line with the thesis that "God is love" his theology became far less legalistic than Campbell's. Illustrative of this less legalistic approach to Christianity is Stone's attitude toward baptism by immersion and toward what is now called "inclusive" or "open" membership.

In his autobiography Stone relates the early confrontation of the Cane Ridge and Concord congregations with this problem. Stone himself and several others had reached the conclusion that "believer's baptism" by the rite of immersion was the correct and scriptural form. The congregations met to face the question honestly. Here is Stone's account of the meeting.

> The brethren, elders, and deacons came together on this subject [baptism]; for we had agreed previously with one another to act in concert, and not to adventure any thing new without advice from one another. At this meeting we took up the matter in a brotherly spirit, and concluded that every brother and sister should act freely, and according to their conviction of right—and that we should cultivate the long-neglected grace of forbearance towards each other—they who should be immersed, should not despise those who were not, and *vice versa.*[19]

Although Stone had become convinced of the correctness of immersion as had many of his fellow members of these two churches, the bond of union was not the "forms and practices of the New Testament church" as in the case of the movement led by the Campbells and Walter Scott. Rather the bond of union was "brotherly love" or what might be described as a return to the "spirit" of the New Testament church.

This seemed illogical and "dodging" to Alexander Campbell. Consequently he took Stone to task in an editorial in the *Millennial Harbinger.* (It is pertinent to remark here that Stone not only believed in immersion but had practiced it five years before the Campbells were baptized. In 1804 he ceased to practice sprinkling or pouring. In 1807 he was immersed.) Stone replied,

Mr. C. [Campbell], observes, "The Editor of the Christian Messenger has, it seems, contended for the *theory* of immersion, for the remission of sins, when "well guarded"—guarded, I hope he means only by *faith in the subject*," (this is my meaning). He adds "To contend for it in *theory*, and give it up in *practice*, is only to treat the authority of the Lord with contempt. Of this I hope he is not guilty." No; I assure Mr. C. and all others, of this I am not guilty. I both contend for it in theory, and practice it, from a firm conviction of its truth. Between Mr. C. and myself I see no difference on this subject, in theory or practice. The only apparent difference is, that I am not yet prepared to reject from fellowship all, not immersed for the remission of sins. If I understand him, he does. Should I reject all not immersed for the remission of sins, I should reject the greater part, even of the reforming Baptists; for very few of them were baptized for the remission of sins. I should myself be rejected, for when I was immersed it was not with this understanding.[20]

In the same issue of the *Christian Messenger* is to be found Stone's reply to a letter from James Henshall. Among other things Stone says,

I confess if I am holy and pious now, I was so before I was immersed. If I was not so then, I am not now.

My dear brother: Zeal for a favorite sentiment has carried many beyond the boundaries of truth, charity, and forebearance. I have known many so zealous for *(the doctrine of the)* trinity, that they have esteemed it the sum of all truth, and considered all as destitute of faith, who did not receive it. I have seen others who seemed to view the opposite doctrine as the very touchstone of truth, and view all who denied it, as unbelievers on the way to hell. I have equal certainty with you, that we are bound to believe everything God has revealed. But where is the man that can say he understands infallibly everything God has revealed; the Pope of Rome excepted? If all may err, is there not a possibility that my brother may have erred also?

"Oh for more of that mind that was in Jesus!"[21]

Similarly in the *Christian Messenger* of October, 1835, we again find Stone trying to release baptism from its legalistic trappings. In a reply to a certain Will S. Gooch, Stone writes,

On the subject of baptism we have been induced to write so often, and so much to satisfy enquirers, that I deem it unnecessary to reiterate the arguments already used. But well knowing that many in the "Far West" and South have not enjoyed the same privileges as others, I will again endeavor to satisfy you and them on the particular topics introduced by you in your letter to me.

We are agreed on the doctrine of baptism for remission of sins, and for the gift of the Holy Spirit. That this is the plan of heaven we all admit. We all agree that when a penitent, reforming believer is baptized, he does receive the remission of his sins, and the gift of the Holy Spirit, for God is faithful who has promised.

Your *Opinion,* deduced from this truth, is, that no unimmersed person, however penitent or believing can be saved, or have his sins remitted, or can receive the gift of the Holy Spirit. You deny present and future salvation to all that have not been immersed; for you say: "How can a person have a good conscience without submitting to immersion? And how can a person enjoy the future salvation without a good conscience?" You further remark: "Say that a man may enjoy these privileges without obedience (Immersion) and all my hopes are blasted. I am like a man standing on a pillar of smoke."

These are your opinions—*opinions* I call them, and am happy in the thought, that they are not Bible truth. You have indeed carried the doctrine to the extreme, as far as any of our bitterest opposers have ever imputed to us and farther than the most zealous among us ever dared. Though we agree in the doctrine of baptism, I dissent from your opinion. Did I believe as you do, then I must of necessity conclude that my former experience was a delusion—that I never was pardoned, or had my sins remitted—that I had never received the Spirit—that I never loved God, his service, nor his people. Were I convinced of this, I should be shut up in desperation, for I have received nothing new in experimental religion since I was immersed, unless it be the satisfaction received since I complied with what I was convinced was my duty. For this expression you, with others, have blamed me. To exculpate myself I will now fully state my reasons.

1st. Before I was immersed, I saw myself a sinner, and that the very seat of sin was in my heart. In my great distress I honestly sought the Lord, endeavored to reform and obey, as far as I was instructed by my teachers. After a long struggle against corruption, I found myself unable to conquer it. I, a helpless sinner, submitted to the Lord, believing that he alone could save me—in Him I trusted, and by Him was sealed with that Holy Spirit of promise—I was as conscious of love to God, and to His people, and to His ways, as I was of my own existence; and this not as a blazing meteor, but of growing continuance. It was by this Spirit I believed I was a son of God. I knew I loved God, . . . and this love of God led me to keep all His commandments. Had I then known that it was the will of God I should be immersed, I would with all readiness, and humility of soul have submitted. Now, if it be proved that this is not Christian experience—that a person may have all this, and yet not have the Spirit, have not remission of sin, neither present, nor future salvation—that it is all delusion—prove this from Scriptures, and then skepticism and despair must succeed.

I, with millions of the fairest Christian characters on earth, would be doomed to hell forever; why? Because we had not been immersed; and this we could not have done, because we were ignorant of it as a duty! Had I such views of God's character, I could not serve Him with cordial love.

2d. Another reason why I dissent from your opinion, is that you leave no room for mercy to those, who do not know, understand, and perform every command required by God. On this principle you would condemn the Apostles themselves. God commanded them to go into all the world, and preach the gospel to every creature. They did not understand the command and for ten years they did not obey it—that is they did not preach the gospel to the Gentiles till Peter was expressly sent to Cornelius. Were they guilty? Had any of them died before the command was understood and obeyed, would he have been excluded from heaven? Their prejudice prevented them from understanding it. Yet did not God bless them abundantly with His Holy Spirit and fellowship, while they were living in disobedience every day—every hour? How many pious, holy people there are who are ignorant of the command, 'Be immersed,' and consequently do not understand nor obey it? Shall we say, 'God will not bless them—that he cannot do it, because they live in disobedience?' Then say, he could not bless the Apostles in their disobedience; and thus contradict a matter of fact.

. . . .

3d. Another reason for rejecting your opinion is, because they who profess this doctrine are no better than those condemned by them. We see no more fruits of the Spirit in them—no more holiness in their lives—no more humility and self-denial. If all others besides themselves are deceived, are yet in their sins, surely we should expect they would shine pre-eminently bright, and conspicuous as lights in the world. But alas! is this true? Do we not see as much conformity to the world manifested—as much pride—as much injustice—as much avarice?[22]

The spirit and approach of Stone is nowhere better shown than in this short statement, "But to denounce all not immersed as lost, and to cut them off from salvation however holy and pious they may be, appears to dethrone charity and forebearance from our breast. If I err, let it be on the side of charity!"[23]

The Present Situation

As the two movements merged (1832), churches founded by ministers and laymen of each group tended to preserve the typical approach to the doctrine of man and salvation inherited from the early leaders of each movement (Christians and Reformers) which united to form what we now know as the Christian Churches or Disciples of Christ. As a consequence there is and has always been tension at this point as well as at other points—such as the basic approach to Christian unity, open membership and open communion—as the two streams of thought have now run parallel, now intermingled, and at times run against each other in the history of the Christian Churches.

The result has been that there has been from the first, and now is, considerable diversity of opinion among Disciples as to anthropology and soteriology. It may run to one extreme as that expressed by an old elder in the first church which I served as a minister following my graduation from college in 1932. As we were preparing for a baptismal service, he rather anxiously admonished me, as a young minister, to be sure that "every hair was under water"; otherwise the converts would not "be saved." Or it may be seen in a diverse viewpoint held by some churches which admit not only people baptized other than by immersion to full membership, but members of the Society of Friends who have never undergone any kind of water baptism. I know of at least one church which admits converts to full membership without baptism of any kind in cases of severe physical disability.

Similarly, doctrines of man held by various Disciples may range all the way from a severe Augustinianism to that of religious humanism.

In the writing of a paper such as this, one is forced to reflect upon his own experience in hearing Disciple preachers and evangelists over a period of forty-five years including sermons which my father preached, and those I have heard from my youth in conventions, in evangelistic meetings, institutes, and so forth. As I recall most of the preaching it was my lot to hear as a boy in Kansas and Nebraska, the emphasis was upon sin as a positive attitude and action, not as an inherent nature. I do not recall as a boy ever hearing the phrase "original sin." Plenty was said about sin—lying, whoring, unbelief, drunkenness, "taking the name of God in vain"—and the sinner had best repent. The preaching took for granted that the sinner could make a response to the invitation. Thus the characteristic theology I remember was distinctly Pelagian, rather than Augustinian. (Since Pelagius, as an Irishman, was a "British Christian" and British Christianity had not yet been Latinized by the monk Augustine and his missionaries and thus was more Eastern than Western in thought, I suppose this means that to some extent Disciples have been de-Latinized and show some affinities with early Eastern thought.)

The process of salvation we were told was to hear the gospel, believe it, repent of our sins, confess Jesus Christ as Savior and Lord, and be baptized. If we did, we would have remission of sins and the gift of the Holy Spirit. This was to be followed by living the Christian life.

Baptism for the remission of sins almost always carried the implication that the waters of baptism in some way washed away sins. Poor mistaken souls who had been baptized with only a little water could not possibly have had much cleansing done. Certainly for many Disciples the Baptist accusation that Disciples really believed in "baptismal regeneration" was a valid charge. Acts 2:38 was a text popular among the preachers.

In our time, undoubtedly for most laymen among Disciples and for a large number of ministers the Christian faith is viewed largely in legalistic categories of thought. The Bible is viewed in some sense as God's "law book" and God himself is conceived primarily as a judge, and the plan of salvation is set out in terms remindful of the process of law. Quite frequently, even today, one hears sermons by Disciple preachers on baptism in which the emphasis is on what is called "obedience to the gospel." This legalistic concern has resulted in two divisions among Disciples of Christ, for in its history on two occasions groups of members and churches left Disciples. Their ground for doing so was the conviction that Disciples were no longer following God's law book nor obeying its precepts.

At present, Disciple anthropology and soteriology, already diverse, is being influenced by ministers and teachers whose theology has been molded by contemporary fashions in theology according to the prevailing winds in the universities and theological schools these ministers and teachers attended. The extent of this influence is yet to be seen. It would seem that Disciples have been less influenced by neo-orthodoxy and existentialism than have those churches with more direct connections with European traditions in theology and polity. Disciples seem to be reluctant to take flights off the ground very far in either metaphysics or theology and prefer to walk more slowly on the ground. This is undoubtedly due to the initial cast given to Disciples by the English tradition in philosophy rather than the German. Locke and his English successors still influence the majority of Disciples. This influence, combined with the early and traditional ideas about man and salvation held by Disciples, seems to cause Disciples to be wary of prevalent fashions in theology. This is a source of dismay and frustration to some of our theologians and a source of joy to others.

All of which is to say that from the very beginning of our "movement" until this day there is no such thing which could be characterized as "Disciple anthropology" or "Disciple soteriology," for from its very beginnings there has been considerable diversity of thought in these areas. All that one can do is to designate the major streams of thought which can be discerned. Like other areas of Disciple thought this means a lack of unity in doctrine which sometimes causes our representatives in ecumenical meetings some frustrations. Yet there are some values which cannot be ignored in this very fact. Chief of these is the plasticity and freedom possible with real potentiality for growth and creative development. A clash of doctrines is not a disaster, but an opportunity.

NOTES

1. Campbell, A. & Owen, R. *A Debate on the Evidences of Christianity* (A. Campbell, Bethany) 1829, Vol. I, p. 115.
2. *Ibid.*, p. 59.
3. Campbell, A., *The Christian System,* 2nd edition, 1839, p. 26.
4. *Ibid.*, p. 29.
5. *Ibid.*, pp. 29-30.
6. *Ibid.*, p. 31.
7. *Ibid.*, p. 55.
8. Idem.
9. *Ibid.*, p. 56.
10. *Ibid.*, pp. 53-58.
11. *Ibid.*, p. 58.
12. *Ibid.*, p. 64.
13. *Ibid.*, p. 66.
14. Ware, Charles Crossfield, *Barton Warren Stone* (St. Louis: The Bethany Press, 1932), pp. xi-xiii.
15. Stone, B. W., and Rogers, John. *The Biography of Eld. Barton Warren Stone* (Cincinnati: J. A. & U. P. James, 1847), pp. 10-11.
16. *Ibid.*, p. 11.
17. *Ibid.*, pp. 30-31.
18. The story and quotations are to be found in pages 31-33 of the same source.
19. *Ibid.*, p. 60.
20. *The Christian Messenger,* Vol. IV, No. 12, December, 1830, p. 272.
21. *Ibid.*, p. 270.
22. *The Christian Messenger,* Vol. IX, No. 10, October, 1835, pp. 220-223.
23. *The Christian Messenger,* Vol. IV, No. 10, September, 1830, p. 236.

PART TWO

THE HISTORIC CHURCHMANSHIP OF DISCIPLES OF CHRIST

8

Reasonable, Empirical, Pragmatic

The Mind of Disciples of Christ

W. B. Blakemore

On September 12, 1958, at the dedication of the cenotaph in the forecourt of the Phillips Memorial Library at Nashville, Tennessee, which now houses the Disciples of Christ Historical Society, the dedicatory prayer was given by our great historian, Winfred Ernest Garrison. Toward the close of his prayer he used approximately these words, ". . . and may we remember, O Lord, that there is yet more light to break forth from thy word and thy world." With these words W. E. Garrison rang a change upon the classic utterance of the Reformer, John Robinson, that there is yet more light to break forth from God's holy word. It was not the first time that I have heard W. E. Garrison speak as he did, for Dr. Garrison belongs among the "liberals." But the whole issue for Disciples of Christ lies in the validity or the invalidity of Dr. Garrison's extension of John Robinson's phrase. Does the light which illumines Christian faith come only from the word or does it come also from the world?

The thesis of this paper is that for the main stream of Disciple thinkers—conservative, middle-of-the-road, and liberal alike—there has never been any question regarding the sole validity of a reasonable and empirical approach to all the questions of religion. The only question has ever been, "What shall be admitted as data?" In technical theological terms, the central issue in our midst has been that of special versus general revelation. Despite the fact that sometimes in our history there has been an argument carried on in terms of natural versus revealed religion, I will show that even when couched in those terms, the argument has actually been one between general and special revelation rather than between natural and revealed religion as those terms are normally defined.

The Temper of Reasonableness

All Disciples of Christ have believed in reasonableness in so far as they have rejected mysticism and spiritualism on the one hand and rationalism on the other hand. Robert Milligan would be looked upon by most of us as a good example of conservatism. He is today regarded by the conservatives as one of their champions. Milligan was educated at Bethany College and felt that in his teachings he was accurately duplicating the teachings of Alexander Campbell, and I have no reason to believe that in the area of methodology this was not the case. Milligan left behind two extensive documents. One is *The Scheme of Redemption,* which is very widely read and is a systematic theology paying no attention to methodology. After seventy-five years, it is still being reissued. But Milligan wrote another lengthy book which has no such continuing popularity. This book is his *Reason and Revelation,* which deals with his theological method. It is interesting to turn to this book and quote it at some length. The methodology which Milligan endorses is an empirical method to be applied to the scriptures, primarily the New Testament. In so far as the opening passages present an empirical method, the passage would be affirmatively endorsed by Disciples of virtually every theological stripe.[1]

My theme is The Province of Reason in matters pertaining to Divine Revelation. On this, as on most other questions of great practical importance, mankind have long been divided. Some run to one extreme, some to another. The Mystics, for example, constrained by their false system of philosophy, have generally assigned to Reason a very low and subordinate place in the investigation and discovery of truth. With them, the *Inner Light* (lumen internum) produced by the immediate and direct operation of the Spirit of God on the sensibilities of the human soul, is the guide of life. Without this, Reason, in their estimation, is blind; and the Bible is a sealed book, an inexplicable enigma.

The Rationalists, on the other hand, give to Reason all authority. Whatever they can explain rationally, *i.e.*, according to their approved system or systems of philosophy, they receive as true; but whatever they cannot so explain and comprehend, they reject as false and absurd. And hence it follows that the Bible has no more authority with them than a heathen classic. Its miracles are either wholly ignored as false, or treated as myths. And its remaining portions are constantly tortured and perverted in the ever-varying crucible of whatever may happen to be the popular system of philosophy.

Here, then, as in many other cases, extremes meet. The tendency of both Mysticism and Rationalism is to greatly diminish, if indeed not to wholly destroy, the authority and influence of Divine Revelation. The former does this, by degrading Reason; the latter, by unduly exalting her. The former makes her the mere slave of feelings; the latter deifies her, and makes her the sovereign arbiter in all things pertaining to human life and human destiny.[1]

It may be useful at this point to consider how fully most of us, and most Disciples, would agree with Milligan that mysticism and rationalism are extremes, and that somewhere between them there is a valid middle ground of reasonableness. Consider how many things akin to mysticism have been given almost no standing amongst us. We take a dim view of mysticism in the more technical sense of the term, but equally we are skeptical of anything that smacks of spiritualism. We use no holy trances; we induce no visionary states; we ask no dreams, no prophet ecstasies, no sudden rendings of the veil of clay. The clairvoyants and seers in our midst, such as Cayce and Ford, may pique our curiosity, but in no wise command our faith. We are not overly given to seasons of prayer and vigils, nor even are we great devotees of positive thinking. All of these things are found in our midst, but around the edges. They may be central to other religious bodies but for us they are the periphery, the fringe. We do not even these days expect strange exercises or speaking with tongues to accompany revivals and conversions. If anyone's conversion is accompanied by more of an emotional disturbance than a few fond tears upon the part of his mother and aunts, we send for the psychiatrist. In these days we faint not, neither do we fast. So far as our religious temperament is concerned, we are all-American Gothic. I speak not of any one breed of Disciples but of our general temper whatever our theological shading. We are joyful enough, but fundamentally sober-sided. It is true that as recently as twenty years ago there were a few renowned Texas preachers who always worked themselves up to tears when they preached, but our great latter-day Texas preachers do not do that.

We are still of the mind which sees rationalism as the other extreme. If Robert Owen were to return with another set of "self-evident" propositions such as he offered as the ground of debate a century and a quarter ago, we would still be as suspicious now as our forefathers were then. We still understand deism for what it was: the deductive outworking of a strictly mechanically cause-effect presupposition with respect to the universe. Similarly, we have rejected that kind of Calvinism which, starting with a rigid definition and assumption regarding the sovereignty of God, proceeds with rather wooden logic into a view which reduces all else to automata moving at his behest. In general we are skeptical of the soundness of such systems as Thomism and Hegelianism, believing that logical perfection rarely mirrors the realities of existence.

The temperate attitude of Disciples of Christ has often misled historians and sociologists in their attempt to classify our movement. From the standpoint of the more rationalistic sects we appear to belong to that stream of pietistic sectarianism which produced so many groups in the late eighteenth and nineteenth centuries. Whatever of revivalism we took on during the nineteenth century would seem to confirm that view. On the other hand, from the standpoint of pietism ours looks like a very intellectual religion, and at an early date is was asserted that it was "a head" and not "a heart" religion. Sidney E. Mead says that it is wrong to classify Disciples as a pietistic sect, and that it is much closer to the truth to realize that they are a rather rare phenomenon—a rationalistic sect with more resemblance to Unitarianism than to Moravianism or Methodism.

The Empirical Approach

Precisely because of our traditional attitude toward rationalism, we Disciples have obviously not been at home in the midst of the theologism which has swept over Christendom this last quarter century in the wake of the revival of continental and Reformation confessionalism. Our sense of strangeness in the midst of the most recent theological period is not to be wondered at. We would not have been true to our genius if we had been able to effect a juncture with neo-orthodoxy and the revival of Reformation theology, for they have been markedly deductive in method, and Disciples have always declared for the sole validity of the inductive method.

Here again I turn to Robert Milligan to quote a passage, which so far as the fundamental methodological idea is concerned would be endorsed alike by Alexander Campbell, Isaac Errett, P. H. Welshimer, and E. S. Ames. These men would argue regarding the data appropriate to religious discussion but they would agree methodologically with Milligan regarding "Methods of Study" as he presents them in *Reason and Revelation:*

There are two distinct methods by which Scripture topics have been investigated. These are

1. *The Dogmatic.* This method consists in reflecting upon a topic until it assumes in the mind a distinct form, supposed to be in harmony with the general teachings of the Scriptures on other subjects; and then resorting to the Scriptures to find evidence of its correctness. In this way, many theological systems have been con-

structed. But its bad effects and evil tendencies are very great and very obvious. The chief disadvantages of this method are the following:

(a) *It is presumptuous.* It proceeds by first consulting human reason on a topic on which God himself has seen fit to speak. It exalts the human above the Divine, making the latter merely confirmatory of the former.

(b) *It is incomplete.* It is not at all probable that all the premises of a Scripture topic should be within the reach of the unaided human intellect. God does not speak unnecessarily; and the very fact that he has made a revelation on a given theme, is a strong presumption that man needed such a revelation—that the truth revealed was not, at least, wholly within his reach. But no man is prepared for true conclusions on any subject, till all the premises necessary thereto are fully possessed by his mind.

(c) *It is unsafe.* The incompleteness of this method makes it necessarily unsafe. For although from incomplete premises a man might, by chance, derive a correct conclusion, it is most likely that his conclusions will be incorrect. This method not only exposes the student to this danger; but it also leaves him without a remedy, which he might find in the statements of the Scriptures. For, as he searches the Scriptures only to find proof of his theory, he is likely either to overlook or underrate the importance of those passages which, judiciously used, would serve to correct his errors.

2. *The Inductive Method.* The method is laborious, too much so for any but the devotedly earnest student; but it is the only one which right reason approves, and which promises safe results. Its process is very simple, consisting, *first,* in collecting all the statements of the Scriptures upon the given topic, and adopting these as conclusions; *secondly,* in deducing from these such other conclusions as are *necessarily* implied in them.

The advantages of this method are briefly these:

(a) It brings before the mind, first of all, that which God has seen fit to say on the subject, every word of which must be accepted, and which, indeed, is generally all that is important for man to know in reference to it.

(b) It causes the Scripture *to form* our theory on the subject, instead of being made, as under the former method, *to conform* to the theory.

In the practical application of this method, this caution must always be observed, namely, that a partial induction of Scripture statement on any subject must always be unsafe. For, although the

Scriptures never contradict themselves, yet their varied statements on the same subject very greatly modify our conceptions of the whole subject, and each of its parts; so that the omission of a single statement from our collection might very greatly modify our conclusions.[2]

It should be remarked that the dogmatic method as here presented by Milligan involves only the process of deduction from concepts derived reflectively, whereas the inductive method includes both the process of inducing generalizations and then the deduction of inferences from them. Where the dogmatic method allows nothing but inferential truths, the inductive method allows both induction and deduction.

One senses here a reflection of the Disciple method as it can already be found in the pages of the *Declaration and Address,* which constantly calls for the examination of scripture in order to discover express commands and approved precedents, but allows also that propositions fairly inferred from scripture premises may rightfully be called scriptural though they may in no wise be demanded as terms of fellowship within the Christian church.

At the same time, Milligan's writing of 1870 seems to foreshadow the methodology of Clinton Lockhart in 1901, when his *Principles of Interpretation* was published by the Christian Index Publishing Company of Des Moines, Iowa. The subtitle of Dr. Lockhart's book was: *The Laws of Scripture Treated as a Science, Derived Inductively from an Exegesis of Many Important Scripture Passages.* That subtitle could have been espoused, with the appropriate changing of only a single word by many a Disciple author. For instance, J. W. McGarvey could not have objected if his *Evidences of Christianity* had been subtitled *Apologetics Treated as a Science, Derived Inductively from Important Scripture Passages.* By 1910 some further changes would have been necessary to paraphrase Lockhart's subtitle for E. S. Ames' *Psychology of Religion: viz, Treated as a Science, Derived Inductively by the Observation of Many Important Religious Experiences.* E. S. Ames, of course, was amongst those who allow the world as well as the word to be used in inducing religious generalizations. It is interesting to comment in passing that while Milligan and Lockhart alike would describe their methodologies as "treatment of the topic as a science, deriving inductively from the Scriptures," one came to be looked on as the spokesman of conservatism, and the other was early marked as a liberal and a center of controversy.

I should like to persist in my thesis that the common mark of Disciples has been the espousal of the inductive method, and that the line of division is the boundary of what they consider acceptable data, by reference to an article which I wrote for *The Christian-Evangelist* a number of years ago. The article compares the preaching of P. H. Welshimer and E. S. Ames. Later it was quoted at length by Dr. Granville Walker in his book on *Preaching in the Thought of Alexander Campbell.* Dr. Walker accepted my thesis that from Alexander Campbell onward there has been a rational-empirical base beneath the preaching of most Disciples and that, despite their seeming differences, methodologically E. S. Ames and P. H. Welshimer were one, reflecting a Disciple tradition. He says, "Although they differ widely in theology, P. H. Welshimer and Edward Scribner Ames were authoritatively described as both displaying certain characteristics that were decidedly 'Campbellite.' "[3]

Granville Walker quotes a paragraph in which I demonstrated how both Welshimer and Ames, in preaching, avoid what Milligan calls "the extreme of mysticism," that is, emotionalism and sentimentalism.

> . . . while the preaching of each man has for its purposes the arousal of true emotion, they are alike devoid of sentimentalism. Neither resorts to the use of the touching story; neither exploits human interest in the old revivalistic sense; neither is given to the use of emotionally fraught verbiage. The preaching of both men tends to begin, not with the relating of human interest stories, nor with colorful illustrations, but with propositions and facts. . . . The process by which emotion and drive are accumulated during a sermon is almost identical in the two men. The greater part of the

sermon is devoted to the steady, relentless piling up of fact upon fact, proposition upon proposition. In both cases the appeal is primarily intellectual, calculated to produce conviction of mind as the only reasonable and sure foundation and guide for the emotions. Each man in his own way, is a brilliant example of the "head religion" which characterizes the Disciples as over against the "heart religion" of sentimental appeal. It is a different set of ideas which is developed in each case. But the manner of presentation of those ideas is strikingly similar.

Walker then quotes from a paragraph which illustrates how Ames and Welshimer alike avoided what Milligan called the "extreme of rationalism."

Their sermons tend to proceed for many minutes in the manner of a platform lecturer presenting impersonal scientific fact. As the sermon proceeds, however, there emerge the characteristics that reveal the religious intent. The ultimate aim is not to communicate knowledge but to produce the type of conviction that brings commitment implying action. But this action is not to be random, nor even an activity motivated by diffuse feelings, however strong they may be. It is to be actively given direction by virtue of an intellectual illumination, the groundwork of which is solidly laid in the early stages of the sermon. The factual mood gives way increasingly, in the sermons of both men, to the actual mood. As the latter mood develops, the impersonality of fact gives way to the warmth of the preacher's own personal conviction. This strong personal feeling then acts like a spark to ignite fire into the well-laid facts in the listeners' minds.

Walker concludes by saying,

They are what Blakemore calls "new-style preachers in the Campbellite sense" representing preaching of Disciples of Christ at its best. In this respect they embody one of the finest legacies of the movement: their religion, though poles apart in theology, is alike in being an appeal to reason and common sense. Loyal to that noble tradition the preaching of the brotherhood has stood since the days of Alexander Campbell.

Disciples of Christ do not realize, perhaps, that from the standpoint of many other denominations, Campbellite reasonableness makes all Disciples "liberals." Many years ago, I was sitting at dinner with several Disciple seminary students discussing the then-current controversies between our conservatives and liberals. The discussion was sharply punctuated by the remark of a southern Presbyterian in our midst who suddenly said, "All breeds of Campbellites are liberals." When pushed for the meaning of his statement, the speaker revealed that in so far as Disciples appealed inductively to scripture instead of declaiming deductively from a standard confession, such as the Westminster, they were from his viewpoint "liberals."

For Disciples of Christ the standard position is that revelation is given by God and appropriated by reason. Faith is belief in testimony. The only real issue between Disciples is with respect to what may be accepted as testimony. Some allow only the life of Jesus Christ. Others point to the whole New Testament. These two positions form two variations of "special revelation" teaching. Others say word and world alike are the vehicles of God's revelation to man. All the disputes that have ever broken out within the Campbellite fellowship can be seen at the theological level in terms of different views regarding what may be admitted as data or revelation.

It should be remarked parenthetically that Disciples of Christ have often differed with respect to their theories regarding the way in which reason operates, and have even differed in their theories regarding what the founding fathers said about the way in which reason operates. For instance, for many years F. D. Kershner tried to insist that A. Campbell espoused the doctrines of the Scottish school regarding the operations of reason. Dr. Kershner's assertion, which he never backed up with empirically derived proof, and which Leslie Kingsbury has only partially substantiated with his Edinburgh Ph.D. thesis, always seemed to me to be invented primarily to try to discredit the Garrison-Ames-Chicago discovery of Campbell's staunch adoption of the Lockean theory of the way in which reason operates. Other Disciples obviously hold other theories regarding the operation of reason. These different theories about reason do not divide Disciples, for they are held within the more general theory that God gives the revelation which reason appropriates. Division does not come over the subjective question of the operation of reason, but over the objective question of what shall be received as data.

Campbell's own doctrine regarding the operation of reason has been frequently recapitulated in our literature. It can be found in Chapter 5, "The Reasonableness of the Revelation" in Granville Walker's *Preaching in the Thought of Alexander Campbell,* or in Chapter VII, "Campbell's Theory of Knowledge" in R. Frederick West's *Alexander Campbell and Natural Religion,* published in 1948 by the Yale University Press of New Haven. Or, if one prefers the fountainhead, he may turn, *inter alia,* to the essay entitled "Foundation of Christian Union" in *The Christian System.*

In this next section of the paper, I shall deal with the question of natural versus revealed religion in Disciples thought. Actually, there has never been in Disciple history a natural versus revealed religion controversy in the ordinary sense of the term. What has happened in the course of Disciple history is two instances when dispute was carried forward under the terms "natural" and "revealed" but only because in one instance a very peculiar definition was given to "natural religion" and in another instance a very peculiar definition was given to "revelation." We shall examine these two interesting instances briefly.

The first instance was the Campbell-Owen debate. Mr. Owen asserted that he was arguing the case of a natural religion, the chief tenets of which were the "laws of human nature." However, when one examines Mr. Owen's "laws" and his deductive method of using them, it is obvious that he belongs not within the fold of what is ordinarily called natural religion, but within the fold of rationalism. Mr. Owen was a lately-come Deist, but since he called himself a defender of "natural religion," Mr. Campbell stated his own case as being that of "revealed religion." Actually the argument was between a set of rationally conceived "laws" and the biblical story of man's creation and development.

The second instance was the liberal's rejection of the term "revelation." Somewhere in his book *The Prophetic Voice in Protestant Christianity,* Ralph Wilburn makes the point that the real issue between liberalism and the newer theological mood is the issue of "revelation." It is certainly true that on many occasions liberals spoke as if they had no use for the term "revelation" at all. At other times, they spoke as if the relevant issue were general versus special revelation. Let me approach the problem through relating an episode.

Many years ago, Dean Shailer Mathews was present at a Tuesday noon luncheon at Disciples Divinity House in Chicago. I remember that Professor E. S. Ames, Professor W. E. Garrison, and perhaps Professor W. C. Bower were in attendance on this occasion. During the discussion a student said, "Dean Mathews, you call yourself a liberal, and these other professors call themselves liberals. What do you consider your common distinguishing mark as liberals?" After only a moment's hesitation, Dean Mathews said, "It is that we have never called anything a revelation," and glancing at his fellow liberals, he received the nods of approval which he expected of the characterization of them all which he had put forward. In actuality, those who knew these liberals knew that they were not arguing against "revelation" if it were used with the traditional Campbellite meaning of the term, *i.e.,* that which has been given for us to appropriate through reason. They were rejecting the term "revelation" in so far as it had come to mean either (1) private or esoteric knowledge (what Milligan called the extreme of mysticism), or (2) God-given generalizations from which all other religious items must be reduced.

However, these liberals had come to believe that the term "revelation" could never be divorced from these two latter meanings—either of which allowed for an authoritarianism. They cared to abandon the term and espouse the term "natural religion," but would have acknowledged that nature was a "given" to be understood by reason. In this sense, not only the word, but also the world are "revealed" and are to be appropriated by reason. Or rather, the world is that which is revealed while the word is the best understanding of it so far achieved, and achieved precisely because of some special character in Jesus of Nazareth.

The Pragmatic Attitude

At the outset I indicated that I wished to add the term "pragmatic" to the title of this paper. Disciples cannot be understood without recognizing the important role which the pragmatic attitude has had amongst Disciples of Christ from the earliest days of the movement.

In another connection, I have pointed out that so far in our Disciple history there have been three syntheses: the original Campbellite synthesis represented by *The Christian System;* the conservative synthesis represented by Robert Milligan's *Scheme of Redemption,* and the liberal synthesis represented by such books as Garrison's *Affirmative Religion* or E. S. Ames' *Religion.* Milligan's synthesis represented the high watermark of an unchallenged biblicism in the sense that the word provides the data of revelation. But already in Milligan's day, modern biblical criticism was destroying that inerrant New Testament which could be used as the Campbellites had been using it. When the liberal synthesis came, it involved not only the appeal beyond the word to the world. The liberal synthesis picked up another typically Disciple note and made it integral to the liberal point of view. Liberalism laid hold upon the principle of expediency which was already a well-established principle amongst Disciples and recognized its implications for a pragmatic criterion which theology must acknowledge.

At their origins, Disciples were asserting, "Where the scriptures speak, we speak, and where the scriptures are silent, we are silent." These words are ascribed on the cenotaph at Nashville to Thomas Campbell. There is no doubt that at times Campbell used the words, but it can be seriously questioned whether they were original with him. The words have caused us trouble enough. Actually, it might be very well if we said, "Where the scriptures speak, we don't have to speak because God has; where the Bible is silent, we have to speak because God has not." In truth, the latter is the way in which we have had to behave—and had to behave from a very early date.

Long before Thomas Campbell was dead, both he and his son had discovered that they could not, where the Bible is silent, keep silent. They were forced to speak, and to control their utterances they had discovered the law of expediency. The law of expediency is that it is necessary to act in order to achieve some desired end which is inherent in the kingdom. As defined in Chapter 27 of *The Christian System,* the law of expediency must be used with respect to all those things wherein no "Thus saith the Lord" has been given, but which are of vital importance to the well-being and prosperity of the kingdom. Furthermore, the law of expediency is the law of adopting the best discernible present means of attaining any given end, or of adopting the most promising means for the discovery of what our aims should be.

The doctrine of expediency has been with us ever since the early Campbellites discovered the *lacunae* in biblical precept, and, true to their rejection of dogmatic and deductive procedures, chose to augment their inductive approach with acts of expediency. Nothing is more indicative of the real freedom of the Campbellite mind from creedalism and confessionalism, from authoritarian dogmatism.

Expediency has played an important role in our midst. It has been used to settle problems that could never be settled by reference to the biblical text. Isaac Errett appealed to "expediency" more often than he appealed to scripture. Whenever Thomas Campbell was confronted with a practical problem, he would "search the scriptures." Issac Errett was much more likely to apply the law of expediency. He invoked it particularly with respect to the organ controversy. This pragmatic attitude was maintained by the *Christian Standard* long after Isaac Errett's death. In recent years it was present in a feature page headed "It Worked for Us," in which all sorts of religious educational and ecclesiastical procedures were reported and approved—not because they met some biblical standard or were read either inductively or deductively off the pages of holy writ, but rather because they "worked" with respect to the aims of the kingdom.

When the Chicago liberals, a generation ago, insisted on emphasizing the pragmatic dimension of Disciple mentality, they were only pointing to something typical of the whole brotherhood in all its parts. In the present theological moment with its greatly renewed emphasis upon historic confessions and the Bible, pragmatism is under a very considerable cloud. It is even scorned and is somewhat of a whipping boy. But most Disciples would still say we are a practical rather than a speculative people.

The first two Disciple syntheses—the Campbellite and the Milliganite—were based on a view of biblical authority which, by the end of the century, was seriously challenged by biblical criticism. Other denominations had already faced the challenge. To be frank about it, most denominations were like Disciples in resisting the extreme of mysticism on the one hand and the extreme of rationalism on the other hand. When biblical criticism swept away an inerrant New Testament, they did not succumb to one or another of the relatively subjective types of religious thought. By and large, Americans and Protestant thought found their objective controls either in history or in nature, and even when they appealed to religious experience, they were not doing so in any individualized subjective sense. The early part of the century saw a development of both historicism and naturalism in religious philosophies throughout

Protestantism. Disciple liberalism participated in both of those movements. But there was something else in Disciple liberalism which was unique and came out of the life of a practical people. Disciple liberalism was historical, naturalistic, and pragmatic, and through its pragmatism it added, as virtually no other Christian body has ever done it, the judgment of the future upon our present scene. One might say that the historical attitude sees the validity of facts regarding the past for the determination of religious thought and conduct. Naturalism adds the dimension of the present; it asserts validity of the facts regarding continuing states of affairs for the determination of religious thought and conduct. Pragmatism adds the dimension of the future, and asserts that emergent facts have their place in the validation of religious faith and conduct. This Disciple recognition of the validity of the pragmatic gave our people an eschatological character. They have deeply sensed that consequences are undeniably part of the criteria of judgment of anything, even religion. It is to be hoped that the scorn and calumny which the present age pours upon pragmatism will not deflect Disciples from this futurist dimension which has been with them from the beginning, and that they will continue to believe that their practices must be judged not only by biblical and historical criteria but also by whether or not they "work."

In another connection, and dealing specially with the possibility of merger between Disciples and some other denomination, I have said:

> We have a continuum of judgment with past, present, and future as sources of criteria. Not only must any merger respond to the Will of God out of which it came, and the laws by which the church prevails; it must also respond to the judgment of its consummation of very specific items of progress in missions, benevolence, social influence, the spirit of intelligence, and an increase in our capacity to love God and our fellow man.

It may be well to point out that there may be a distinction between the motivation of the Stoneites and the Campbellites toward unity. The Stoneite ideal is largely expressed in terms deduced from the notion that eventually there should be a single church organization. Therefore, to "die the death" and "sink into union with the Body of Christ at large" is the aim deduced from this idea of the ultimate character of Christian unity. Christian unity is, from this point of view, to be a unity of sects. The Campbellite aim is rather the unity of Christians. If one again uses phraseology from the propositions in the *Declaration and Address,* the aim of Christian unity is that Christians may be without uncharitable divisions, that they may receive each other as Jesus Christ has also received them, walking by the same rule, minding and speaking the same thing, perfectly joined together in the same mind and the same judgment. I think it would not be right to make too much regarding a difference between Stone and Campbell at this point. Both of them were concerned for unity in their day, and the difference in their way of stating the ultimate aim was only a nuance at that time. However, in our own day we should recognize that there is a distinguishable difference between those who think of a single "Coming Great Church" and from that ideal seek to determine next steps for Christian unity, and those who understand Christian unity to mean fundamentally the unity of Christians without any prejudgment regarding the ultimate ecclesiastical questions.

It has already been pointed out that Disciple thought did not fall in line with the theological revival of the late 1920's and early 1930's. Neo-orthodoxy was, for Disciples, too speculative in mood, too rationalistic in its method of rooting thought systems in confessions or a few dominant conceptions. Only more recently, with the emergence of a biblical theology, have Disciples been able to feel at home with the current theological climate. Biblical theology once again established a basis of detailed data upon which the mind can go to work empirically. To do it requires the acceptance of a special status for the biblical writings, and of some specialization in the revelation. All of these matters require that eventually we must arrive at some understanding of biblical authority and of the nature of revelation. At this point, we are concerned only to raise those issues which our history brings to the fore.

The Nature of Faith

There is one further point which I would like to discuss, or reopen for discussion. It is a point which has come up several times in the deliberations of this Panel of Scholars and was given considerable elaboration by Dwight Stevenson.[4] The issue centers in the problem of faith as belief in testimony and faith as personal commitment. Disciples of Christ were early characterized as having a "head religion." We understand the accusation. It arises not only from a definition of faith as belief in testimony. It came about because of the sobriety of early Disciple preaching. The sermons of early Disciples were markedly free from manipulation of the sensibilities of the hearers. But Disciples have often felt their approach to religion to be too intellectual, and over against their definition of faith as testimony they have adopted also a definition of faith as personal commitment, or as personal loyalty to Christ, or as loyalty to the person of Christ. As Dwight Stevenson pointed out, an early instance of this way of speaking about faith is to be found in Robert Richardson's *The Principles and Objects of the Religious Reformation, Urged by A. Campbell and Others, Briefly Stated and Explained.*

One of the major points of the book is that faith is to be understood not as doctrinal but as personal, not as centering on doctrine, but on a person. Stevenson showed that this view as expressed by Richardson is in accord with Thomas and Alexander Campbell and Walter Scott. So far as that is concerned, practically all Disciples have accepted this way of stating the case. I have frequently heard it said that what we call the believer to is the acceptance of a personal Savior. I wish I had a dollar for every occasion upon which I have heard a Disciple say, "Faith for me consists not in what I believe, but in whom I believe." I wish I had a dollar for every time I have heard myself say it. The person of Jesus Christ was the heart of every sermon ever preached by Burris Jenkins. Time and again I used to hear E. S. Ames speak of Christian faith as personal loyalty and commitment to Christ. He would invoke Luther to emphasize the double meaning of faith as belief and as trust. Dwight Stevenson stands in a noble tradition when he wants to develop the kind of Christology implied in his paper.

First we should disabuse ourselves of the illusion that this way of handling our religion is distinctive to the Disciples. Robert Richardson wrote,

> But we differ from all the parties here in one important particular. to which I wish to call your special attention. It is this: That while they suppose this Christian faith to be *doctrinal,* we regard it as *personal.* In other words, they suppose doctrines or religious tenets to be the subject-matter of this faith; we, on the contrary, conceive it to terminate on a *person,* THE LORD JESUS CHRIST HIMSELF.[5]

So wrote Richardson in 1853, offering this personal definition of faith as the distinguishing mark of Disciples. Such an identification of a "distinguishing mark" proves an embarrassment, however. It tends to show that Robert Richardson did not really understand the religious world in which he lived. In the first half of the nineteenth century there were many who were making the statement that Christianity was for them a personal rather than a doctrinal matter. It was exactly the sort of thing being said in the 1830's by Horace Bushnell. It was the sort of idea which was leading to a complete rethinking on Bushnell's part of the nature of Christian nurture. A decade ago I wrote a short article entitled "Campbell Out-Campbellited." I quote briefly,[6]

> I have found Campbell out-Campbellited because a nineteenth-century Anglican succeeded in saying with magnificent precision exactly what Thomas and Alexander never quite succeeded in saying so clearly. Here are Maurice's words:
>
> "The Church is a body united in the acknowledgment of a living *Person;* every sect is a body united in the acknowledgment of a certain notion."

This quotation is from Maurice's *Kingdom of Christ* (1858), Vol. II, p. 338, and appears on p. 209 of A. P. Vidler, *Witness to the Light; F. D. Maurice's Message for Today* (Scribner's, 1948).

"The church unites around a person; a sect unites around a notion." Was there ever a more accurate way of stating just what the Campbell's wished to say? . . .

Maurice was among the most beloved of nineteenth-century Anglicans. In the midst of High, Broad, and Low church parties he stood above the tides of doctrine and grasped the essence of the unity of the church in the person of Jesus Christ. His insight is applicable far beyond the bounds of Anglicanism.

It is important to note that Maurice was writing more than twenty years ahead of Robert Richardson. It is important also that in our day, every Protestant group has preachers and theologians, and they are of every "school," who ring some change upon the idea that "God sends us not a 'what' but a 'whom.' " The idea that "faith centers on a person" is not the peculiar position of any one branch of Christendom because it is of the very nature of Christianity itself.

It might seem, therefore, that the idea of a "simple personal confession of faith" might be accepted by all as the basis for church membership. This, however, is not the case, for each man understands this basis differently. For the rationalist, faith centers on the Christ, but the articulation of the faith comes in terms and concepts—and faith can speak to faith only through terms and concepts. From this point of view it is only as there can be a common acceptance of a conceptual expression of faith that unity can be discerned, and a creed becomes the prerequisite of unity. For the Roman Catholic, no less than for the Quaker, faith centers on the Christ, but, for the Catholic, faith reaches self-understanding in the individual only through the assistance of the church at the center of which Jesus Christ stands, while for the Quaker an inner illumination is necessary.

I am quite sure that one of the reasons why Disciples like this "personal" definition of faith is that it seems to restore to them a concrete and historic basis for religious thinking, to wit, the historical Jesus. Furthermore, our weekly practice of communion enhances our sense of the "personal Christ," or of Jesus Christ in a very personal, or human way. At communion we remember his life, his work, and his sacrificial death. The emblems are not for us a portion of some divine substance, but the provocation of our memories and the church's memory of a concrete earthly existence. Communion is a memorial and, to many Disciples, nothing more. We are left with the impression that this personal Christ to whom we are committed we can grasp empirically, reasonably. When Disciples speak of faith as personal trust in Christ, they really mean Jesus Christ as a historic person—the Nazarene, the Galilean living out his days in loving service and teaching, and dying sacrificially for us. This exemplary Christ is today everywhere exemplified in Sallman's *Head of Christ.* His intense popularity Disciples share with many another denomination. This is the most widespread form of popular Christianity in Protestantism today. But it is not Christianity. It is rather a religion of the good man, the "dedicated" man, the prototype of all those "dedicated" souls who make today's world of business and organization, art and fashion, diplomacy and good works go round. It is not Christianity, but Christ*ism,* a religion which begins and ends with Christ Jesus of Nazareth. This Christ often appears in some "modernized" form. But that is not the difficulty. The historical Jesus and the modernized Christ are alike inadequate if they have become the objects of religious devotion, if they stand at the center of what James Hastings Nichols very aptly calls a "unitarianism of the Son." Such a "unitarianism of the Son" is precisely the character of much modern-day religion including much Disciple religion—and it is so just because we have too uncritically tended to give up our understanding of faith as assent to testimony in favor of faith as personal trust. This popular religion misidentified Christ the Revealer for the God who is revealed in and through Christ.

In classical Disciple thought, the personal Christ is ultimately important because he is datum for constructing our belief about

God, not because the Christ is the object of religious devotion. In fact, the very intellectualism of our earliest formulation, which we so often deplore, is the very character about our understanding of faith which makes us move on beyond Jesus Christ to that of which he is index and datum, namely God himself. Jesus Christ is not that which is revealed for us to worship; he is the Revealer. The revelation is given through the Christ for us to appropriate. In and through him we see and know God, and this knowledge saves us. In so far, God was in Christ reconciling the world unto himself. Jesus of Nazareth stands in the center of the data from which we derive our understanding of God. In this sense our religion is Christological; but in a very real sense it must not be Christocentric, because it must be theocentric. One way of understanding the significance of the good confession by which we accept persons into church membership is to understand it as meaning, "I am committed to seeking God and what he requires of me through the Christ; as I join my fellow men in the eternal search for God, I too accept the New Testament presentation of Jesus Christ as my primary datum."

It is important to remember that toward the end of Dr. Stevenson's presentation the term "God in Christ" becomes more and more frequent, the term "Christ" less frequent. This is a shift in the right direction, but I believe its significance is not adequately stated in Dr. Stevenson's own paper. If it is "God in Christ" who is the object of our loyalty, it is because the Christ bears witness to him, it is because God is manifest in Christ. Our faith in Christ then is our acceptance of him as the testimony to the God in Christ to whom we should be committed. That means that our "intellectualistic" definition of faith does have the priority and importance given to it by our forefathers. Their theology was Christological, based in a knowledge of the Christ. This Christological tendency of Disciples of Christ is important because at base it is reasonable and empirical. It recognizes that there is a realistic base to Christian thought.

Our religion has no validity unless it gives meaning to the history that has been, gives us an understanding of the nature and experience in which we are now set, and awaits expectantly the new light that is to break forth. In so far as religion does truly interpret life, the remaining question is whether all of life or only that particular segment of it which is Judeo-Christian history may be used as the data of religious inquiry. Whether or not, and in what way, both the word and the world are to be data for our knowledge of God still remains a question of high priority for Disciples of Christ.

NOTES

1. Robert Milligan, *Reason and Revelation* (St. Louis: Christian Publishing Co., 1870), sixth ed., rev. and enlarged, pp. 15-16.
2. *Ibid.*, pp. 415-417.
3. Granville Walker, *Preaching in the Thought of Alexander Campbell* (St. Louis: The Bethany Press, 1954), pp. 86ff.
4. *Vide supra*, p. 334.
5. *The Principles and Objects of the Religious Reformation Urged by A. Campbell and Others* (Bethany: A Campbell, 1853), p. 26.
6. W. B. Blakemore, "Campbell Out-Campbellited," *The Scroll*, XLVII, 4 (Dec. 1949), p. 131.

9

The Structure of the Church

Freedom and Authority in Matters of Polity

D. RAY LINDLEY

IT is doubtful if any religious group ever has been more completely stamped with the personality of its foremost religious leader than has the communion of Disciples of Christ. For almost a century and a half now we have been reverberating the tones which Alexander Campbell tolled. Some of them have been clear, true notes. Others have been clanging, discordant tones. We have been marked by the strength of his religious genius, the tragedy of his weaknesses, and the confusion of his contradictions. A movement which began with a joyful plea for the unity of God's church now finds itself fractured into at least four distinct groups, each one claiming Campbell as its authority, and each one finding, in Campbell, ample justification for its claim.

Campbell achieved a profound spiritual insight which led him to wage war on "sacerdotalism" in all its forms. Now sacerdotalism simply defined means "priestcraft." It includes all the rituals and techniques by which the "priesthood" is exalted into a so-called "sacred" order, and looked upon as being in possession of mysterious powers which are denied ordinary men.

Campbell conceived that God created all men as blood relatives. He said, "God made men, the priests make laymen. Man is the creature of God, a layman the creature of priests." It was this insight which led him to point out that Protestantism had subverted its own doctrine of the "priesthood of all believers." He charged that it did this by its insistence that the call to the Christian ministry is either by the magical succession of grace through the laying on of hands in an apostolic line on the one hand, or the result of an arbitrary act of God's direct intervention on the other. Other ways by which it did this, he held, were by the coercive power by which its ecclesiastical courts thwarted freedom of expression, by the arbitrary use of its creeds as tests of religious fellowship and thereby of religious exclusion as well, and by its heresy hunters being self-constituted as a sort of Gestapo of orthodoxy. Thus, while professing to make men subject to God, he held that Protestantism had succeeded only in bringing them into subjection to the clergy.

Campbell moved from this insight to the conclusion that God's activity is not arbitrary and capricious, but dependable and impartial; that the experience of redemption is not a consequence of magical Mumbo Jumbo but the natural response of the human life to divine love; that redemption is achieved not through some secret formula of priestly intervention but in the bosom of a Christian fellowship; that the universe is not a chaos but a cosmos, not one of confusion but one of order.

Thus Campbell arrived at the bedrock of his entire faith; that God acts in history, not by shattering history with an arbitrary action which contradicts his dependable laws, but through the inexorable outworking of those laws. The process of history is for God not an enemy to be smashed, but an instrument to be used. As Edwin McNeill Poteat has more recently expressed it, "History . . . is the base on which all sequence rests from digit to doomsday, for without sequence, order is meaningless."

The evidences of this faith on Campbell's part are abundant. He conceived the call to the ministry not as an arbitrary act of God, but as the natural act of the church calling those who are best fitted to serve. His approach to the interpretation of the Bible was to see each book in its historical perspective: "Who wrote it, to whom was it written, what was the occasion and purpose of its writing? etc." Charles Clayton Morrison, in his book, *What Is Christianity?* has expressed it: "The revelation of God in history is not a dictation of truth to men's minds; it is divine action in the field of events. . . . Revelation is not a truth uttered, but a deed done. God does not perform the deed and in addition dictate man's response to the deed."

Campbell would say, "The world is the field of God's redemptive action. God works through the world, not apart from it. God works through his natural laws, not in defiance of them. God speaks to us through our human senses, not by disconnecting them."

At long last here was a religious faith from which all magical concepts had been stripped. Here was a conception of God's action from which had been weeded out all pockets of cosmic irrationality. "Christianity," said Campbell, "is a sensible, a reasonable religion." Man's response of faith and obedience to God's love is not an unnatural but a natural and a normal response. Christianity is a religion of sense rather than of nonsense.

Campbell thus affirmed the psychophysical unity of life. He saw the visible and physical world as the only known medium of expression of the spiritual world. This psychophysical unity is seen in his insistence that the mind could gain no knowledge except through the organs of the body, that the Spirit could operate only through the word in appealing to the mind of man, and that the visible act of baptism was one with the spiritual decision in accepting the lordship of Christ. It is specifically affirmed in Volume VI of the *Millennial Harbinger* as follows:

> The animal frame, the five senses, like the five mechanical powers, are but the machinery through which and by which the mind acts and is acted upon. The material universe enters the soul, or acts upon the mind only by the medium of sense; and no other universe can enter the soul but through the material universe. So that the Great Spirit operates upon the human mind through the material universe.[1]

Inevitably this means that Christianity takes on every conceivable hue in its flow through human society. Instead of being disturbed that it finds different forms of expression, we should take cognizance of the fact that its coloration is as varied as are the wide ranges of human life.

Dr. Kenneth Scott Latourette has called our attention to the fact that in its march through the centuries and around the belted globe, Christianity makes itself at home in every environment, in each culture, and, in so doing, it inescapably takes on the color of that culture. Yet, Christ has never been contained in any single culture. As Charles Gilkey says, "When we begin to look upon Him as our exclusive possession, and our house as His permanent home, He moves on out beyond us."

Campbell thus conceived the church as having its existence only in a social context. He specifically repudiated the idea of any "invisible church." Therefore, the only authority which the church recognizes is that which inheres in the nature of the church itself.

It is important to remember that the Campbells' belief in Christian union issued out of their conception of the ecumenical nature of the church, and that their goal of the restoration of the New Testament church was in their minds the first step toward achieving a united church. The beginning point, therefore, of their mission was neither restoration nor union, but it was the question, "What is the nature of the church?" The answer to that question was that the church is an inclusive fellowship, one which is determined not by questions of belief, but by the nature of the fellowship itself.

In his defense against N. L. Rice, Alexander Campbell said,

> The gentleman complains that our foundation is too broad—too liberal. It is indeed broad, liberal and strong. If it were not so, it would not be a christian foundation. Christianity is a liberal institution.[2]
>
> Mr. Rice could not, were he and I both to try, find as great a variety amongst us, of character, preachers and doctrine, as I can find in the New Testament complained of by Paul and his

associates. So that the argument is as strong against Paul and the primitive church, as against myself and my brethren.[3]

The question, for example, Would you receive a Universalist, a Unitarian? We respond, not *as such*. Nor would we receive a Trinitarian *as such*.[4]

. . . We can neither justify nor condemn a man for his unfortunate education, for his peculiar organization or his eccentric opinions. Treat him rationally. Treat him rationally, treat him humanely, and in a christian-like manner, and all these opinions will evaporate or die within him. Receive him not as a Calvinist, a Papist, a Baptist or a Universalist; receive him as a *man* and as a *christian*.[5]

We have ignored the obvious meaning of the words of Thomas Campbell when he said, "The church of Christ on earth is essentially, intentionally, and constitutionally one." It was not an invisible church that he saw as one, but the church on earth, and as Morrison has pointed out, "It was not a future union which he envisaged, but a present and actual union—the church *is one*." The one church which Thomas Campbell conceived was not an *absentee* church, but an *actual* church.

The Unity of the Fellowship

This meant the recognition of an essential unity underlying all our divisions. We have tried to imply that God is present in our midst when correct doctrine is believed, and is absent when false doctrine is present. We have ignored the fact that God is present in the *koinonia,* the organic fellowship of the Christian community.

It was this insight that made it possible for Campbell to speak in one breath as if all authority was in the Bible, and in the next for him to cry, *"vox populi, vox dei."* He believed the church to be free, but it was a freedom in Christ, not a freedom from Christ. This dictum, "The voice of the people is the voice of God," was not intended to imply that the *majority* is right. Rather it is a clue to Campbell's conception of the church as being the incarnation of Christ; it is his body.

This inevitably meant a creative democracy in which the locus of strength and authority lay in the heart of the fellowship itself. It meant a respect for the dignity of the least member of the church. As a religious institution Disciples of Christ *are* the religious counterpart of the American ideal of a free society. No religious group is in a more desirable vantage point to reflect the Christian concept of the dignity of human personality than are Disciples of Christ. Far more important than the particular decisions we make as to how we ordain our ministers, how we are represented in our conventions, and how we initiate our members, is the faithfulness by which we adhere to this basic concept of the priesthood of all believers. Our error has been the interpretation that this means the priesthood of *every* believer. The idea of the priesthood of *every* believer leads inescapably to ecclesiastical anarchy. The idea of the priesthood of *all* believers puts the seat of authority at the point of the *fellowship,* the spiritual body of Christ. Before there ever was a New Testament, Christ was the authority, and before there ever was a New Testament, Christ had returned and was glorified as authority in his church, his spiritual body. To deny the authority of the church is to deny the New Testament concept that the church is the spiritual body of Christ. The New Testament gets its authority from the church just as much as the church gets its authority from the New Testament. The error of Roman Catholicism was that it made, not the whole church, but the hierarchy the authority. The error of Protestantism has been its attempt to extract the Bible from the church as an authority when the Bible is a product of Christ's spiritual body, the church.

C. C. Morrison says,

> The basic error which has dogged the history of the church since the early centuries is its subordination of the *koinonia,* the organic fellowship of the Christian community, to the claims of doctrine, or organization, or Bible, or personal experience. . . . It is the church, the historical community revealing the wisdom and grace of God in the organic fellowship of all believers, which gives to doctrines, and sacraments, and orders, and organizational agencies and personal experiences their Christian meaning.[6]

Paul saw this clearly when he conceived the church to be the body of Christ. In his early ministry Paul shared with the early church in looking for the Lord's return. Then he became overpowered with the conviction that Christ had already returned, that he is here in the life of the church. He, therefore, began to characterize the church as the spiritual body of Christ. It is in this sense, and in this sense only, that the church is a saving institution. It is in this sense, and in this sense only, that there is no salvation outside of the church. The person who shares in the church's fellowship is a cell in Christ's body, and as such participates in the healing alchemy of Christ's body.

John Knox says,

> The words 'the life of Christ' mean for us the career of Jesus of Nazareth, but for Paul they would have meant something quite different—the present reality and lordship of the risen Son. Romans 5:10, "For if while we were enemies we were reconciled to God by the death of his Son, much more, now that we are reconciled, shall we be saved by his life." The "life of Christ" is not the remembered life that preceded His death, but the life which followed it, the present life of the Son of God.[7]

Disciples of Christ have been accused of not believing in the Holy Spirit, but here is the ultimate of faith in the Holy Spirit. The Holy Spirit is Christ alive now in his church. As Holy Spirit, Christ returned on Pentecost, and he saves us today by receiving us into the fellowship of his body. Canon Wedel says, "Churchmanship is integral to the gospel. Christ must be met as the living Lord, as the power of the living Spirit, or there can be no death of the sinner nor resurrection, and the Spirit is Christ in His body, the church."

It is this concept which was fundamental to the career of the Campbells. It was often expressed in Campbell's frequent quotation of the dictum, "The voice of the people is the voice of God." By this he meant that the church in action is Christ in action. This concept of the whole church as the creative and free functioning of the body of Christ is a part of the genius of the faith of Disciples of Christ.

This faith about the church is indispensable to its being an effective instrument of God's redemptive grace. The church is more than a genial, social fellowship. The very fact of being a part of that fellowship, I say, is fundamental to all else. We read and hear a lot of nonsense about the unworthy motives which draw men and women into this fellowship. I doubt if any human being ever came into this fellowship with a motive which is worthy. It is here that we are saved by God's grace, that his grace is sufficient for us; even though our motives are unworthy, God's saving grace is at work in the fellowship of the body of Christ.

Congregational Independency

The abiding sin of the church is the sin of fragmentation. If Roman Catholicism fragmented the church by making a fraction of the church, the papal system, the authority; and if Protestantism fragmented the church by extracting the Bible which tells of the incarnation, from the life of the church which is a continuation of the incarnation; the sin of Disciples has been that of imputing to the local congregation, which is also a fragment of the church, an authority which properly belongs to the whole church. We have emphasized independence at the cost of an essential interdependence.

In his early career, the issue of Campbell's opposition to all forms of ecclesiastical control was his affirmation of the autonomy of the local congregation.

In the earlier days of his crusade against religious tyranny, this autonomy seemed to be complete, and the justification for it was what Campbell conceived to be the New Testament pattern. "An individual church or congregation of Christ's disciples is the only ecclesiastical body recognized in the New Testament." Campbell was as jealous and as zealous in guarding what he conceived to be the freedom of the individual believer. His campaign against creeds was at once an attempt to free the living church from a dead church, to liberate the local church from an ecclesiastical hierarchy, and to emancipate the individual believer from priestly presumption. His opposition to the doctrine of apostolic succession was of a piece with the foregoing, and his denial of a "direct" call of the Holy Spirit to preach, apart from a social contract with the church, was an attempt to rid the church of what he considered to be the arrogance of the clergy. All this was in the direction of what he felt would be an untrammelled and unfettered freedom of inquiry, first, on the part of the individual believer, and second, on the part of the local congregation. The only restraint whatever allowed by him in his *Christian Baptist* days was his conception of what was "written" in the scriptures. The conflict of his literalistic approach to the scriptures with his reverence for free inquiry is nowhere more clearly evident. The two following statements rather uniquely point up this conflict:

> Weak minds are the slaves of old times, and of old customs. They need the crutches of antiquity, and human authority. But men of vigorous minds ask, *what is truth?* not *who* says it.[8]
>
> I am opposed to all innovations. Innovations, with me, are not the creations of last year, last century, nor of the last millennium. Innovations are customs, usages, rites, doctrines that commenced one year after John wrote the word amen at the end of the Apocalypse.[9]

As if the issuing of these two statements from the same lips were not enough cause for amazement, the occasion of their saying is stranger still. If the popular idea of Campbell's earlier "literalism" and his later "liberalism" be accepted, we would at least expect to find the second statement is the *Christian Baptist,* and the first toward the end of his career. But the fact is that both statements were made not only when he was at the very peak of his power, but in the very same speech, in his debate with N. L. Rice.

If Campbell did not get away from his "literalism-liberalism," he at least did change in the area of his ecclesiastical atomism. At the time of his revolt from Baptist associations he specifically rejected all forms of supralocal church gatherings which either legislated, decreed, ruled, directed, controlled, or assumed the character of a representative body in religious concerns. This rejection was categorical at the time, whether the gathering was composed of clergy or laity, or both, and whether it was called a session, a presbytery, a synod, a general assembly, a convention, a conference, an association, or an annual meeting.

Campbell no sooner sowed the wind of a loose autonomy than he began to reap the whirlwind of a rampant independency. Individual disciples who embraced his pleas for religious liberty were too completely emancipated. Many soon became neither responsible nor accountable to the church as a whole. Entire congregations were led into error and factionalism by leaders who gloried in their irresponsibility.

For a time it appeared that Campbell, after having wandered into the far country of a wild independency, having almost squandered his movement in riotous factionalism, and having fed on the husks of a barren and incompetent local church leadership, must arise and go back to his early ecclesiastical house.

The Principle of Cooperation

He escaped this dilemma by developing his "principle of cooperation." The same faith which Campbell posited in the "brethren" with regard to the administration of the affairs of the local church was posited in the aggregate of the local churches in the administration of the larger affairs of the kingdom. Just as surely as all "supralocal" organizations were deterred from coercing the local congregation, so all local congregations were under an imperative to combine voluntarily their joint counsels in making plans for the general good. The very nature of the church demanded this. In discussing the "Body of Christ," he pointed out what he considered to be such necessity:

> This institution, called *the congregation of God,* is a great community of communities—not a community representative of communities, but a community composed of many particular communi-

ties, each of which is built on the same foundation, walks according to the same rules, enjoys the same charter, and is under the jurisdiction of no other community of Christians, but is to all other communities as an individual disciple is to every other individual disciple in any one particular community meeting in any given place.[10]

Campbell here laid the foundation of his conception of the relation of the local congregation to the world church, and this foundation was the same as that upon which the individual believer was related to the local church. Joint action was required, not by virtue of any authority having been vested in a specially called set of men, but by virtue of the nature of the Christian religion. Love was the very heart of his "law of expediency." All methods of procedure were to be settled according to the law of love and the will of the enlightened majority. In speaking of this principle of church polity, Kellems says:

Campbell falls back upon a principle which is uniquely his own, his unswerving faith in the correct judgments of the enlightened common mind. In a word, the majority of those who love the Lord must always decide such questions, and the minority, as in all social compacts must quietly bow to its will.[11]

An interesting thing to note about Campbell's position is the fact that he not only affirmed the "right" of the common mind to be expressed, both in the affairs of the local congregation and in supralocal affiairs, but he affirmed the "rightness" of the decisions the common mind would make. Here is the ultimate of faith in the democratic principle.

The period of the early days of the *Millennial Harbinger* was comparable in the history of Disciples to the period of the Judges in Hebrew history. "Every man did that which was right in his own eyes." Moore says of this time: "In pleading for liberty the Disciples came perilously close to anarchy, and it required all the tact and ability of the leaders of the movement to bring order out of this confusion."

The first volume of the *Millennial Harbinger* was relatively quiet on the whole question of church organization, as if Campbell were allowing his readers time to forget some of the things he had said in the *Christian Baptist*. But the second volume began to ring with the plea for the cooperation of churches.

He reflected disappointment over the incompetent leadership which had sprung up under his "no clergy" program. He began to flay what he called the little independent "popes" with as great abandon as he previously had the "ecclesiastical popes."

Another type of problem which began to occasion alarm was the rapid spread of "general agencies" such as church publications and church colleges, which came into being as private enterprises appealing to the church as a whole for support, but accountable to nobody except their founders. Campbell began to decry the multiplication of such agencies, and his growing conviction that whatever concerned the welfare of the church as a whole should be accountable to the church as a whole was a large factor bearing upon the development of his conception of the cooperation of churches. He began to advocate the need of such agencies as church colleges, missionary societies, publication societies, and benevolent agencies, but only when such agencies were created under the joint sponsorship and authority of the churches of an area, of a state, or of the nation.

Campbell was quick to call upon the scriptures in justification of a regional plan of organization of the churches:

The churches had their angels, messengers or ministers, from its first organization. It has its Lukes, its Marks, its Barnabases, its Phillips, its Timothies, its Tituses, its Aristarchuses, its Aquilas, its Appolloses, &c., employed as itinerants and local evangelists. It had its local heralds and its traveling heralds, sent out by one church, and by pluralities of churches and brethren. They had districts of churches, and provincial fields of labor. They had churches through all Judea, in Syria, in Galatia, Macedonia, Asia Minor; churches of the Gentiles, churches of the Jews, churches of the Samaritans—churches whose public character was known and appreciated throughout the world.

Districts intercommunicated with one another; not only churches in one and the same district, but churches in different districts.[12]

This regional plan was to include the total of local congregations in the region, and every individual congregation was under a moral and spiritual imperative to share in conjoint effort, counsel, and cooperation.

The "church" district was to be commensurate with the geographical, or political district. That is, the "milicu" was to determine the size and extent of the district:

The churches were *districted* in the age of the Apostles.

This is evident from the classifications so frequently mentioned in the Epistles. For example: "The churches of Galatia," . . . "The churches of Macedonia," . . . "The churches of Judea," . . . That they were so districted with a reference to some object, or for some cause, must be obvious. The question now is, For what cause were they so districted? This we answer in the form of a separate proposition—

The churches planted in those districts of country, because of some local and discriminating interest, as well as because of the co-operation for certain specified purposes, were denominated from the districts of country in which they lived.

That churches of certain districts had peculiar interests, arising from their own peculiar circumstances, is evinced on sundry occasions.[13]

As the churches of an area were under an obligation to cooperate, so the several areas, districts, or states, were under an obligation to cooperate together, and so on in an expanding circle, until provision was made for the entire needs of the kingdom:

But as we, individually, or a particular church individually, cannot intercommunicate with all the churches in the world, we are not compelled to do so. But as far as we can intercommunicate with all the churches in a country, a province, a state, or an empire, in the fulfillment of our social duties, so, and only so far, are we bound to do so. The measure of our duty and privilege is the opportunity vouchsafed to us.[14]

This regional organization of churches, according to Campbell, was to include all the factors essential to a "perfect system of cooperation." He enumerated these factors as follows.

1. Statistical knowledge. 2. Joint consultation or counsel; not *a council,* but *counsel.* 3. Co-operation, or working together by an executive board. 4. Ordinary or stated meetings in one place. 5. And occasional meetings extraordinary on special emergencies. I do not mean ecclesiastical courts of *oyer and terminer,* or judicial tribunals; but deliberative, co-operative, and executive meetings.[15]

In order to emphasize the nature of these "stated meetings in one place," Campbell designated them as "conventions." The convention was the medium by which the churches were to cooperate, and therefore was responsible to and under the control of the aggregate of local congregations.

The local churches were to be represented at these conventions by "messengers," for which Campbell found New Testament precedent in the "great convention in Jerusalem, when the apostles, the elders, and the whole church in Jerusalem assembled to decide an existing strife between Jewish and Gentile Christians." Thus the convention among the disciples from the beginning has consisted, for the most part, of delegates from the more distant churches mingling with a mass assembly of members from the local churches.

Perhaps the focal point of disunity among the dissident groups who have looked to Campbell and his co-workers for leadership has been our failure to recognize the place and function of the convention. On the one hand, there has been too great a tendency on the part of the so-called "agencies" to believe that the convention belonged to them, and that its principal function was to serve as an avenue of propaganda and promotion. On the other hand, there have been those independent agencies which have despised or been indifferent to the convention, refusing to be accountable to it. A general recognition on the part of the total movement that the convention properly belongs to the churches, that it is the effective medium through which the churches are to cooperate and pool their efforts in the cause of the larger interest of the kingdom, might have transformed our entire history. If, "The hand cannot say to the eye I have no need of thee," then no fragment of the church can say to any other fragment of the church, "I have no need of thee." The church as the spiritual body of Christ can function as an effective organism only when the many parts are fused together into unity. The proper seat of authority is the church, and the many fragments which comprise the local congregation can express the voice of the whole church only through the convention. The proper attitude of any general agency or agent therefore is neither to ignore the convention nor to seek to control the convention, but to see in the convention the avenue through which its marching orders are received from the churches, and the occasion on which it gives an accountability of itself to the churches.

NOTES

1. *Millennial Harbinger,* Vol. VI, April, 1835, p. 152.
2. Alexander Campbell, *A Debate Between Rev. A. Campbell and Rev. N. L. Rice on Christian Baptism* (Lexington, Kentucky: A. T. Skillman & Son, 1844), p. 808.
3. *Ibid.,* p. 810.
4. *Ibid.,* p. 811.
5. *Loc. cit.*
6. Charles Clayton Morrison, *What Is Christianity?* (Chicago: Willett, Clark & Co., 1960), pp. 263-264.
7. John Knox, *Jesus Lord and Christ* (New York: Harper & Row, Publishers, Inc., 1958), pp. 206-208.
8. *Campbell-Rice Debate,* p. 608.
9. *Ibid.,* pp. 609f.
10. Alexander Campbell, *The Christian System* (Cincinnati: H. S. Bosworth, 1866), p. 73.
11. Jesse R. Kellems, *Alexander Campbell and the Disciples* (New York: Richard R. Smith, 1930), p. 392.
12. *Millennial Harbinger,* Vol. III, No. 6, June, 1853, p. 302.
13. *Millennial Harbinger,* Vol. II, No. 5, May, 1831, p. 238.
14. *Millennial Harbinger,* Vol. III, No. 6, June, 1853, p. 305.
15. *Ibid.,* p. 307.

10

An Evaluation of Our Ministry

In the Light of our History

CLARENCE E. LEMMON

THE movement known as Disciples of Christ began in the minds of ministers. Thomas Campbell came to America in 1807 bearing credentials as an Anti-Burgher Seceder Presbyterian minister. Although a year later he withdrew from the Presbytery of Chartiers to which he had been assigned, he never relinquished his position as a minister of the gospel. When his son, Alexander Campbell, joined him in 1809, he soon decided to become a minister. During the period of his preparation he once wrote to a person who offered him an educational position, "However honorable and important, in my estimation, a collegiate department may be, I have not the least inclination of devoting myself to that business. I conceive one calling to be enough for one man: I have made my choice and mean to abide by it."[1] Three years after he had joined his father, he was ordained in the Brush Run church and a certificate was issued, signed by his father and attested to by four senior deacons of the congregation. In these days of ministerial beginnings the young Alexander Campbell would affix the letters V.D.S. (minister of the word of God) after his name in order to offset the D.D. so commonly used by the established churches.

There is no need to question the fact that Alexander Campbell held his own ministry of the word in dignity. Even though he was called Brother Campbell, or Elder Campbell, never reverend or doctor, he nevertheless had a rather fierce pride in his status as a minister of the gospel and he was not reluctant to speak with ministerial authority and occasionally with arrogance. There is no question but that he held the ministry in high regard. He believed that preachers should be qualified for their work in character and, if possible, in education and certainly in industry, and that they should be carefully chosen. He did not hold for any mystical "call" to the ministry, believing that character, inclination, talents, and commitment were sufficient credentials for ordination. He came to believe in a paid ministry and urged upon the churches the support of pastors and evangelists.

Despite this, however, Alexander Campbell and the movement that he espoused became fiercely anticlerical. This anticlericalism, stemming as it did from Campbell, became a tradition among Disciples and though much mitigated, still has its influence in the life of the brotherhood.

After his ordination in 1812 Alexander Campbell spent the next few years in uneasy fellowship with the Redstone Baptist Association attacking the pretensions of the clergy, and gradually stirring up enmity among the leaders of the churches. Certain differences began to develop between the Baptists and the Reformers, one of them as to the ministry, which Garrison describes:

> The difference in view in regard to the nature of the ministry and the distinction between clergy and laity cannot be briefly and accurately stated. It is enough to say that, whereas other denominations considered the Baptist view of the ministerial office sadly loose and low, the Baptists thought the Reformers' view looser and lower.[2]

It was during this period that Campbell was preparing to start publication of *The Christian Baptist*. Richardson in the *Memoirs* describes Campbell's developing anticlericalism:

> So great, at this period was the antagonism between Mr. Campbell and the clergy that he was induced to animadvert with great severity upon their claims and their proceedings. Having entrenched

himself in the position that "nothing was to be admitted as a matter of faith or duty for which there could not be produced a divine precept or a Scripture precedent," he made from this impregnable fastness many a sharp foray into the territories over which the clergy had so long exercised almost undisputed sway. That caustic sarcasm and playful irony to which he was naturally disposed, but to which decorum forbade him to give utterance as a *preacher,* found expression through the pen of the editor, and much of the earlier numbers of the paper was devoted to lively sketches of the working of the clerical machinery in the manufacture of the preachers; in the securing and enlarging of salaries; in the obtaining of high positions and of pompous titles, and in the extending of authority by means of "confederations in the form of general councils, synods, assemblies, associations and conferences."[3]

So bitter was this attack on the clergy that his father, Thomas Campbell, "alarmed at the adventurous boldness of his son in handling so roughly things and persons hitherto considered as sacred by the people, expostulated often, and sought by contributing milder essays to soften or extenuate censures whose substantial justness he could not but acknowledge."[4]

This anticlerical attitude became a traditional feeling among the Reformers. One of the points of difference between the Stone movement and the Campbell movement which were joined in 1832 was that the Christians, under the leadership of Stone, considered that only an ordained minister was qualified to administer the ordinances, whereas the Reformers under Campbell believed that either minister or laity was so qualified. This was not unnoticed at the time, for a correspondent in the *Millennial Harbinger*[5] complained of the Christians' clergy as "the hireling system—the called and sent—the rulers." This, says Garrison, "was certainly an exaggeration . . . and a gross injustice to call any of their preachers 'hirelings.' "[6]

Alexander Campbell did not accept compensation for his preaching. He married a woman of considerable wealth, conducted a profitable farming operation, soon had a thriving publication business, and did not need compensation. His example was followed by many of the leaders who drew their compensation from teaching or farming. The word "hireling" was bandied about in those early days, and many local groups did not believe in paying preachers. Campbell sought to reverse this trend, arguing that preachers were "worthy of their hire" and that they should be relieved of secular burdens so that they might give their time and thought to the ministry. It is interesting, however, to note that as late as 1860 Campbell permitted the publication of an article in the *Harbinger* by one J. Epps, a layman and a physician, to the effect that he had made a careful examination of the whole subject and had come to the conclusion that ministers should not be paid.[7]

In 1868 friends of Isaac Errett, who was then a Detroit pastor, presented him with a silver doorplate bearing the inscription "The Reverend Isaac Errett." The cry of "priest-ridden" rose up and this little episode created quite a tempest of publicity.[8]

Reasons for Anticlericalism

It is not enough to document the fact of anticlericalism in Disciple history. It is also important to examine the reasons for it. No one explanation will suffice.

First: This attitude was a natural reaction from the sectarian feeling of postrevolutionary days. It is difficult for us to imagine the intensity of feeling that attended the various divisions of Christendom. The minister of each of these sectarian groups had a vested interest in perpetuating the doctrines, church forms, and rituals, of his own particular segment of Christianity. Much of this ecclesiastical baggage had come over from the Old Country and had legitimate historical background but was not relevant to the actual life and conditions of the primitive American people. This anticlerical reaction was bound to come and, if the Campbells had not sparked it, would have come anyway. It was a part of the feeling of the day. Thomas Jefferson and Thomas Paine had written in the same tenor. It was in the air in the early days of the nineteenth century.

Second: Campbell's anticlericalism may have stemmed from his own psychological make-up. This is discussed by D. Ray Lindley in his *Apostle of Freedom.* Campbell was quick to take offense at any affront to his person. Says Lindley,

> The trial of Thomas Campbell is often thought of as an incident, however important, in the life of Alexander Campbell. It would better be thought of as the key to his career. Coming as it did at the very time when the decision as to his lifework was being made, and being of such a nature as to outrage his sensitive spirit, it launched him on his career.[9]

That the trial of his father rankled in his soul, was an affront to his spirit, and carried over in his lifetime attitudes could be one of the determining factors in his anticlerical bias.

Third: This depreciation of the ministry also stems from the philosophical background of the later colonial and early national period of our history. The writers of the Declaration and the Constitution were steeped in the writings of John Locke, British philosopher, who contended that government was a social contract with the governed. It was natural that this political category should be transferred over into a new community of Christians forming on the American continent. To Campbell and his followers the "social contract" was between the local congregation and the minister. There was no presbytery, or connectionalism, to which the clergy had obligation. Thus any congregation might ordain a minister, without much regard to fitness, education, or, at times, even character. This premise for securing and ordaining ministers left the whole matter to congregational individualism and gave free play to the personal ambitions of individual preachers.

Garrison points out a difference here between the Reformers and the Christians of Barton W. Stone.

> The Christians, perhaps remembering their orderly Presbyterian background even while repudiating the authority of presbyteries and synods, had at least the beginnings of a method of obtaining a re-

sponsible ministry. Reports from the churches carefully distinguished between "elders" (meaning ordained ministers) and "unordained preachers." Stone criticized those who thought that a church could "induct into the ministerial office"; he considered that function as belonging to the "bishops and elders." . . . The idea was that the ministry as a whole, or by conference groups, should have power to protect the churches from erratic or unworthy ministers. There is no evidence that such control was actually exercised, but even the idea of such control was alien to the Disciples. At the time of the union, the Christians seem to have had a somewhat "higher" conception of the office of the ministry and less fear of "clerical domination."[10]

The domination of the Reformers over the Christians after the merger has not always worked out to the good of the brotherhood.

Fourth: The anticlericalism in the tradition of Disciples also has a sociological basis. While our movement began with a vehement protest against sectarianism, one feels that we were soon captured by our opponents. It was not long until the Restoration movement was quite as sectarian in spirit as the movements against which it railed. Indeed it was quite impossible for us to escape the sociological influences that surrounded our beginnings and early growth.

Such analyses as those of Elmer T. Clark in his *The Small Sects in America* and Richard Niebuhr in *The Social Sources of Denominationalism* would contend that Disciples have been powerfully influenced by the normal social trends which affected the development of all religious bodies of America. Indeed Clark uses Disciples of Christ as an example of such sectarian beginning and, with the rise of culture and education and economic status, of subsequent gradual moving into conventional denominational status. He says "the sects are usually looking backward; in their own minds they are recovering primitive Christianity, maintaining the integrity of the Bible, preserving true religion and the experience thereof, or restoring the church to pristine purity."[11]

Clark indicates that the problems of the passing of the sect into the denomination are illustrated by Disciples who lost the more sectarian segment of their fellowship by the defection of the Churches of Christ. One wonders if most of our present problems are not merely the refusal of certain groups within the brotherhood to pass from the sectarian to the denominational status.

One of the characteristics of the sect is anticlericalism. As Alexander Campbell and his followers began their somewhat primitive movement from the hills of West Virginia, the anticlerical emphasis seemed natural and persuasive. Depending upon a ministry quickly chosen, inadequately educated, and often considering preaching as an avocation instead of a vocation, they found in anticlericalism an appealing message. It was a kind of straw man which the early preachers could knock down with vehemence. This is true of cult religion as well as sects. The most vehement sessions of the otherwise placid mass convention of Jehovah's Witnesses recently held in New York, were those in which the clergy were attacked. Anticlericalism, while held in sincerity by the early leaders, was a natural and popular note to have sounded in a primitive society such as marked the beginnings and early days of our movement.

Fifth: It is only fair to say that the original emphasis of Disciples on "where the book speaks" gives a valid basis for being wary of clerical pretensions. One has only to read such Hebrew prophets as Amos and Micah and follow the controversies of Jesus with the Pharisees and the episodes of driving the money changers out of the temple to feel the antiecclesiasticism that runs throughout the prophetic portions of the scriptures. Religion is always in danger of being tinctured by ecclesiastical pretensions and clerical assumptions. In moving away from the dangers of anticlericalism we must not be blind to the dangers of clerical presumption.

Mitigating Influences

As over against this anticlerical tradition, there have been developing through the years certain mitigating influences.

There was, first of all, the need for leadership. It was not long after the beginning of the Reformation that this need appeared. Except for a few highly intellectual and well educated leaders, most of the early preachers were primitive exhorters. There were few congregations able to support a settled ministry. These preachers were farmers or tradesmen or teachers. Many of them were poorly educated and somewhat illiterate. The concept of an unpaid ministry worked against the idea of settled pastorates. In the 1830's Campbell was pleading for a better ministry and by 1840 he had established Bethany College with the important purpose of training ministers. The influence of this school began at once to be felt in brotherhood life. When W. T. Moore edited his first volume, *Living Pulpit of the Christian Church*[14] in 1868, he drew upon 29 of the most prominent preachers for sermons. Of this number, twelve were graduates of Bethany College. That was a good score for the first 25 years of the college. It is interesting further to note that two of these twenty-nine preachers had M.D. degrees, one had collegiate training in the University of Virginia, one in the University of Missouri, one in Nashville, and one in Washington College in Pennsylvania. Ten of the 29 had no college training.

At the time Bethany College was established, college training was the goal for ministerial preparation. Theology, as such, was frowned upon, but the Bible was used as a textbook. There was no thought of advanced graduate work for the preparation of the ministry. The first mention we have found of seminary training was an observation by Isaac Errett made in 1856: "Our pulpits do not furnish evidence of much intellectual or spiritual growth, *nor of adaptedness to the times. . . .* The spirits that hunger and thirst for righteousness, will seek elsewhere for sympathy and encouragement—broad views of humanity—elevated views of the spiritual are rare."[12] "There should be," wrote Isaac Errett, "a school of prophets—a theological school—where men of learning, and wisdom, and large experience, could impart the sum of their knowledge, from books, from life, and from their own souls, to the young and prepare them for wise and faithful labors."[13]

"A dislike for theological seminaries developed very early in Disciples of Christ history," says Dr. Riley B. Montgomery in his *Education of Ministers of the Disciples of Christ.*

> This attitude came about as a result of Mr. Campbell's condemnation of the clergy as sectarian leaders, who stood in the way of union and were hostile to his efforts to restore primitive Christianity. He came to feel that their opposition was to be traced to the doors of the seminaries, where they had been indoctrinated in sectarian tenets.[14]

Liberal arts colleges, similar to Bethany, began to spring up over the nation, sponsored by Disciples, most of them making as their chief apologetic the development of ministerial leadership for the churches. Some of them were of short duration, but even these did much to lift the general level of ministerial education.

It is interesting to note that when W. T. Moore edited his volume, *The New Living Pulpit*, in 1918, fifty years after the first, out of twenty-eight preachers only two had no college training, eight had college training but no degree, eight had stopped with A.B. degrees, five had Masters degrees, two had Bachelor of Divinity degrees, and two had Ph.D. degrees. The college distribution indicated that by this time Bethany College had much competition for there were only five from Bethany, three from The College of the Bible, two each from Eureka, Wooster, and Drake. There was one each from Abingdon, Chicago, Culver-Stockton, Butler, Hiram, Kentucky University, and Harvard College.

It is also significant to note that in 1868 Moore had only ten pastors contributing sermons out of the 29 sermons while in 1918 twenty of the 28 sermons were from active pastors on the field. Whereas the earlier churches had a two-level ministry, that of fine intellectual strength contributed largely by educators and writers with a much lower level of itinerant evangelists and local preachers, fifty years later the intellectual level of the pastors had greatly increased and Moore did not need to use so many educators for his symposium of sermons.

The first school for specialized training for the ministry was The College of the Bible at Lexington founded in 1865. The bias against seminaries has rapidly diminished. Disciples now have five full-fledged seminaries offering B.D. degrees in addition to fifteen colleges, three schools affiliated with large universities offering seminary training, and several schools of religion affiliated with large universities. Besides this, our ministers are being trained in such recognized seminaries as Union, Chicago, Yale, and Harvard.

The point I am making here is that the building of these institutions was not so much a thirst for culture as the recognized necessity for trained leadership.

The second mitigating influence against anticlericalism has been the general rise in the cultural level of the American people. Far larger numbers have been attending our secondary and higher schools. A congregation that has itself developed a higher level of culture will naturally demand a higher grade of ministerial preparation. The old-fashioned primitive church has almost gone with the old-fashioned primitive society. The entire nation has been suddenly urbanized so that even in a country church it is not unusual to find several college graduates. Such lay leaders naturally look for a higher level of preparation on the part of their ministry. Thirty years ago Dr. Riley Montgomery, in the preparation of a doctor's thesis at Yale, made a survey of Disciple ministers' education through the state secretaries. The result indicated that 56.6% had college degrees; 11.1% had postgraduate training; 29.6% had high school with some college training; and only 13.8% acknowledged only grade school education. No doubt the level would be much higher today.[15]

Another mitigating factor in the anticlerical tendencies of the brotherhood has been the example of certain distinguished pastoral leaders strategically placed throughout the nation. In the nineteenth century our intellectual leaders were nearly all educators or writers. An exception to that was one of the most remarkable men Disciples have ever produced—Alexander Procter of Independence, Missouri, who was pastor there from 1860 until nearly 1900 when he died. Procter ran a one-man School of the Prophets. Such men as T. P. Haley, Burris Jenkins, George H. Combs, and many other younger men got their inspiration from him. Intellectually he was a giant and, said George Hamilton Combs, "fifty years ahead of his times." No preacher could talk with Procter, or hear him preach, without being influenced by his mind and his person.

The twentieth century has produced a number of these "anchored men" who, by example, have given dignity and meaning to the ministry of Disciples. Even the most anticlerical members of the brotherhood could not discount the influence of such pastors and leaders as Haley, Jenkins, Combs, and Miller of Kansas City; the Philputt brothers of St. Louis and Indianapolis; George A. Campbell of St. Louis; Peter Ainslie of Baltimore; Power of Washington; Chilton of St. Joseph; Bricker of Atlanta; Powell of Louisville; Medbury of Des Moines; or Goldner of Cleveland. These men gave themselves to the pastoral ministry and the stability of their character, the singlemindedness of their lives, and their eminence in their own communities and in the communion raised the status of the ministry among Disciples.

Disciples ministry has been benefited by the fellowship of our churches in the ecumenical movement. When laymen and ministers found themselves working together in local, state, and national councils, there were many points of comparison with the status of ministers in other communions. A church that has a large place in cooperative Christianity will demand of its own leadership a quality of preparation comparable to those with whom they are associated.

That the anticlerical feeling among Disciples is mitigating is evidenced by the increased financial support of the ministry. William Martin Smith has dealt with this at length in his volume, *For the Support of the Ministry.* In this work he cites an unpublished manuscript prepared by W. R. Warren, who had been a Secretary of Ministerial Relief and was one of the organizers of the Pension Fund. Warren was interested in this relation of Disciples to their ministry and made an interesting chronological classification as follows:

Indifference (1809-1823)
Hostility (1823-1830)
Neglect (1830-1840)
Kindly Interest (1840-1870)
Increasing Concern (1870-1895)

Smith made a survey of the comparative salaries of full-time ministers of Disciples in 1925 and arrived at the figure of $2,317 plus parsonage. Thirty years later, 1955, the average had almost doubled, $4,030.86 plus parsonage.[16] There is no better success story among Disciples than the development of the Pension Fund, started in the depression of the early thirties and in a little over three decades accumulating assets of more than $35,000,000. If it is true that people appreciate what they pay for, it can be said that there is a growing appreciation of Disciples ministry on the part of the churches.

While the employment of the minister remains on the "social contract" basis with the local congregation and there is no presbytery or ministerial organization, there is an increasing concern being shown for the ministry in the organized life of the communion. In 1935 the San Antonio Convention appointed a "commission on ordination." In 1944, under the leadership of the Home Missions Planning Council, a Committee on Effective Ministry was set up under the chairmanship of F. E. Davison.

This committee prepared a Ministerial Code of Ethics which was widely publicized and has considerable influence. It seeks to establish the ethical relationship of the minister to his family, his congregation, his brotherhood, and the church universal. In that same year and also under the chairmanship of Dr. Davison, a Conference on Ministerial Recruitment met in extended sessions and made recommendations to subsequent conventions. No doubt this has had a beneficial effect. The United Christian Missionary Society maintains a national Director of Ministerial Services who has played a major role in developing the Disciples Guidance and Recruitment Service.

While it is still true that many local congregations will ordain, employ, and discharge ministers without reference to any outside agencies, there is a growing tendency to consult the state secretary. In the last twenty years in Missouri, it has been unusual for a minister to be ordained without the presence and participation of the state secretary. In many instances, an ecumenical note is sounded also in the inclusion of some minister or official from another communion or some council of churches in the ordination service. An increasing number of states has developed an effective commission on the ministry, and ordination is now commonly the joint action of several congregations through an ordination council, rather than a unilateral action.

In ministerial placement there is a tendency to consult the state secretary. The effectiveness of his counsel depends upon the character and viewpoint of the secretary himself, who can have much influence in the theological coloring of the ministry of his state. On the whole this is beneficial and many of our state secretaries are adept in this counseling of the local church board. It is interesting to note that the opposite tendency is at work in such a strictly connectional system as the Methodist Church. While the bishop has complete appointive power, there is a growing habit of consulting the local congregations in the appointment of ministers. As we move toward the Methodists, they move toward us.

There is a danger implicit in this system of consultation which probably cannot be avoided but should be faced. The tendency on the part of state secretaries is to place a premium on conformity. They are happier recommending the man who will go along with the organization. As was pointed out in William Whyte's *The Organization Man,* it is easy under the system of ecclesiastical guidance to put a premium on the *organization preacher.*

Another tendency which is subject to scrutiny is the use of a questionnaire evaluating ministers. These questionnaires deal, for the most part, with the surface qualities of the minister and his wife, and do not penetrate into the basic convictions which make a minister responsible to his Lord. When one reads a questionnaire coming from a state office, he reflects on the fact that it is the best way to eliminate genius. One feels quite sure that such a questionnaire would have eliminated the Apostles Peter and Paul. One doubts if such remarkable but somewhat eccentric leaders as Burris Jenkins or E. L. Powell could have passed muster. The questionnaire method is not the way to develop prophets. It tends to rub off all the corners and leave the preacher a perfectly smooth, conforming individual.

One regrettable fact is that while the state secretary may be called for consultation in the ordination or placement of a minister, he is less often consulted when a minister is dismissed. Congregations rather thoughtlessly terminate their contract with a minister without consultations with any outside parties. If that dread word "hireling" is ever applicable, it can be appended to the situation of the minister who is rather ruthlessly cut off from his congregation and his living without recourse or appeal to any larger body of brethren.

A further influence in a developing self-consciousness of the Disciple ministry as a group is in the growth of state ministerial associations. These associations create fellowship among the ministers, provide inspiration, and refreshment of their professional attitudes, and are generally helpful to the profession. In a few of the states, notably Missouri and Texas, local churches are contributing to lectureships, usually in the name of some distinguished Disciple leaders. These annual contributions are usually for several hundred dollars and are providing lecturers of good calibre.

The Pension Fund breakfast, held each year at the International Convention, brings together as many as a thousand ministers and adds to the meaning of the ministry in the eyes of the brotherhood.

In the evaluation of the ministry there is always the equation of the offce and the man. A Catholic priest, by virtue of his office and the doctrinal support given it, is held in reverence without much regard to his personality. This is true of the Episcopal clergy to a lesser extent. The Presbyterian system tends to exalt the ministry as an office. The connectional system of the Methodist Church gives some status to the preacher. In the more evangelical churches, however, reverence for the profession as such is secondary to the qualities of the man himself. The evaluation of the ministry is largely with the man and not his office.

The writer would go along with the Disciple tradition in this regard. We believe that a minister should be evaluated first as a man and then as a minister. A man in the ministry should earn respect by the quality of his preparation, the firmness of his dedication, and the stability of his character, and not primarily by the nature of his office.

NOTES

1. Robert Richardson, *Memoirs of Alexander Campbell* (Cincinnati: The Standard Publishing Company, 1868), Vol. I, p. 310.
2. Winfred Ernest Garrison and Alfred T. DeGroot, *The Disciples of Christ, A History* (St. Louis: The Bethany Press, 1948), p. 163.
3. Richardson, *op. cit.,* Vol. II, pp. 54-55.
4. *Ibid.,* Vol. II, p. 56.
5. *Millennial Harbinger,* 1832, p. 191.
6. Garrison and DeGroot, *op. cit.,* p. 215.
7. *Millennial Harbinger,* 1860, pp. 388-389.

8. Oliver Read Whitley, *The Trumpet Call of Reformation,* p. 143.
9. D. Ray Lindley, *Apostle of Freedom* (St. Louis: The Bethany Press), p. 16.
10. Garrison and DeGroot, *The Disciples of Christ,* p. 210.
11. Elmer T. Clark, *The Small Sects in America* (Nashville: The Abingdon Press), p. 21.
12. *Millennial Harbinger,* 1856, p. 491.
13. *Ibid.,* p. 550.
14. Riley B. Montgomery, *The Education of Ministers of Disciples of Christ* (St. Louis: The Bethany Press, 1931), p. 46.
15. Montgomery, *op. cit.,* p. 46.
16. William Martin Smith, *For the Support of the Ministry* (Indianapolis: Pension Fund of the Disciples of Christ), p. 30.

11

A Critique of the Restoration Principle

Its Place in Contemporary Life and Thought

RALPH G. WILBURN

THE purpose of this treatise is to offer a critical analysis and evaluation of the restoration principle, in reference to the question: what place, if any, does, or should, this principle hold in contemporary Christian thought? The particular historical and practical references are to Disciples of Christ, but the fundamental concern is a critique of the principle.

The Principle as Construed by the Founding Fathers

The historic source of the restoration idea held by the Disciple fathers lies in the movement for Independency which arose within the Church of England in the late sixteenth century and the seventeenth century, a movement which was generated by the infiltration of Calvinistic ideas into the Church of England. More radical than the Puritans, who demanded reform but who resolutely remained within the established church, the Independents called for radical action, "without tarrying for any," and proceeded to establish independent churches, in order to restore the church of the New Testament.

Alexander Campbell received a theological orientation during the year spent at the University of Glasgow (1808-1809), prior to his journey to America. At Glasgow he came under the influence of Greville Ewing and his associates, who were in charge of the Haldanes' training school for lay preachers. Campbell was evidently deeply impressed by the theological outlook of this movement. Robert and James Alexander Haldane stressed the promotion of pure and simple evangelical Christianity. "At this time their minds were turning more definitely toward the restoration of the exact practices of the primitive church."[1] Campbell also fell under the influence of the writings of Glas and Sandeman, who emphasized the need of restoring primitive Christianity, *in all details*. Many of the basic aspects of Alexander Campbell's restorationism are traceable to the impressions made on him during this year at the University of Glasgow. His biographer, Robert Richardson, says that Campbell's "first impulse as a reformer" was derived from the Haldane movement.

Walter Scott, who was reared in the Presbyterian Church of Scotland, drank from the same theological well as did Alexander Campbell. Scott came under the influence of George Forrester, the pastor of one of "many scattered primitive Christianity congregations which had sprung up under the stimulus of the ideas of Sandeman and the Haldanes."[2] When Forrester died, Scott inherited the leadership of his congregation in Pittsburgh, Pennsylvania, together with Forrester's library, which included the writings of Sandeman, Glas, the Haldanes, and John Locke.

Because of the dominant influence on the Disciple fathers of Independent restorationism in Great Britain, it was not long after Thomas Campbell launched his unity movement in America until the plea for unity was coupled with the method of restoration. The movement received a further thrust in this direction as a result of the difficulty which its leaders encountered in promoting unity within the fixity of the denominational situation then prevailing on the American scene. Hence Thomas Campbell's reform movement for unity within the existing denominational structures underwent a transition. It became less and less distinguished as a "reformation," and more and more understood as a "restoration" movement, developing the separatist, sectarian qualities and attitudes so characteristic of the spirit of Independency. "The idea of Reformation was now entirely abandoned and Restoration became the battle cry of the Disciple hosts."[3]

There was a variety of emphases among the original Disciple leaders, who proceeded to shape the structure of their movement by the restoration idea. Thomas Campbell stressed the *sola scriptura* principle of Protestantism, and organized the "Christian Association of Washington" for the sole purpose "of promoting simple, evangelical Christianity."[4] To him, this meant "the whole form of doctrine, worship, discipline and government, expressly revealed and enjoined in the word of God." Campbell wanted Christians to work together "for the restoration of pure, primitive apostolic Christianity, in letter and the spirit, in principle and practice."[5]

Alexander Campbell amplified and expanded the details of the biblical order to be restored, under the popular slogan "restoring the ancient order of things." He wanted to restore "Original Christianity,"[6] or "primitive faith and measures."[7] His aim was "to reduce to practice the simple original form of Christianity, expressly exhibited upon the sacred page."[8]

He spelled out this order (as he saw it) in considerable detail: local autonomy, rejection of clerical status, the right of the laity to participate in all the functions of the church, a plurality of elders and deacons, weekly celebration of the Lord's supper, immersion baptism, the use of biblical names, weekly fellowship in the offering, and so forth. In 1843 he wrote, "The current reformation, *if conspicuous now or hereafter* for anything, must be so because of the conspicuity it gives the Bible and its ordinances as the *indispensable moral means of spiritual life and health. . . .* The distinguishing characteristic is *a restoration of the ordinances of the new institution to their place and power.*"[9] What are these ordinances? Campbell replied: "They are preaching the gospel—immersion in the name of Jesus into the name of the Father, and of the Son, and of the Holy Spirit—the reading and teaching the Living Oracles—the Lord's day—the Lord's Supper—fasting—prayer—confession of sins—and praise."[10]

According to Walter Scott, the transition from reformation to restoration was effected by three major steps. "First the Bible was adopted as sole authority . . . to the exclusion of all other books. Next the apostolic order was proposed. Finally the True Gospel was restored."[11] Scott felt that by his theology of evangelism, he supplied what was not yet specifically articulated by the Campbells. The ancient *gospel,* as well as the ancient *order,* must be restored. The former is necessary to make disciples, the latter to keep them. In the fall of 1827 Scott spelled out, in detail, the pattern of this ancient gospel: faith, repentance, baptism, remission of sins, the Holy Spirit, and eternal life.[12] More specifically, Scott argued that "faith is to destroy the love of sin, repentance to destroy the practice of it, baptism the state of it, remission the guilt of it, the Spirit the power of it, and the resurrection to destroy the punishment of it; so that the last enemy, death, will be destroyed."[13]

Barton W. Stone received his theological orientation in American Presbyterianism. He escaped from a frustrated attempt at conversion, along the old lines of Calvinism, through the influence of the New Light Presbyterianism of William Hodge, who contended that anyone could forthrightly accept the gospel without waiting painfully for any miraculous working of the Spirit. Stone and his followers (the "Christians") were also concerned to re-establish the sole authority of the Bible, yet they were "less vigorous in their demands for a close observance of the New Testament pattern."[14] This is evident in Stone's warning against adopting a rigid view toward the immersionistic form of baptism. He wrote, "none of us are disposed to make our notions of baptism, however well founded, a Bar of Christian fellowship."[15]

He warned all "reforming Baptists" that should they make their own peculiar views of immersion a test of fellowship, "it will be impossible for them to repel, successfully, the imputation of being sectarians, and of having an authoritative creed."[16] Stone's major emphasis was to restore the *spirit* of New Testament Christianity. He felt that the use of the New Testament alone, as a creed, would "bind together all who live in the spirit of it."[17]

The two main foci, it seems, of the restoration idea are: (1) loyalty to Jesus as Lord and Christ, and (2) loyalty to the interpretation of this Christ-reality, as written on the pages of the New Testament. The problem encountered by the movement, however, was how to retain and maintain this theological ellipse. The Stoneites tended to de-emphasize the latter of the two foci and stress the former; while in large areas of the Campbellian tradition, the New Testament principle became a legalistic norm, which threatened to supplant the authority of Christ himself and to mitigate the personal element in faith. The question is: were not the fathers actually operating with the two ultimates, the objective authority of the Bible, and the transhistorical authority of Christ's own lordship? This duality in the idea of religious authority generated a basic theological problem for the entire history of the movement.

Intellectual Developments Bearing on the Restoration Plea

Valuable and valid as some elements of the restoration ideal are (as we shall later indicate), the growth of insight during the past one hundred years has generated new perspectives on Christian truth, which expose fundamental errors in the restoration plea. As a basis for indicating these errors, let me first describe briefly three of these intellectual developments: (1) the scientific development of biblical criticism; (2) a new understanding of the historical character of human existence; and (3) the theological growth of ecumenicity.

Developments in Biblical Criticism

Space permits only the briefest indication of the character of this modern science. In the eighteenth century Lessing, Semler, and Herder developed a feeling for history, and accordingly abandoned the traditional view which made the Bible a canon. Studying the biblical literature historically, they were led to abandon the idea of the unity of the Bible. They also abandoned the notion that to understand the Bible one needs some special exegetical method unnecessary to the understanding of other historical documents. These achievements in the modern scientific approach to biblical studies firmly established the conviction that the biblical writings were human products of particular historical situations and must be so understood.[18] The "historical approach" was worked out in considerable detail during the nineteenth century, giving to the church an understanding of the Bible of which she had been grossly ignorant, due to her almost exclusively canonical interest in it. The aspects of this historico-critical approach to the Bible which have a bearing on the restoration plea are as follows:

1. *The historical character of the Bible.* By a comparison of the mythological thought-forms of the biblical writings with those of Judaism and Hellenism, the conviction was now established, beyond further question, that the biblical writings are historical, human products, the form of which was shaped and determined by the relative forces of the age and culture out of which they came. This conclusion shatters the orthodox notion of an infallible book. Neither the text, nor the process of selection of books to be included in the canon, nor the theological concepts of scripture can any longer be viewed as orthodoxy viewed them, namely as a compendium of absolute truth insulated from the relative currents of history. Whatever part the apostles play in a theology of biblical authority, their life and thoughts must now be seen as an integral part of the flow of history.

2. *Variety of church organization in the New Testament*

period. Historical research has brought to light the fact that when restorationist groups operated on the basis of the belief that there was a uniform local pattern of organization in the early church, their ecclesiology rested on an illusion. It is now fairly well agreed by all, except our Catholic brethren, that this belief in ecclesiastical uniformity is false. Dean Stephen J. England writes, "The evidence from the New Testament does not indicate that there was a uniform local pattern of organization in the earliest days. The conclusion that there was such a uniform pattern can be reached only by an unwarranted generalizing of the examples given us in the New Testament records."[19]

3. *The illusion of a golden age in the past*. Historical study has also exploded another basic aspect of restorationist theology, namely the notion of a golden age of the church in the past, to which many have looked back with restorationist longings. It is now quite clear that the idea that the actual church of the primitive period was a perfect model for all subsequent periods of the church's historical career is a grand illusion. Even if we regard the church during the apostolic age as a unity, its life and thought can hardly be regarded as a normative model for all subsequent ages. The imperfection of the thought of the primitive church was, in part, due to many foreign elements which yet characterized the mind of the church, since *only gradually* did Christianity emerge out of Judaism, and *only gradually,* in the midst of its Hellenistic environment, did Christianity assume its definite character.

4. *The historical Jesus now a problem*. Biblical criticism has brought to light the fact that both the Fourth Gospel and the synoptics give us a picture of Jesus which was wrought out in the Christian community in its development from the fourth to the seventh decades after the death of Jesus. It has also shown that this Jesus picture was determined and shaped by the church's belief that Jesus was Messiah and Son of God; and the portrait was drawn to present this fact and to prove it to be true.[20] Thus in many respects, this testimony of faith

is not the record to which the actual history would lead; but in various ways, one must say that faith actually engendered or created, and embellished this history, which was used, of course, to substantiate it. For example, biblical critics are fairly well agreed now that this faith of the Christian community placed some words in Jesus' mouth which it is hardly reasonable to believe that Jesus actually said; it told of deeds performed by him which he probably did not perform. It is difficult to escape the conclusion that the tradition of the Christian community constituted a dominant determining factor in the creation of the history of Jesus in the gospels.

The quest for the real historical Jesus was an effort to get behind these limitations and distinguish clearly between the real "historical Jesus" and the "Messias picture" of the believing community so as to supply Christianity today with a basic historical residuum of words and deeds of Jesus about which faith could orient itself anew. But as Erich Dinkler says,[21] these efforts have been in vain, for Mark and Q are also *missionary books* which have faith in Jesus Christ as a basic presupposition. Says Dinkler,[22] there never has been an objective biography of Jesus or collection of his words not determined by the writer's presuppositions. Historical information and confession are inseparably bound up with each other in the gospel portrait. Every word and every history of Jesus must therefore be critically questioned for its historicity. Critics press forward with the help of critical methods of refinement which, above all, the *Formgeschichteschule* has given us, and penetrate more and more into the history of the Jesus tradition, before our oldest sources. But we find ourselves here in an area about which many things must remain hypothetical and uncertain.[23]

In short, the entire question as to whether the Bible, or the teachings of Jesus (so central an element in the Lockean-Campbellian plea for a "simple gospel") can, in any sense, be regarded as *an authority* has become problematical. This belief, in the old orthodox sense, is no longer possible.

The Historical Character of Human Existence

The first novel thing here, in regard to its relevance to the restoration idea, is the modern doctrine of historical relativism. The absolutist rationalism of the Enlightenment has given way to a new existential awareness of how profoundly all human thinking is enmeshed in and determined by the processes of history. All thinking is colored by one's point of view, which point of view is shaped by the time and space and condition of the individual, enmeshed in a particular historical context.[24]

The growth of science itself, and more particularly the philosophy of science, has also been a major force in bringing to light an awareness of the relativity of man's knowledge of his world. This is especially evident in the science of physics and Einstein's theory of relativity, by which he demonstrated that the truth of a scientific judgment is not absolutely but only relatively true, depending on the perspective in the time-space nexus from which the judgment is made.

Furthermore in the discipline of epistemology it has been demonstrated that the perceptual act itself is beset with subjective limitations; and this significantly modifies Locke's theory of perception as a totally organized body of *sensa* ready made for the perceiver.[25] John Dewey called for such modification when he demonstrated that an organism, by the direction of its attention, is determining its response or its failure to respond to external stimuli. That is, whether one responds and the measure of the response are determined, in part, by the inner state of the organism itself. Dewey felt that Locke unjustly minimized the significance of "native activities"[26] in human nature. All conduct, Dewey argued, "is *interaction* between elements of human nature and the environment, natural and social."[27] And individuality "always colors responsive activity and hence modifies the form which custom assumes in its personal reproductions."[28]

If, now, we concede the findings of biblical criticism to the effect that the biblical writings are a genuine product of history and if all history is, by definition, this interminable and forever changing flow of finite forces and if we concede the validity of the modern epistemological thesis that subjective factors play a determinative role in the cognitive act, must we not now significantly modify the view that the gospel mesage written on the pages of the New Testament constitutes a cozy deposit of absolute truth? In the light of these intellectual developments, can we any longer regard the New Testament as a compendium of objective religious truth regarding belief, polity, and ethics, a datum insulated against and unaffected by the forces of history? Does not the truth of historical relativism render untenable Alexander Campbell's notion of "purely supernatural communications in the Bible?"[29] Even if, with C. H. Dodd[30] we boil the *kerygma* (the apostolic preaching) down to a six-point compendium of apostolic belief, can even the *kerygma,* so construed, check the floodtide of historical relativism?

To be sure, Christians cannot cast aside their belief that God's word of salvation comes to us somehow *through* the biblical writings. These writings must still be regarded as authoritative in some basic sense. The Bible is certainly indispensable. Yet intellectual integrity demands that we no longer cling to a *theory* about the Bible which *identifies it absolutely* with the infallible word of God, and that we arrive at a truer understanding of the relation between God's living word of revelation and the biblical writings, an understanding which no longer obscures from our vision the fact of their genuinely historical, human character. The Bible is both a divine *and* human book. To cling to the restoration ideal is, in fact, to *deny* the *genuinely historical* character of the simple gospel we are seeking to restore.

The Ecumenical Movement

A third movement which has a direct bearing on the restoration plea of Disciples is the ecumenical movement.

The Disciples' ardent plea for unity undoubtedly constitutes one of many forces in Christendom which, during the past 150 years, have generated the ecumenical reformation of the church.

As William Adams Brown suggests, in the unwillingness of Thomas Campbell and others of similar mind "to be satisfied with any half-way stage to unity, we have the direct antecedent of the faith and order movement."[31] Yet growth in ecumenicity can hardly be said to be the product of Discipledom. Many streams of influence have converged to make it possible.

Although the growth of the ecumenical movement may be said to represent a measure of fulfilment of the *major aim* of Disciples, namely, to realize the church's unity on earth, it is not precisely the kind of fulfillment which Disciples were led by their forefathers to expect. Unity has not been achieved through the method of restoring the ancient order of things. It turns out, thus far at any rate, that it is a unity of faith in Jesus as Christ and Lord, including a *vast variety of orders* of things. It is a unity which comprehends a much greater diversity of theological beliefs and ecclesiastical orders than the Campbells would have thought was possible.

Must we not say, then, that their restoration method failed to achieve their noble purpose? They did not succeed in their plea for all Christians to unite on "the ancient order of things." What they did achieve by means of this restoration plea was the establishment of another denomination which, of course, was the last thing on earth they wanted to do. This evidently means that God himself was unable to make much use of the Disciple restoration plea, and that he was obliged to look elsewhere for insights which could implement a greater growth in unity. Subsequent history seems to show that the Holy Spirit frowned upon the Disciple restoration method, yet he surely must have smiled benignly upon the deep longing in the Disciple heart for the oneness of God's people. Disciples can perhaps find comfort in the Pauline truth of justification by faith.

We do not forget, of course, that the restoration idea became deeply entrenched in Disciple thought, over a number of decades, at a time when the other denominations still seemed unconcerned about unity. Hence the situation was such that it did not offer any serious challenge to the validity of the restoration ideal. "If only these divided groups were interested in unity, they would quickly recognize the soundness of the restoration plan" —so the early Disciple leaders thought. Today the situation has greatly altered. The majority of groups *are* very much interested in unity, and they *are* making real strides toward its realization, but along routes other than that of restoring the ancient order of things. Indeed, to the consternation of Disciples, the confessional pathway to unity is enjoying far more success than the restoration plea.

Fundamental Errors in the Disciple Restoration Plea

In the light of these recent intellectual developments we are now able to perceive several basic fallacies in the restoration theology of Disciples.

A False Presupposition of the Orthodox View of the Bible

In the main, the Campbellian restoration plea presupposed the validity of the orthodox view of the Bible, at least the New Testament, as a body of infallible objective truths anchored to the "facts" of the gospel. The documents make this quite clear. Alexander Campbell expressed his belief in the competence of the inspiration in the testimony of the apostles "to make them infallible teachers of the Christian institution."[32] He argued that the New Testament "needs no reformation, being, like its author, infallible."[33] John Rogers, enthusiastic popularizer of the union between the "Christians" and the "Reformers," declared, "We . . . are determined to test every sentiment we hold, by the infallible word."[34] J. W. McGarvey contended that "all Protestants agree that the Bible is the only infallible rule." and that "if a man denies any part of the Bible . . . he is to that extent unsound in the faith."[35] In view of the conclusions reached by recent biblical criticism, theological integrity calls upon Discipledom for a more forthright abandonment of this false belief in an infallible book, a belief which, to a great degree, obscured from the view of the fathers the fallible, historical character of the documents of the New Testament.

The Failure to Deal Critically with the Problem of Biblical Interpretation

The theoretical attempt to make the apostolic testimony the sole basis for union was coupled with a failure adequately to perceive what this norm meant when practically applied. Distinguishing sharply between faith and opinion, and erroneously thinking that none of their opinions was involved in *their discernment of the meaning* of biblical testimony as to terms of church membership and church polity, they were somewhat blinded to the fact that what they actually did was to interpret the meaning of these writings and their significance for them,[36] the process of interpretation itself being determined by their historical and cultural situation on the American frontier.[37]

The theological ambiguity which resulted from this failure to realize that they were *interpreting* Scripture is evidently one of the major sources of the numerous divisions which the movement has spawned. From 1823 to 1830 Alexander Campbell was himself opposed to Sunday schools, for he could not find them in the scripture. At that time Campbell still believed that Christians should "discard from their faith and their practice every thing that is not found written in the New Testament."[38] The Churches of Christ cannot find organs in the New Testament; they are, therefore, persuaded that the Disciple wing represents a "digressive" movement. Missionary societies, located pastors, individual communion cups, Sunday school literature, a paid ministry, open or closed communion, open or closed membership—dissension and division which developed over such issues indicate that the pattern idea of restorationism opened Pandora's box and out came a host of mischievous theological spirits which have wrought havoc in the unity of the unity movement itself.[39] In the light of this fact, must it not be conceded that there is some truth in Philip Schaff's statement when he wrote that "those sects which reject all creeds are as much . . . exposed to controversy, division, and change, as churches with formal creeds."[40]

It may be asked how it was possible for such great minds as those of the Disciple fathers to adopt this uncritical biblicism. Could it be because they were laboring under the spell of Lockean epistemology, with its *tabula rasa* idea of the mind, and proceeded to carry this erroneous belief, that the mind is a passive recipient in the cognitive act, into their theory of religious knowledge? Alexander Campbell reacted strongly against the subjectivistic views of faith which were rampant in his day. He contended that "the efficacy of faith is always in the fact believed, or the object received, and not in the nature or manner of believing";[41] and he explicitly correlated this idea with the Lockean *tabula rasa* concept. He argued that "all the pleasures and pains of sense; all the effects of sensation, are the results, not of the manner in which our five senses are exercised, but of the objects on which they are exercised." Then he added, "Passing from the outward to the inward man, . . . we shall find no exception to [this] law. . . . It is neither the faculty of perception, . . . nor the manner of perception, but the thing perceived, that excites us to action."[42] Operating with Lockean epistemological principles, the fathers believed that if we sit down before the "facts" of scripture, like little children, we *will* all see it alike. It appears to us that it would hardly take a philosopher to perceive that this just is not so.

It should be remembered also that the rationalism of the Enlightenment made its contribution to the illusion of objectivistic biblicism, for this rationalism was still unhistorical in its bearings. It failed to recognize the existential involvement of human reason. Enlightenment rationalism left out one important factor: the individual. As Paul Tillich says, "Enlightenment and rationalism confuse the essential nature of reason with the predicament of reason in existence."[43] Hence, to borrow Langdon Gilkey's apt statement, rationalism said that the mind of man "can easily, accurately, and with no historical influencing, grasp and believe what is clearly True if the evidence warrants it. Thus in the human reception of this Truth, there is no need of interpretation."[44]

Such rationalistic biblicism is no longer possible for us today. Immanuel Kant has demonstrated that the mind itself, with its *a priori,* epistemic forms, is a determinative factor in the cognitive act, along with the casual influence of sense data. Sigmund Freud has shown that subrational forces are at work determining the content of reason. Existentialists like Heidegger and Sartre have shattered metaphysical rationalism and developed the belief that the existing individual is *the sole source* of the content of reason. And the destructive use of reason in modern totalitarianism shows clearly that man often sees what he *wants* to see. To be sure, theology cannot yield to the radical subjectivism of the atheistic existentialists; that way leads to theological suicide. Yet modern theology cannot ignore the insights of modern epistemology which show undeniably that subjective as well as objective factors are of determinative significance in *all* man's knowing. To be sure, we must maintain vigilance against a theological method which seeks to overcome the weaknesses of restorationism by an irrational *fideism*. The dangers of rationalism are not to be overcome by resorting to antirationalism, but by a more sober use of reason and by a critical awareness of its historical and existential limitations.

Inadequate Awareness of the Historical Character of the Church

The fallacious assumption here was threefold, the belief (1) that there is a fixed pattern essential to the well-being of the church, (2) that this original pattern is laid down in the New Testament, and (3) that this pattern was perfectly exemplified by the apostolic church.

"Were we then," Thomas Campbell wrote, "in our Church constitution and managements, to exhibit a complete conformity to the Apostolic Church, would we not be in that respect as perfect as Christ intended we should be?"[45]

George Plattenberg repeated this same illusion of a golden age in the past when he argued that faith in Jesus as Messiah gathered and fused heterogeneous materials and widely discordant elements of the ancient world into "one perfectly articulated and compacted body."[46] The New Testament records do not substantiate this high claim. The negative orientation of the fathers toward theological concern caused them to neglect the task of thinking through the problem of the nature of the church, critically."[47] Consequently, as usually happens when critical thought is lacking, traditional patterns of thought took over and structured Disciple ecclesiology. The Calvinist tradition, with its pattern idea of the church, was perpetuated by Disciples in a form modified by conditions and needs on the American frontier.

We have already seen how modern scholarship has disclosed that this pattern idea of the New Testament church is an illusion.[48] The restoration view of the church rests upon a misunderstanding of the relation of church and world. In terms of content, the church cannot be defined apart from the world. The organic relation of church and world is basic, though of course not exhaustive.

This means that early Disciple ecclesiology was not yet sufficiently historical in its view of the church. It failed to see with sufficient clarity that at *no* time in history has the inner, permanent element of the church's being existed apart from transient, structural elements; it therefore failed to see that the mere fact that something was or was not done in the apostolic age of the church's life is not sufficient theological reason for doing it or not doing it at the present time.

The Separatist Attitudes of Sectarianism

Time has demonstrated that the restoration method not only did *not* effect the goal of unity but has actually served, in several ways, to perpetuate and even to further the disunity of God's people. We must, of course, be sympathetic in making this negative judgment, for it has been *subsequent* intellectual developments in biblical understanding, philosophy of history, and epistemology which enable us today to perceive the basic weaknesses in the restoration method. Yet the divisive effect of the plea for the restoration of the ancient order of things is evident in a threefold attitude of the group-mind which it produced.

1. *Theological self-centeredness.* In a fairly short time, the restoration plea changed the character of the movement from a uniting union movement to that of a sect, a grouping with definite separatist qualities and attitudes. Once this transformation was accomplished, this sect proceeded to behave like all sectarian "come-outer" groups: it issued a call to members of other groups to "come out from among them and join us," since we have a corner on the truth.[49] The restoration program had scarcely been launched when some of its more perceptive leaders became sadly aware that it was producing this insidious evil. Walter Scott, for example, perceived that the restoration method was proving to be divisive rather than unitive in its effect. He was loathe to say so publicly, but in a letter to P. S. Fall he wrote, "When you express your doubts of the matters connected with the recent Reformation I sympathize with you, for the thing has not been what I hoped it would be by a thousand miles. We are indeed 'a sect' differing but little, of anything that is good, from the parties around us. Alas! My soul is grieved everyday."[50]

Many other leaders who followed were not blessed with equal theological discernment. Isaac Errett, for example, for all his gracious spirit, boldly called on all Christians of other groups "to come out from all party organizations, to renounce all party names and party tests, and seek only for Christian union and fellowship according to Apostolic teaching,"[51] by which he really meant, "according to Apostolic teaching *as interpreted by us*." Moses E. Lard seems to have been disastrously dimsighted in his failure to realize the extent to which he himself was caught in the grip of this uncharitable spirit. He wrote:

> Let us agree to commune with the sprinkled sects around us, and soon we shall come to recognize them as Christians. Let us agree to recognize them as Christians, and immersion, with its deep significance, is buried in the grave of our folly. Then in not one whit will we be better than others [as if Christians could legitimately desire to be such]. Let us countenance political charlatans as preachers, and we at once become corrupt as the loathesome nest on which Beecher sets to hatch the things he calls Christians. . . . Let us agree to admit organs, and soon the pious, the meek, the peaceloving, will abandon us, and our churches will become gay worldly things, literal Noah's arks, full of clean and unclean beasts.[52]

2. *The loss of feeling for catholicity.* The success of the restoration program resulted in the loss of a feeling for the catholicity of the church, the loss of a sense of oneness with the total, historic continuum of the church throughout twenty centuries. Thereby also the ideal made for disunity, rather than unity.

At this point the restoration movement even represents a break away from the Protestant Reformation itself. The great sixteenth-century reformers regarded Protestantism as essentially one with the historically continuous church. But the restorers developed a more negative attitude toward the total Christian tradition. They thought of their restoration movement as "a break with the historical church and a junction with the true church of the New Testament, which was lost in the medieval darkness of Romanist domination."[53] C. C. Morrison correctly argues that "In one [the Reformation], the church is felt as *given* in history and is perennially reformable; in the other [the Restoration], it is felt as *given* in the New Testament and is re-created according to a fixed norm or pattern by evangelism, including proselytism, and often by rebaptism."[54] The loss of feeling for catholicity among the restorationists resulted not only in an inability to appropriate their total Christian heritage, but it also created a blind spot, a tragic ignorance of the numerous ways in which the theology and ecclesiology of the restorers themselves were actually shaped by forces operating in the process of the church in history. Their theology proved itself to be much too unhistorical to be true to fact. Disciple restorationism therefore had within it the seeds of fragmented individualism.

3. *A deposit of ecclesiastical lethargy.* The restoration ideal generated a spirit of self-complacency and lethargy, which at the present time constitutes a somewhat difficult problem for Disciples of Christ, as their leaders attempt to guide the communion into larger ecumenical relations. Despite their talk about having "no creed but Christ," their biblicism was such that they fell prey to creedalistic fixations, which formed the basis for the institutional morale of the denomination, and inspired its members to take pride in its denominational uniqueness. The resulting deposit of denominational lethargy shows that two conflicting impulses were operating in Discipledom: (1) the original, wholesome impulse to unity, and (2) the restorationist orientation which, to the extent that it was promoted, has made for sectarian separation and disunity. Hence by uniting the plea for unity to the mistaken belief that they had found the basis for it in the ancient order, they paradoxically promoted disunity by intensifying their own sectarian religious consciousness, thereby blunting and distorting the ecumenical impulse at the outset of the movement.

The Neglect of Theology

The emphasis on noncreedalism, and the demand for liberty in the realm of opinion have, paradoxically, produced both good and evil results. These elements yielded a good result, in so far as they restored liberty to the individual conscience. This provided room for growth, for which freedom of inquiry is always the essential prerequisite. At the same time, however, one is made to wonder whether the movement has adequately fulfilled the theological responsibility which is the counterpart of such intellectual liberty. For the result of the slogan "in faith unity, in opinions liberty" was that the emphasis fell on the realm of faith, the unitive principle, the given in the New Testament, while the other realm of opinion, the realm where creative theological effort might be exercised, tended to be neglected.

Here, evidently, lies one of the reasons why Disciples have not infrequently been theologically weak, and why the movement has not infrequently fallen prey either to the vagaries of naïve biblicism or to the theological anemia of pietism. Hence the charge of some historians that Disciples of Christ should be categorized as pietists has in it a measure of truth. Even William Robinson feels obliged to confess, "With regard to the great doctrines of Christianity—the doctrines of God, the Person of Christ, and the Atonement—there is need to say little; for it is not here that Churches of Christ made their greatest contribution to religious thought."[55] This aspect of the movement evidently accounts for the fact that Disciples are today in a quandary, theologically, not knowing precisely what they do believe about God, Christ, the Holy Spirit, the Bible, eschatology, and so forth. The confusion is embarrassing as they seek to respond to the call for confessional interchange with other Christian groups in ecumenical conversation.

Elements of Truth in the Disciple Restoration Plea

As Disciples today move toward theological reconstruction, seeking to extricate themselves from the errors of restorationism and to build on more secure foundations, they should not fail to appreciate the elements of truth in the plea, distorted though they were by the restoration idea.

The Christocentric Ground of Unity

The movement emerged out of an impulse to look beyond the church divisions which were generated and sustained by the authoritarian use of confessions, and to bring to the light of day the fountainhead of the Christian religion. By so doing, it was believed that it would be possible to find the true and effective basis of unity. This restoration impulse contained a theologically sound directive. The insight into the significance of this directive was perhaps more adequately perceived, and more clearly expressed, by Thomas Campbell and Barton W. Stone than by the other leaders of the original grouping.[56] The insight which they endeavored to articulate stemmed from a deeply religious impulse to destroy the grip of external human authorities, so as to make possible an effective realization of the lordship of Christ. That this was the direction in which the initial impulse pointed seems clear from the early slogan of the movement, "no creed but Christ." Thomas Campbell expressed this insight eloquently when he wrote, "Resume that precious, that dear bought liberty, wherewith Christ has made his people free; a liberty from subjection to any authority but his own in matters of religion."[57]

Viewed in historic perspective, this means that these men were seeking to recover for Protestantism the spirit of the sixteenth-century Reformation, which was distorted and corrupted even before Luther completed his life's work. Even as Luther dedicated his life to liberate the church of his day from the authority of pope and church councils by directing the conscience to the living Word of God, so Disciple fathers sought to remain true to this Reformation principle and to free the Christian conscience also from the authority of the Protestant creeds. As the Disciple movement developed, this Christocentric impulse became weakened and distorted by the influence of Protestant orthodoxy itself, with its norm of literalistic biblicism. Yet with a degree of fairness, the initial Disciple impulse may be said to represent a recovery of the *sola scriptura* principle, as construed in the classic period of the Reformation.

Luther meant to use the principle of *sola scriptura* to liberate the Christian conscience from external church authority. Furthermore, Luther did not intend that scripture should be distorted into a similar external authority, for he insisted that *sola scriptura* is to be correlated with *sola fide*. Luther's central norm of "justification by faith" (Christ experienced) made possible a free and creative use of scripture, as a human instrument, used by God in his self-communicating activity, in his mode of being as the Word. For Luther, scripture was an authority of a sort (though no ultimate, infallible authority), but only in so far as it "drives Christ into the heart";[58] that is, scripture is an authority only in correlation with faith. Protestant orthodoxy, however, distorted this principle of *sola scriptura* by twisting it into an infallible authority, *independent of the realm of faith.* And it proceeded to support this authority of scripture, so construed, by developing a rigid theory of mechanical inspiration. But since it is absurd to hold that every Christian must *actually know* all the multitude of infallible truths in scripture, orthodoxy proceeded to draw a distinction between those truths, a knowledge of which is *essential* to salvation, and those which are *unessential.* At this point, the authority of the creed came into being, as a necessity to define explicitly what the essentials are. Creed and scripture are logically inseparable and mutually dependent in orthodoxy.

It was at this point that the Disciple fathers became dissatisfied. Their dissatisfaction initiated the impulse to break the back of this authority of orthodoxy and make possible, once again, a correlation of *sola scriptura* and *sola fide*. Whatever the eventual outcome, the Disciple founders once again *attempted* to make use of the apostolic principle of reform, in its original Protestant sense.

Thomas Campbell saw that Christianity *is* grounded ultimately, not in any human doctrine, but in the lordship of God in Jesus Christ. What he and his colleagues did not yet adequately see is that the biblical writings also must be subsumed under the category of fallible, human documents, however necessary they are, *as a medium of revelation,* and that Christ alone is Christianity's only ultimate authority. As a result of this theological deficiency, the new Christocentric impulse was blunted at the outset, by a perspective which permitted the spirit of orthodoxy to reassert itself and claim the Disciple mind also.

Historical Character of Revelation

Fallacious in many ways as the restoration plea was, it contained a valuable insight in regard to the historical character of the Holy Spirit in the Christian revelation. If the Christian faith in Jesus, at its very heart, is true, the redemptive working of God is anchored to a particular focus in historic process, namely the mighty act of God in Jesus as Christ.

Genuinely Christian unity is something more than mere unity in human, moral values, valuable as the unity of humanism is. It is too indefinite merely to say: "Let us all be one, regardless of what we believe." Such a basis is too broad and loose to serve to develop genuinely Christian unity, which must be structured by its Christological impulse and motif. Sharing in the Holy Spirit is *grounded* in the *historic community,* whose origin and character is determined by the influence of Jesus. It was this insight which correctly led Disciples to adopt a strongly negative attitude toward the subjectivism of enthusiastic spiritualists and individuals in religion.

The historical character of the event of revelation was stressed by Alexander Campbell in terms of the togetherness of Word and Spirit. As Campbell put it, " the 'word alone' system is as far from the equator of truth as 'the Spirit alone' theory."[59] Again, Campbell wrote, "The Word of God is but a special embodiment of the Holy Spirit. It is veiled Spirit, or . . . grace; and hence the Spirit works only through the word upon the understanding, the conscience, and the heart. . . . We speak to God in words, and he speaks to us by his word."[60] One feels certain that Campbell would heartily agree when Luther contended that such a subjectivist in religion is really an enemy of the divine order of the church,

> when he gaps and cries, "Spirit, Spirit, Spirit," and at the same time tears down the bridges, ladders, paths, and roads by which

the Spirit comes to us, in the objective divine order of things, in the institution of baptism, in the signs and the written word of God; and when he teaches not how the Spirit comes to us, but how we are to find the Spirit; when he teaches that one should travel in the clouds and ride on the wind, and says nothing about how or why, where or what, but only that one should experience it, as he has.[61]

The Motivation of Love

A third abiding value which lies at the heart of the restoration plea of Disciples is found in the heart throb of Christian love. Many things were wrong with the *method of procedure* in the restoration plea; but who can fail to see beneath this problematical *method* the thrilling *motive* of Christian love? The goal sought was "that they may all be one." Perhaps the truest and noblest thing about the life and thought of Discipledom is the upsurge of Christlike love which it represents. Peter Ainslie sensed this and called for a de-emphasis on "*formal* Christianity" and a re-emphasis on "love among Christians, which has to do with *vital* Christianity."[62]

The healing, unitive power of the kind of human togetherness where love and liberty have their way can be seen at work throughout the history of Discipledom, blocked and weakened though it has often been by forces of a divisive nature. Indeed, the original union of the "Christians" and the "reformers" was a product of this kind of community. As W. T. Moore says, "it is impossible not to recognize the fact that it was a union where love was the predominant factor rather than theological definition. . . . There were substantial doctrinal differences and some practical differences, but all these gave way before the all-conquering power of Love."[63] This original union, as John Smith reminds us, was not a unity by absorption. The Campbellites did not join the Stoneites, nor *vice versa*. The two groups yielded their autonomies to let God remake them. "In love and liberty [they] became one body; not Stoneites, or Campbellites . . .; but Christians . . . children of the same Father who is God over all and in all."[64]

It was this same power of the *agape* quality of Christian community, combined with liberty, which constrained Alexander Campbell to qualify the absolutist view of the immersionist mode of baptism, even though his own studies had led him to a very strong conviction that this was the New Testament teaching on baptism. The famous Lunenberg letter reflects this freedom of Campbell from theological narrowness, even when the matter dealt with a belief about which he held deep convictions. He wrote that "there is no occasion . . . for making immersion . . . absolutely essential to a Christian—though it may be greatly essential to his sanctification and comfort."[65]

In my opinion, W. T. Moore was using the word "theological" in an unjustifiably narrow sense, but he was really stating a valuable theological position when he wrote, "The way to Christian union is by putting all our theological differences into the hot crucible of love, and if they are allowed to remain there long enough they will be melted and easily made to conform to a united Church."[66] It may be doubted just how "easily" they will be restructured, in line with the idea of unity; but Moore was correct; if Christlike love is at work, this realignment of doctrinal beliefs *will* take place.

A REBIRTH OF INDIVIDUAL LIBERTY

The latitudinarian spirit was at work, generating the distinction between the realms of faith and opinion, and coining the slogan "in faith unity, in opinions liberty, in all things charity," evidently a rewording of the old phrase of Rupertus Meldenius, "in essentials unity, in nonessentials liberty, in all things charity." Time has proved this distinction to be not nearly so clear-cut and unambiguous as it seemed to the Disciple fathers. Doubtless much which they came to regard as faith was really their opinion, or interpretation, of scripture. But problematical though the slogan was, it did, theoretically, throw open the field of theological inquiry for freedom of thought, and it did contribute to the Disciple mind the spirit of progressive and free thought, which, in large measure, accounts for the fact that, on the whole,

Disciples have been able to assimilate new insights, and adjust themselves to new perspectives brought into view by continual change in the cultural situation.

As we have seen, there were two major forces which have handicapped Disciples and prevented them from *exercising* this new-born liberty as they might have done.

(1) Their failure to come through with an adequate theological understanding of the nature of biblical authority resulted in the fact that large numbers among them lapsed into the old orthodox way of thinking of the authority of the Bible. But since the only practical way of making use of an absolute Bible is to implement its usage with a creed (as orthodoxy discovered), and since it was impossible in Discipledom to write a creed, the result was that numerous unwritten creeds were forthcoming—a phenomenon which has been the source of much dissension and division.

(2) Since unity was the predominant ideal, and this was to be achieved only on grounds of faith, the realm of opinion (presumably the realm of creative thought) was permitted to slide into the background. This tended to generate, once again, the spirit of seventeenth-century pietism, a spirit which neglects or deliberately shoves aside the responsibility of constructive theological thinking. Hence, the progressive spirit of liberty in Discipledom has been somewhat impeded, theologically, by biblicistic absolutism on the one hand and by the obscurantism of pietism on the other.

Nevertheless, the thrust of liberty was a significant one in the impulse which generated the movement. To a degree, "the right of private judgment" was restored.

The Principle of Comprehension

A fifth positive value in the Disciple plea has to do with the fact that they adopted the principle of comprehension as a basic aspect of the unity they were out to achieve. Unity was coupled with the diversity of liberty.

To be sure, there was ambiguity here, arising from the ambivalent nature of Thomas Campbell's idea of authority. He was operating with two concepts of authority, the lordship of Christ and the objective biblicism which he inherited, and from which he never extricated himself. Nevertheless, the new idea of a unity which comprehends differences was set to work. As a result, there have never been lacking Disciple voices which have opposed the unity of dead uniformity, in favor of the idea of an organic kind of togetherness, which makes room for diversity. They have sought to avoid unity at the expense of diversity, for they have seen that this has led orthodoxy to a dogmatism which destroyed the spirit of charity. Yet they also see that diversity without unity cuts the vital bond of the church's life with her Lord, the Christ.

Had it not been for this early vision, which brought the principle of comprehension into play, it is doubtful that so many Disciples today would be able to press forward in ecumenical endeavor, insisting that their diversity of witness must be made *within* the larger fellowship of the church universal, so that fragmentary perspectives on the truth of the gospel can be complemented and corrected by cross-fertilization with the perspectives of other individuals and groups.

Suggestions Toward Theological Reconstruction

In the above analysis and evaluation of the restoration principle, we have already made numerous suggestions toward theological correction. It is perhaps appropriate, however, to conclude this essay with a more explicit summary of these suggestions.

ELIMINATE "RESTORATION" FOR "TRANSFORMATION"

The restoration idea is basically a false concept. Because of the numerous errors which have become part of the meaning of the word and because recent intellectual developments knock the props from under the plea as originally formulated by the Disciple fathers, it would seem wise to abandon the use of the term altogether. In view of the growing tendency today to speak of the "ecumenical reformation," it might be advisable to reorient the positive values associated with the restoration idea about the concept of "reformation." In so doing, one could recover the sound impulse of the movement at the beginning, when the fathers were still speaking of it as a "current reformation" and thus reaffirm Alexander Campbell's prophetic insight that the spirit of reformation should never be lost.[69]

The modern understanding of history has led us to see that the church is never restorable, for every event in historic process is unique; it is unrepeatable and irreversible. We should rather think of the church as perennially reformable, or perhaps better still, perennially transformable. To be sure, there must be a clear grasp of the principle of transformation, or the abiding source of the church's continuing transformation. This source is found in the motif of the gospel. This is the transhistorical, transrelative norm, by which a continuous process of transfiguration of the historical being of the church is to be realized. It is clear thus that more adequate understanding of the nature of the *kerygma* is called for.

Reorient the Unity Impulse About the Christological Motif

To give to the movement a fresh and more adequate Christological reorientation, forthrightly freed from restorationism, will put it at the center of the whole drift of the "ecumenical reformation." It can make possible a creative forward thrust, and help to free the movement from the separatist attitudes and tendencies generated by the restoration complex.

There can be little doubt that the shift from standards of orthodoxy to the authority of Christ is the major development which has made possible the recovery of the feeling of catholicity in Protestantism. Freeing the Disciple movement from the illusion of restorationism will help make it possible for Disciples to take their proper place in the ecumenical movement with more consciousness of their at-homeness in it and with stronger resolve to bear their ecumenical responsibilities. Nor would a decisive move in this direction be an entirely new step. Ever since Barton W. Stone there has been a strand of feeling which is not expressed in the pattern concept of the church. Edward Scribner Ames describes it as "the exaltation of the spirit of Christ, rather than a set of rules and forms."[70] Many another has agreed that the pattern idea is too mechanical and legalistic in its bearing to express the true genius of the Disciple movement. The time is past due for this strand of feeling to assert itself with theological rigor and to reshape the entire theological outlook of Discipledom. To do so calls for critical reconstruction in Disciple Christology, which is vital nerve of this strand. Christology must be rescued from the vagaries of sentimental pietism, and developed with such clarity and force as to reshape basic religious and ecclesiastical attitudes and relations.

Develop an adequate Understanding of the Bible

In the light of biblical criticism, serious and highly significant revisions are called for in traditional Disciple theology about the Bible.

First, it must be frankly admitted that the fathers were building on a fallacy when they construed the apostolic testimony as an absolute truth-datum. There is no such datum in historical thought forms. Disciples must banish the illusion of an unhistorical scripture and face up to the relativity which characterizes the *historical aspect* of the givenness of the biblical writings in general, and of the *kerygma* in particular.

Secondly, Disciples must face up to the similar historical conditioning in our own act of faith, which appropriates the meaning of scripture. Both the apostolic givenness and our faith-reception of scripture are historically conditioned. This relativity and variability in our response to the call of God in

Christ is quite proper when it is due to the finite, historical character of the human mind, and not to willful caprice. There is no presuppositionless study of the Bible. Yet a sincere study of the Bible, in faith, will modify one's presuppositions.

The church has persisted in history because her members believed that they have a gospel which represents not merely the best thinking of her members, but that it is a gospel which comes through the revelation of the Eternal One, who transcends the relativities of historical time. With the recent movement of biblical theology, we must now inquire anew: what *is* this gospel which the church feels it to be her mission to proclaim? If we can no longer identify this eternal gospel with any of the relativities of history, with the creeds, with the Bible, with the teachings of Jesus, what is it? And how can this gospel, which the church believes to be perennially relevant to human existence, be communicated from one historical context to another?

All this means that Disciples must work out a more valid understanding of the nature of religious truth. We suggest that religious truth has to do, primarily, with man's living personal relation to God, rather than an objective body of propositions to be believed. The biblical writings, will then be seen as the *historical witness* to the living faith of those who saw the initial shining of the Light; but a historical witness which, like the entire proclamation of the ongoing church, serves as a means for the continuing fulfillment of God's act of self-revelation in Jesus Christ. *In its essence,* however, religious truth will be seen neither as subjective feelings, as in Schleiermacher and mysticism, nor as an objective quantum, as in orthodoxy, but as a *vital, primal relation* with the living God. The new center of gravity will thus be, not the Bible *per se,* but the divine activity in history, the creative and redemptive working of God, as it becomes existentially real through faith.

C. C. Morrison offers an intriguing reinterpretation of the slogan "in faith unity, in opinion liberty." He suggests the categories of the church's "constitution" and its "fellowship." The constitution is the sphere of authority; the fellowship the realm of liberty. Morrison contends that standardized bodies of belief, special interpretations of the Bible, and the Bible itself, all belong, not to the constitution, but to the fellowship of the church. "The constitution of the church is forever determined by Christ himself. In him alone and in his Lordship the church has its sole constitutional authority."[71] In the main, Morrison is suggesting a correct perspective, though the regulative function of the apostolic witness, in the continuing act of God's self-revelation, is not adequately dealt with in Morrison's argument. To discover and state this regulative function of the apostolic witness calls for a more critical treatment of Christ's actual exercise of his authority, in and through his body, the church.[72] It is certainly true, however, that we must maintain a clear distinction between Christ, Word of God (*logos tou theou*), God himself in his self-revealing mode of being, and the relative forms through which this "Word" comes to us, and is interpreted by us, in history. The final authority in Christianity is to be distinguished from all external authorities; it is eschatological in nature. Christianity is anchored to an authority which is more than any of the historical forms through which it is expressed and realized. At this point Disciples need to dig in on the problem of Christ and history, and the function of the biblical witness in the experience of the living Lord.

Appropriate the Fullness of the Historic Heritage

Disciples are called upon to shake themselves loose from decades of accretion of separatist feelings and claim their rightful place as an organic part of the universal church. The original impulse (1804) of the Springfield Presbytery to "sink into union with the Body of Christ at large" was soundly catholic in its spirit, though the rigidity of the denominational situation which then obtained prevented the fulfillment of the impulse at that time; to achieve this ecumenical sinking, in any sense, at that time, imposed the un-Christian demand to forfeit one's liberty.

Behind the Last Will and Testament of the Springfield Presbytery, however, lies a problematical assumption regarding the nature of Christian unity. If the idea of the fathers was that we should all give up our distinct groupings, founded on confessional individualities, determined by diversified cultural situations, and become one universal, monomorphic church, we should have to register dissent, for that would be an unrealistic concept of unity. But if by such "sinking" they meant to banish the illusion that a denomination is the church (to borrow Morrison's argument), or if they meant to overcome the separatist attitudes of the denominations so that, in a truly catholic spirit, we could achieve unqualified mutual recognition, we would contend that this was a theologically sound will.

It is an occasion for deep gratitude that Disciples *are* now executing the will of the Springfield presbytery, in so far as they are vigorously promoting a vast variety of interdenominational, cooperative endeavors, frequently called "ecumenical." Such cooperation *becomes* truly ecumenical when those cooperating no longer think of their task as mere denominational cooperation, but as a task of the one church, which they are seeking to fulfill together, *as brethren,* in a full and unqualified sense.

It is doubtful that Disciples will encounter a great deal of further opposition to their objection to the use of creeds as instruments of exclusion. This warning should, of course, be kept alive, in the name of freedom. Disciples, however, must correct their excessively negative attitude toward historic confessions. The creeds have also exercised a wholesome influence which is fourfold. (1) They have a liturgical significance; they were made to be sung or chanted in the sanctuary; there is a hymnic quality about them. As great hymns of the church, their significance has been positive and beneficial. Although not clearly conscious of the fact, Disciples of Christ have themselves tacitly admitted this positive value of the creeds, in principle, in their own liturgy, by using such confessional forms as the Gloria Patri, the Doxology, and the Lord's Prayer. (2) As Walter

Harrelson reminds us, the creeds served as "banners of the faith";[73] they proclaimed to the world the faith of the Christian community. Such proclamation must, of course, always be made in some language other than a bare recitation of Scripture. (3) The creeds have had a positive value in the church's teaching and preaching task; they served as summary statements of the faith, in the instruction of new members—a wholesome theological function, surely. (4) The creeds helped to preserve the theological integrity of the church. They were useful in view of the ever-present danger of misrepresentation by the whims and fancies of cantankerous individuals.

The historic significance of the Apostles' Creed, in particular, is very great. It kept before the mind of the church the fact that man's redemption is wrought through the mighty act of God in Jesus as Christ; it taught the church to make its theology dependent on the redemptive deeds of God, and it reminded the church that it could understand what God had done only by making distinctions between Father, Son, and Holy Spirit. In view of the tremendous flux of religious and philosophical currents in the second century of Christianity's life, how very different indeed the development of the mind of the church might have been without the background of this guiding formula!

In short, Disciples must develop more truly catholic attitudes in their thinking and feeling about the church. They must grow in ecumenical stature and appropriate the fullness of their historic heritage, even as they have appropriated the heritage of the Campbellian tradition.

Develop an Adequate Functional Theology

Abandoning the orthodox belief in the Bible as a legal authority, Disciples can scarcely any longer defend their practices of baptism, the Lord's supper, and liturgical order simply by quoting Acts 2:38, 42.

It is not within the province of this paper to develop an adequate theology regarding all the issues relevant to church union.

But we feel obliged to point out that if the main arguments of the paper are sound, Disciples are called upon to abandon the restorationist biblical basis upon which they established and perpetuated their peculiar practices. They are now called upon to rework their doctrine on these points of issue, in the light of a more adequate understanding of the church, as a continuing community amidst the relativities of history, generated and continually renewed by the living word of God. The symbols of this continuing community should therefore reflect, and proclaim, the central redemptive facts of the gospel, particularly the life, death, and resurrection of Christ, his exaltation as Lord, his abiding presence as the corporate Spirit of the community, and the promise of the fulfillment and consummation of his reign. And Disciples must rework their doctrine on these practical issues on a more defensible use of the biblical witness to the gospel. If the Bible can no longer be regarded as an authority on these points, in the old orthodox sense, in what sense, if any, *can* it be regarded as authoritative in these areas of concern?

In his famous Lunenberg letter, Alexander Campbell pointed in the proper direction when he distinguished between the *absolute* center of the faith, found in man's affirmative response to God's call in Christ, and the *relativity of the forms* of this response—"according to the measure of one's knowledge of his will," said Campbell. Ecumenical greatness is reflected in this Campbellian principle of comprehension which can enable Disciples to overcome certain fixations on some of these points, and move toward greater unity with others, even though their forms of response are not identical with those of Disciples.

True advance toward unity must be made *through and in terms* of denominational and confessional variety; neither the Disciple pattern for unity nor those of other denominations can legitimately be regarded as the ideal structure of unity. We must quest for it together, under the leading of God's Spirit.

It is to be hoped that in Disciple thought the principle of expediency will eventually be given full recognition and intelligent application, in matters pertaining to church structure, an application which must therefore be based on clear and sound theological understanding of the nature of the church and her mission. The principle of expediency says that whatever forms are appropriate to achieve the church's redemptive task, in a given situation, are the forms to be adopted and utilized. Precisely what these forms to be adopted are must, therefore, be determined by the method of democratic pluralism, under the guidance of God's Spirit.

At this crucial point, however, the theological perspective of Discipledom may need further revision, at its deepest level. It may be questioned whether the essential limitation of all idealisms has been clearly perceived. Has it been adequately understood that God is always attempting to lead us to a fulfillment which reaches vastly beyond anything that our limited ideals are able to envisage, at any given time? Has not failure to understand this limitation often resulted in the idolatrization of our ideals? No human mind or group of minds can grasp all the complexities of God's redemptive purpose, which are required for its fulfillment. Always we mortals see "through a glass, darkly." As H. N. Wieman says, "all human effort to work out an ideal order must be characterized by an underestimate of the importance of many factors and an overestimate of others. Many requirements of living are left out. . . . This limitation in men's idealizing ability can be overcome only in small part by the exercise of our greatest intelligence and by the utmost generosity of the heart."[78] This limitation in man's vision of the truth inevitably means that our religious ideals are abstractions. "They cannot by their very nature include the total concrete fullness of actual existence nor all the new possibilities emerging out of unique situations."[79]

This means that theology should never be allowed to become static and final. We must recognize the primacy of our experience of God over our theologies about this experience, vitally important as our theologies are. Our religious beliefs and practices should be functionally conceived. We should never give our *ultimate* religious commitment to any of our religious ideals or theologies, but only to the creative and redemptive working of God, which works at levels vastly deeper than human intelligence and purpose. Hence the urgent need for a willingness of heart and mind *to be continually transformed,* lest we be found blocking the very working of God as he seeks to bring about fuller realization of the beloved community on earth.

Give Theology Its Proper Place

Too long have Disciples clung to the Campbellian prejudice against theology. Gradually, however, the foundations of the rationalistic biblicism, on which the restoration movement was originally based, have been eaten away by the acids of modern criticism. These foundations have crumbled. And unless critical and constructive theological effort is given its proper place, so as to rebuild on more secure foundations, the movement may find itself adrift, without chart or compass, and hopelessly exposed to the infiltrations of modern culture, which always threatens to reduce the church to just another culture group. For example, a recent excellent study by Harold Lunger reveals that a large percentage of the ethical decisions which are made by members of Protestant groups, and particularly by Disciples of Christ, are the expression of operative centers of authority other than Christian, such as the secular press, the public opinion of an entire city or section of the country, radio, TV, the impulse to self-preservation, personal desire or inclination, tradition, reason or common sense, etc.[80] The urgent need of the church for an adequate theological basis for Christian ethical decision is obvious.

If critical theological effort is not given its proper place and function in the life of the church, only two possibilities would seem to remain open; either the church will be hopelessly exposed to the various philosophical and social currents which beat upon it, by virtue of its involvement in the cultural situation, currents many of which threaten to make a shipwreck of the church; or she will vainly attempt to retreat for safety to the corroded anchors of orthodoxy, as many fundamentalists are evidently doing. The church must, in many ways, be identical with the cultural situation in which she realizes her being. Church and world are bound so closely that either would cease to be if the other were not. Yet if the church is to be the church, she must also maintain her prophetic distinction from the world. This is the dialectic so essential to the being of the church; both identity with, and distinction from, the cultural situation. But for a clear grasp of the principles and issues which such a dialectical existence involves, creative theological effort is always the indispensable requirement.

NOTES

1. Winfred Ernest Garrison and Alfred T. DeGroot, *The Disciples of Christ, A History* (St. Louis: Christian Board of Publication, 1948), p. 142.
2. *Ibid.*, p. 180.
3. William Thomas Moore, *A Comprehensive History of the Disciples of Christ* (New York: Fleming H. Revell Company, 1909), p. 334.
4. Thomas Campbell, *Declaration and Address,* p. 4.
5. John Allen Hudson (ed.), *Great Pioneer Papers,* n.d., p. 55.
6. *Ibid.*, p. 39.
7. *Ibid.*, p. 40.
8. Alexander Campbell, *The Christian System* (Cincinnati: Standard Publishing Company, n.d.), p. XII.
9. *Christian Messenger,* VII, 39.
10. *Christian System,* p. 174.
11. Hudson, *op. cit.*, p. 15.
12. *Ibid.*
13. *Ibid.*, p. 16.
14. Moore, *op. cit.*, pp. 273-4.
15. *The Christian Messenger,* V, 109.
16. *Ibid.*
17. *The Christian Messenger,* VI, 6-8.
18. One should not fail to note that Alexander Campbell's orthodox view of the Bible was somewhat loosened by this historical method. Speaking of the inspiration of the biblical writers, Campbell wrote, "In all matters purely supernatural, the communication [from the Holy Spirit] was made in words. . . . So that, as Paul says, 'We speak spiritual things in spiritual words,' or in words suggested by the Holy Spirit. But a very small portion of both Testaments are of this character. Communications purely supernatural occupy by far the least portion of the sacred books. In the historical books of both Testaments, and in the epistolary part of the New, there are many things presented to our minds which did not originate in heaven. . . . The sense or sentiment of all the sacred books is of divine authority. The words and phrases were in all instances, except the communications purely supernatural, of the selection of the writer." (*The Christian Baptist,* St. Louis: Christian

Publishing Co., 1828, p. 499); see also Alexander Campbell, *The Christian System,* p. 3.

19. Stephen J. England, *The Apostolic Church* (Eugene: Northwest Christian College, 1946), p. 81. See also B. H. Streeter, *The Primitive Church* (New York: The Macmillan Co., 1929), pp. 49, 52, 56.

20. Cf. Martin Dibelius, *The Message of Jesus Christ,* trans. Frederick C. Grant (New York: Charles Scribner's Sons, 1939), p. 128.

21. Erich Dinkler, *Bibelautorität und Bibelkritik* (Tübingen: J. C. B. Mohr [Paul Siebeck], 1950), pp. 19, 20.

22. *Ibid.,* p. 20.

23. See Albert Schweitzer, *The Quest of the Historical Jesus* (New York: The Macmillan Co., 1956), pp. 398-399.

24. Ernest Troeltsch forcefully described this universal law of historical relativism in his *Christian Thought, Its History and Application* (New York: Meridian Books, 1957), p. 44.

25. J. A. St. John (ed.), *The Philosophical Works of John Locke* (London: G. Bell & Sons Ltd., 1916), p. 205.

26. John Dewey, *Human Nature and Conduct* (New York: Henry Holt and Company, 1922), p. 106.

27. *Ibid.,* p. 10.

28. *Ibid.,* p. 84.

29. *The Christian Baptist,* 1828, p. 499.

30. Dodd sums up the New Testament kerygma by saying that "it recounted in brief the life and work of Jesus Christ, His conflicts, sufferings and death, and His resurrection from the dead." (C. H. Dodd, *Gospel and Law.* New York: Columbia University Press, 1950), p. 9.

31. William Adams Brown, *Toward a United Church—Three Decades of Ecumenical Christianity* (New York: Charles Scribner's Sons, 1946), p. 20.

32. *The Christian System,* p. 88.

33. *Ibid.,* p. 128.

34. Moore, *op. cit.,* p. 266.

35. J. H. Garrison (ed.), *The Old Faith Restated* (St. Louis: Christian Publishing Co., 1891), p. 45. E. Scribner Ames, it seems, indulged in a bit of wishful thinking when he argued that this plea for a restoration of primitive Christianity involved merely "the exaltation of the spirit of Christ, rather than a set of rules and forms;" and when he added that "all external authority was rejected," he was far from the mark (Edward Scribner Ames, *The Disciples of Christ,* Chicago, 1943, p. 10). W. E. Garrison renders a sounder judgment when he says that the Disciple emphasis on the New Testament enabled them to assimilate Old Testament criticism with a fair degree of tranquility. But "a frank facing of the problems raised by critical New Testament scholarship would compel a re-examination of some of the assumptions embodies in the phrase 'loyalty to the New Testament' " (Winfred E. Garrison, *Whence and Whither the Disciples of Christ.* St. Louis: Christian Board of Publication, 1950, pp. 39-40).

36. Garrison and DeGroot, *op. cit.,* p. 553.

37. Cf. W. B. Blakemore, *The Cornerstone and the Builders* (Toronto: University of Toronto, 1955), p. 6.

38. *The Christian Baptist,* p. 133.

39. According to West's count, the movement has divided and subdivided into more than twenty groups. Most of these divisions, West contends, "have occurred over conceptions of the form of church organization," that is, over the ecclesiastical nerve of the restoration idea (Robert Frederick West, *Alexander Campbell and Natural Religion.* New Haven: Yale University Press, 1948, pp. 219-220).

40. Philip Schaff, *The Creeds of Christendom* (New York: Harper & Brothers, 1919), I, 9.

41. *Millennial Harbinger,* 1833, p. 343.
42. *Ibid.,* pp. 344-5.
43. Paul Tillich, *Systematic Theology* (Chicago: The University of Chicago Press, 1951), I, 80. Copyright (1951) by the University of Chicago.
44. *Ecumencial Study Series,* Vol. IV, No. 1 (Indianapolis: Council on Christian Unity, 1958), p. 23.
45. *Declaration and Address,* p. 10.
46. J. H. Garrison, *op. cit.,* p. 340.
47. Cf. Garrison and DeGroot, *op. cit.,* pp. 538-9.
48. Cf. Howard E. Short, *Doctrine and Thought of the Disciples of Christ* (St. Louis: Christian Board of Publication, 1952), p. 24.
49. Cf. Garrison and DeGroot, *op. cit.,* p. 553.
50. From the P. S. Hall collection.
51. Isaac Errett, *Our Position* (Cincinnati: Standard Publishing Company, n.d.), p. 9.
52. *Lard's Quarterly,* April, 1865.
53. Charles Clayton Morrison, *The Unfinished Reformation* (New York: Harper & Brothers, 1953), p. 136.
54. *Ibid.*
55. William Robinson, *What Churches of Christ Stand For* (Birmingham: The Berean Press, 1929), p. 91; cf. Garrison and DeGroot, *op. cit.,* pp. 537-8.
56. Through the Christocentric focus was a dominant aspect of the perspective of the entire movement. Alexander Campbell, for example, wrote that "the church of Christ is an assembly of believers, or of saints called out of the world and constituted by his authority" (*The Christian Baptist*), p. 163.
57. *The Declaration and Address,* pp. 14-15.
58. As Luther expressed it in his preface to the Book of James.
59. *Millennial Harbinger,* 1836, p. 232.
60. *Ibid.,* 1851, pp. 483-4.
61. Martin Luther, *D. Martin Luthers Werke,* bearbeitet von G. Buchwald und G. Käwerau (Weimar: Hermann Böhlaus, 1886), IV, 169.
62. Peter Ainslie, *The Message of the Disciples for the Union of the Church* (New York: Fleming H. Revell Company, 1913), pp. 33-34.
63. Moore, *op. cit.,* pp. 274-75.
64. *Ibid.,* p. 259.
65. *Millennial Harbinger,* 1037, p. 411.
66. Moore, *op. cit.,* p. 275.
67. This was one of Campbell's basic criticisms of Protestant orthodoxy: "creeds and manuals, synods and councils, soon shackled the minds of men, and the spirit of reformation gradually forsook the Protestant Church" (*The Christian System,* p. 3).
68. Ames, *op. cit.,* p. 10.
69. Morrison, *op. cit.,* p. 197.
70. For a fuller statement of the significance of scripture as a medium of the continuous aspect of God's self-revelation through Jesus as Christ, see Ralph G. Wilburn, *The Prophetic Voice in Protestant Christianity* (St. Louis: The Bethany Press, 1956), pp. 178ff.
71. Lynn Leavenworth (ed.), *Great Themes in Theology* (Chicago: The Judson Press, 1958), p. 48.
72. Henry Nelson Wieman, *Now We Must Choose* (New York: The Macmillan Company, 1941), pp. 43-4.
73. *Ibid.*
74. A piece of research which Professor Lunger did for the Association of Disciples for Theological Discussion, not yet published.

PART THREE

HISTORICAL INFLUENCES UPON DISCIPLES OF CHRIST

12

The Sociology of Disciple Intellectual Life

Historical Form of Organization for Thinking

W. B. Blakemore

THE appointment in 1957 of the Panel of Scholars is one of the major indications that Disciples of Christ have become participants in the "theological renaissance" which characterizes midcentury American Protestantism. There are large factors in the heritage of Disciples which might have prevented their involvement in the resurgence of theology, and those factors are such that they do and will continue to differentiate the Disciples' attitude toward theology from that of many other denominations.

The term "renaissance" implies a succession of three historic periods:

1. An original period of development
2. A period of decline into obscurity
3. A period of rediscovery and new appreciation, of "rebirth"

The kind of theology in which interest has been reborn was originally formulated during the first two centuries of Protestantism (1517 to approximately 1750). The directions taken by theology in that period were set by such early reformers as Melanchthon, Calvin, and Cranmer. By the end of the period, these original directions had developed into elaborated systems of theology generally referred to as Protestant Scholasticism. For denominations which came into existence in the early years of the Reformation, the contemporary theological renaissance is a return to thought-forms and methods associated with their ecclesiastical origins. For Reformation denominations, the emergence of a neo-Reformation theology was a return to ways of expression with which they were historically identified, and by which they were marked until the revolt against scholastic theology began in the eighteenth century. That revolt was the work of the Enlightenment in philosophy and of pietism in religion. These forces were amongst those which forced classical Protestant theology into an obscurity that lasted till about 1925 when the current renaissance began.

During the period of the decline of scholastic theology, several denominations came into existence. Most of these denominations were, indeed, a vigorous part of the revolt and were characterized by anti-"theological" attitudes because they believed that they had discovered more adequate articulations of the Christian faith than those offered by scholastic theology. Disciples of Christ were such a body. They came into existence midway through the period of decline. Historically they have been against creeds. Alexander Campbell was opposed to all forms of "theology" and would not allow it to be taught in the Bethany College which he founded in 1840. In the realm of biblical studies Campbell belonged already to the critical rather than to the dogmatic school. While Campbell did not progress beyond what is today called lower criticism, the fact that he was even a lower critic meant that he was a radical in his day. He laid a groundwork amongst his followers for a sociohistorical understanding of the scriptures. This kind of critical approach helped Disciples of Christ to be ready for the fuller critical points of view as they were formulated by the end of the nineteenth century. By that time the leading scholars of Disciples had espoused the higher criticism of the Bible. They were pioneers in the analysis of social and psychological influences upon religious institutions and ideas, and they belonged philosophically to the critical lines associated with such names as John Locke and Immanuel Kant.

The emergence of a new theological era beginning during the 1920's felt to most Disciples like a reaction, especially because this theological revival was intimately associated with the name of Calvin and most early disciples had looked upon Calvinism as one of the worst examples of dry and unprofitable speculation. The consequence was that it was not until the 1950's that Disciples of Christ began to participate in the theological revival of this century. Feeling estranged from the theological tendencies apparent in most denominations and in the ecumenical movement, Disciples gave expression to their ecumenical concern through their administrative and service activities rather than through engagement in theological discussion. Even so Disciples of Christ have been outstanding amongst the denominations in the promptness and thoroughness with which they prepared their responses to such major ecumenical reports as came from conferences at Amsterdam (1948), Lund (1952), and Evanston (1954).

The Sociology of Disciple Intellectual Life to 1950

Within the decade of the 1950's there was a remarkable breakthrough in theological activity and interest amongst Disciples of Christ. This breakthrough, with revolutionary rapidity, organized the most extensive and intensive intellectual enterprise in which Disciples have ever been engaged in their one hundred and fifty years. A brief review of the sociology of Disciple intellectual life in the years before 1950 provides an orientation to the later ways in which inquiry is being carried on.

In the period 1830 to 1860 Disciple intellectual life centered in Bethany, Virginia. Alexander Campbell was not only himself an astute thinker; he could also gather and inspire a team or a "school of thought." The *Millennial Harbinger* was not only Campbell's vehicle of communication. It also served his father, Thomas, and such colleagues as Robert Richardson, Walter Scott, and W. K. Pendelton. It nourished a number of lesser lights and even an occasional luminary like Robert Milligan.

With the fading of the Bethany group, the center of activity amongst Disciples tended to move toward certain editorships. Isaac Errett through the *Christian Standard* and J. H. Garrison through the *Christian-Evangelist* exercised a great intellectual stimulation. They were in turn stimulated by those who sent them articles for publication or who wrote to the "Letters to the Editor" columns. These editors, their writers, critics, and commentators constituted a system through which Disciples did their major thinking during the last half of the nineteenth century. At the close of the century the creative range broadened again. There appeared a series of scholarly quarterlies, and the more scholarly men of the brotherhood gathered annually for congresses at which learned papers were read. These congresses served to refresh the preaching ministry in our churches as well as to bring the best minds into relationship with each other.

Shortly after the turn of the century, there developed within American Protestantism an acrimonious division, usually known as the fundamentalist-modernist controversy, which threatened every denomination. Amongst Disciples of Christ the outbreak of argument resulted in a retreat by the modernists and liberals from the public abuse heaped upon them by certain reactionaries. In order to achieve an atmosphere in which they could provide each other the intellectual stimulation adequate to a scholarly pursuit of their concerns, the modernists and liberals retreated into a small and relatively exclusive grouping. The men so banded together called themselves the Campbell Institute. For a number of years they went about their work of rethinking the Christian faith as a closed community. Eventually the creativity and sincerity of their thinking won a deserved recognition. Realizing that a day of acceptance was at hand the Campbell

Institute was opened to any who cared to join and became a public platform for the position usually called "liberalism." The great creative period of the Institute lasted from about 1910 to 1940. It still exists to carry on the very important function of being an open platform from which anything may be said and on which any questions may be raised. In membership the Institute is now too large to be the source of a new and constructive ideology but it is among Disciples of Christ still the paramount symbol of intellectual freedom.

Developments of the Current Decade

It was during the 1950's that an entirely new social structure for the furtherance of Disciple intellectual life emerged. It consists of a large number of small discussion groups scattered throughout the brotherhood and across the nation. These groups have five primary sources.

The earliest of these groups was brought into existence by the World Convention of Churches of Christ at its 1952 Assembly in Melbourne, Australia. A series of theological studies was set up and reported at the Toronto Assembly in 1955 and at the Edinburgh Assembly in 1960. Further studies have characterized the preparations for the Puerto Rico Assembly in 1965.

The second primary source of study groups is the Council on Christian Unity. The Department of Ecumenical Study of the Council originally brought into existence more than a dozen groups, each responsible for a topic which has emerged within World Council or other ecumenical discussions. These groups varied in the intensity of their work according to the urgency of preparation for Disciples to participate in particular ecumenical assemblies. Units existed for the discussion of such topics as baptism, rapid social change, proselytism, the World Council basis of membership, the theology of evangelism, etc. More recently the Department of Study has consolidated into three discussion groups dealing respectively with Theology and Unity, Theology of Mission, and Theology of Christian Social Ethics.

A third primary source of these groups is the Panel of Scholars established in 1957 by the Board of Higher Education and the United Christian Missionary Society. The Panel of Scholars was conceived to number fifteen men (professors and ministers) and to meet semiannually to pursue its program of studies. The focus of these studies was to give guidance (not dictation) to the practical life of the churches and particularly to the agencies which created the Panel. The work of the Panel was relayed out to a large number of study groups across the nation who then sent in their responses. These study groups were also small enough for extensive and intensive discussion. It was originally expected that the Panel of Scholars would be in existence for three years; it was early recognized that the envisioned work would require a five-year span which was approved by the Sponsors of the Panel.

Another source of study groups is the Department of Social Welfare of the United Christian Missionary Society. It has established three groups which annually conduct "Conversations in Theology and Social Ethics." The aim of these conversations is not to reach conclusions but to deepen and extend communication, foster new ideas, and discover new insights. These groups are composed of the heads of major agencies of the brotherhood, seminary personnel, and ministers and laymen known to have an interest in social ethics.

The fifth and newest source of study groups is actually only one group—of about thirty men—known as the Association of Disciples for Theological Discussion. It is composed entirely of men in academic life, teaching in theology or a cognate field. It is able to meet because of financial assistance from one of the denomination's major agencies.

The sum total of the intellectual activity now initiated by these groups is the most extensive theological stimulation ever experienced by Disciples of Christ in their history. Even so, one of the limitations of the present sociology of Disciple intellectualizing is that the groups are all composed of selected personnel. These groups do not yet include any of a strictly voluntary type. However, it must be pointed out that the only way to get creative thinking done is to bring together those persons known to have the discipline necessary to the pursuit of creative thought. To open the door wide means to allow in those who might come only as auditors, or from some motivation other than intellectual. Since nearly all of the groups are subsidized, the divergencies that would be created by mass participation are uneconomic; even so if anyone feels left out, there is nothing to prevent him from finding some colleagues and starting another group. It is out of closely knit intensive stimulating communication of eager minds that new ideas and insights will emerge.

The Significance of Agency Initiative

A most striking feature of this new phenomenon of innumerable small study groups, and one which constitutes a kind of revolution which has occurred within a very few years, is that every one of these study groups grew either directly out of "agency" initiative, or achieved agency auspices in the process of coming into existence. The World Convention, The United Christian Missionary Society, the Christian Board of Publication, The Council on Christian Unity, The Board of Higher Education, the Department of Social Welfare—these have been the stimulating units, not the local churches or even the schools, though the latter provide much of the personnel for the study groups.

Yet there is something true to the genius of Disciples in the fact that these agencies brought the study groups into being. The motivation of these groups has not been in terms of theology for speculation's sake. It has been in terms of dealing with the emergent practical problems, in terms of renewing a sense of direction, and for the sake of the denomination's self-identity as it moves from one period of its life to the next. In so far as the denomination is dynamic, it is intended that study groups will assist in the maintenance of a sense of communication across the generations, and a sensitivity to both the continuities and discontinuities involved in a dynamic movement through time.

With respect to the present study program of Disciples, the function of the agencies is to present problems for discussion. The function of the theological study groups is to identify the issues involved in the problems, and then to suggest to the agencies the various options for action which appear. Ultimate decision lies back with whoever has the responsibility for action. But in one sense, the arms and feet of the denomination have been building for themselves a more representative brain than they had a few years ago. Instead of a few agency personnel sitting down to think through the issues, many more members of the denomination are now caught up into a practically orientated study of theology. In seeking to provide an orientation for the Association of Disciples for Theological Discussion, Dr. Langdon Gilkey, professor of theology at Vanderbilt University and a member of Woodmont Christian Church, Nashville, wrote:

> Believing that theology is most creative when it is the careful thought *of* the churches, rather than an academic discussion of scholars, and that tradition is alive when it is related to the contemporary scene, we propose to begin with our own church life, and to explore both our tradition and contemporary theology from the standpoint of that life. The real theological problem of authority is not so much an intellectual problem for the academic mind as it is a problem for the life of the church.

When the Panel of Scholars was formed, it too, like the later Association of Disciples for Theological Discussion, recognized that it was fundamentally as churchmen that its members had been called together. As their work progresses they more and more clearly understand that their task is to contribute, by God's grace, to nothing less than the renewal of church.

13

Dogmatically Absolute, Historically Relative

Conditioned Emphases in the History of Disciples of Christ

RONALD E. OSBORN

THE earnest intention of Disciples of Christ was to escape from the relativities of the church's history. It was the fond belief of the founders, as it is of many yet today, that they had actually succeeded in doing so. Alanson Wilcox began his *History of the Disciples of Christ in Ohio* with the confident declaration, "The church of Christ began at nine o'clock in the morning on the day of Pentecost succeeding the crucifixion of Christ."[1] The movement for "the restoration of the primitive gospel" was the "greatest since the apostolic age." "Believers in Christ . . . were only asked to lay aside their human appendages and give full obedience to Jesus Christ."[2]

Moses E. Lard stated the position in 1863 without equivocation:[3]

> The reformation for which we are pleading consists, 1st. *In accepting the exact meaning of Holy Writ as our religious theory.* . . . Hence human elements are absolutely excluded from our theory. . . . We accept as our creed the contents of his word without enlargement, contraction, or modification. . . .
>
> 2nd. *In the minute conformity of our practice to the revealed will of Christ.* . . . All practices having their origin in tradition, human reason, or expediency, are utterly eschewed.

Here was an effort to strike off the shackles of tradition, to renounce human creeds and the inventions of men, to repudiate all innovations, to clear away the rubbish of the centuries—such phrases become clichés among Disciples—and to take up things "exactly where the apostles left them," "to contend for the original faith and order, in opposition to all the corruptions of fifteen centuries."[4]

A century and a quarter have elapsed since Alexander Campbell wrote the words just quoted; Disciples of Christ now have a history as well as a position. And the experience of five generations has made quite clear three important facts:

(1) Disciples of Christ today—even those who cling to the restoration ideal—are not what they were in 1835. Crucial dogmatic and institutional changes have occurred in life and thought and ethos.

(2) These changes are obviously to be interpreted as the result or manifestation of particular forces and influences in the history of Disciples of Christ.

(3) The original position must likewise be interpreted as the result or manifestation of historic forces and influences.

The position of Disciples is not so free from environmental taint as they have wished to believe. Their peculiar and cherished emphases have been conditioned by the changing context of their corporate experience. They have liked to think of their position as dogmatically absolute; in fact, it has been historically relative.

It now behooves the author to provide substance for the allegations just advanced. Suggestions for the general trend to be followed in the paper as well as hints concerning specific factors to be discussed have come pre-eminently from three American historians: Frederick Jackson Turner, whose well-known essay on "The Significance of the Frontier in American History" casts a flood of light on the experience of Disciples, though he does not mention them and presumably never investigated them; Arthur Meier Schlesinger, Sr., whose *Paths to the Present* sets the Turner thesis in perspective by suggesting the role of more recent factors such as immigration, urbanization, and the like; and Dan E. Clark who led me through a course at the University of Oregon in "Forces and Influences in American History." All this prepared me to receive with eagerness the plea of the Third World Conference on Faith and Order at Lund that the communions study the social and cultural factors in their history, particularly as these have borne upon division or union—a plea which elicited no very enthusiastic response from most of the theologians. Certainly the dean of church historians among Disciples of Christ, W. E. Garrison, has been mindful of such factors and delivered at Lund a masterful address on the subject with the whimsical opening sentence: "Students of religion have long known that culture, social structure and habits, climate, economic conditions, forms of government, national loyalties and the like affect all religions except their own."[5] Besides Garrison, W. W. Jennings, Henry K. Shaw, R. Frederick West, and various other historians of Disciples have acknowledged the role of environmental influences in the life of the movement. The paper on "The Age of Alexander Campbell" presented at Bethany College by Arthur M. Schlesinger, Jr., also deserves mention in this connection.[6]

The intention of the present paper is to delineate major forces and influences which have affected the corporate life and thought of Disciples, at the time of their founding, in the "middle period," and in the present generation. While it must be conceded that the concept of historical causality has been seriously questioned of late, it may also be affirmed with Sidney Hook that "No historical account that goes beyond the form of a chronicle can be written without the assumption of causal connection."[7] Hook also adds, "Every statement of causal connection is an hypothesis," and my purpose is to suggest a number of hypotheses, some of which we may consider already substantiated, others of which require investigation. In conclusion, I wish to face the issue which all this poses for Disciples and for the church in general, the issue of the church's involvement in the culture and the implications for Disciples' understanding of the nature of the church.

What, then, are the major environmental forces which have given shape to the life and thought of Disciples?

The Original Formulation

We shall begin with the period of the founders.

1. *The understanding of history* which prevailed at the beginning of the nineteenth century must be mentioned first of all. Here is exquisite irony: the belief of the fathers that they could transcend history with all its relativities and by restoring pristine Christianity could reach the absolute form of the church unconditioned by history—this conviction itself was historically conditioned. The point has been well made by Langdon Gilkey in a recent essay, to which only a few comments will be added here.[8] The illusions of a lost Golden Age, of a free, preinstitutional state of nature, of the perfection of pristine society, beguiled the minds of many, especially the leading intellectuals of the late eighteenth century and those who took them seriously. Jean-Jacques Rousseau developed a theory of education from the proposition that a child is good and potentially perfect until corrupted by the depraved demands of human society.[9] The respectable hallucination concerning the "noble savage," uninfected by the blight of civilization, deluded more than one *philosophe* who had grown weary of Paris, Versailles, and Geneva but was untroubled by any of the facts of anthropology. The notion of a primitive church, unsullied by history, and the belief that it was possible to reproduce that perfect church eighteen hundred years later belonged to the same pattern of thinking.

The Lockean theory of knowledge supported the illusion. John Locke (1632-1704), the "Christian philosopher," profoundly influenced Rousseau and his French contemporaries, the generation of great American statesmen and their followers at the time of the Revolution, and Alexander Campbell and his colleagues. Locke had described the mind of the human infant as *tabula rasa,* a blank writing tablet unmarred by innate ideas and ready to be filled up by impressions received through the five senses. In similar fashion, Disciples believed it possible and right for adults to clear their minds of all inherited notions about religious doctrines and practices and upon that blank tablet to receive the simple gospel. So Alexander Campbell urged: "Open the New Testament as if mortal man had never seen it before."[10]

In the body politic, the results of such primitivism proved violent. Edmund Burke said that "the French Revolutionaries went hideously wrong because they supposed that they could abolish history and reconstruct human nature from the foundation; indeed, d'Alembert had said quite explicitly 'let us abolish history.' "[11] That was also the cry of the early Disciples, "Let us abolish history!" and their iconoclasm sometimes attained the same pitch of frenzied idealism as that of the French Revolutionaries. The mood of the *Christian Baptist* in lopping off the heads of the kings and princes of the clergy was not unlike that of Mme. LaFarge in La Place de la Concorde.

2. *The preoccupation with written constitutions.* John Locke and subsequent political theorists had advanced the notion of the social contract, a hypothetical compact between government and people far in the unrecorded and unremembered past, the state of nature. So Englishmen salved their consciences for overthrowing King James, and all at once the English colonists in America, nourished on the same doctrine, turned it against King George. Not content to stake their liberties on political theory (and drawing upon the precedent of the church covenant which had become a historic reality in New England), the men of the new nation drew up a social contract in black and white, the Constitution of the United States. The people of every state that entered the Union likewise wrote a constitution of their own as their fundamental law, and during Alexander Campbell's years of residence in the United States nineteen new states were ad-

mitted to the Union. He himself helped to rewrite the constitution of Virginia. In political life, all the freedoms and the welfare of the people depended on the constitution; it was venerated with a fervor almost religious. The historian George Bancroft hailed the Constitution of the United States the most perfect document ever to issue from the brain of mortal man.[12]

Alexander Campbell habitually thought of the church in political analogies, and what more natural than that the church should require a written constitution? But who would be so blasphemous as to suggest that mere men should devise it or should negotiate a social contract with the Almighty? It stood to reason that Deity should provide a written constitution for the church. Indeed, Alexander Campbell flatly maintained that the Bible is the perfect bond of union because a good and benevolent God would have to give one.[13] Political or ecclesiastical order without a written constitution was inconceivable; so the New Testament was said to be the divine constitution for the church. Campbell rejoiced that all Christians were agreed "in the character of King Jesus, and in the authority of his statute book."[14] From Thomas Campbell's Proposition IV to the most recent editorial in the *Christian Standard* it does not seem to have occurred to the adherents of this view to ask whether the New Testament is indeed a constitutional document. The assumption was postulated as axiomatic, though we must declare it false.

I have made no study to determine who first spoke of the New Testament as the *constitution* of the church. Protestant Reformers from the beginning had appealed to the Bible as their rule of faith and practice. But I propose that the preoccupation with written constitutions in nineteenth-century America was an important factor in the plausibility of the plea of Disciples—it was self-evident—and in the growth of various restoration movements.

3. *The democratic spirit.* The younger Schlesinger takes the democratic spirit as the key to his interpretation of Campbell, whose emphases on simplicity and intelligibility in doctrine, on

the humanizing of faith, on congregational government of the church are all seen as manifestations of that spirit.[15] Democracy was not just a matter of political government. It pervaded the realm of ideology and demanded simplicity, which Disciples offered by dismissing the doctrine of the trinity and other difficult dogmas as unscriptural and hence inconsequential. This sort of treatment was assumed to have solved the problem and was typical of the era: de Tocqueville observed a general tendency of the American masses to deny what they could not understand.[16]

The energetic democrats of the young nation which had made good its revolution against Great Britain also rebelled against the various engines of authority which they believed had oppressed them in the past. A commentator in the *American Monthly* described the mood of Jacksonian democracy while Old Hickory was in the People's Palace: "It declares a war of extermination upon the established institutions of religion and government. It denominates all religion priestcraft, all property a monopoly, and all jurisprudence an organized fraud upon the liberties of mankind."[17] Above all things else, the democrat wanted to get government into his own hands; congregational polity and the repudiation of ecclesiastical courts accorded well with the temper of such people. Turner quotes an early Western appeal for statehood: "Some of our fellow citizens may think we are not able to conduct our affairs and consult our interests; but if our society is rude, much wisdom is not necessary to supply our wants, and a fool can sometimes put on his clothes better than a wise man can do it for him."[18]

The would-be leader of these frontier democrats often sought to play to the gallery; with the adoption of universal white manhood suffrage, the demagogue became a stock character on the political stage. He was, in the language of R. H. Luthin concerning Jackson, "a caterer to the many, the technician of mass leadership . . . , the influential party chieftain who, by vigorous personality and noisy appeal to the crowd, made gross political capital by waging warfare against the affluent minority."[19] One such Western democrat who was linked closely both to Jackson and to Campbell was Richard M. Johnson, brother of the famous preacher John T. Johnson. Disciples have read with pride that Richard Mentor Johnson was vice president of the United States. Few have known what manner of man he was. It may be as diverting as it is disconcerting to read Luthin's account:[20]

> Back in 1812, he had left his seat in Congress to go as a colonel to war against the British. In the battle of the Thames he shot an Indian chief alleged to be Tecumseh. On his return home, Colonel Johnson was presented with a sword, lauded as Tecumseh's killer, and re-elected to Congress. In the House he held forth on the theme "Vox Populi *is* Vox Dei"—the lowly are the only group of consequence. In 1819 he was elevated to the Senate. He became Jackson's satellite in the war on the Bank. The "Workingman's" party took him up as its presidential candidate. "Rumpsey, dumpsey, who killed Tecumsey?" became a preconvention battle cry. At Baltimore in 1834 there was presented a play, *Tecumsey, or the Battle of the Thames,* in which were used the pistol "with which the hero slew his savage foe," the "identical dress worn by Tecumseh at the time of his death," and "the identical flag captured by the Colonel from the British"—all borrowed from the War Department. . . .
>
> Johnson was selected by Andrew Jackson to be Martin Van Buren's running-mate on the 1836 national ticket. Elected vice-president, Johnson registered an unimpressive record. His liberalism disappeared before an obsession for office. His private life proved so embarrasing that the Democrats declined to renominate him in 1840. Some states, however, named him and he took to the stump. In Ohio he opened his shirt to show his scars of war. He boasted: "I was born in a canebrake and cradled in a sap trough." He failed of re-election.

The historian must admit that a similar spirit of demagoguery characterizes the religious campaigns of early Disciples, as of the frontier revivalists generally. Campbell's diatribes against elegant church buildings are an example; apparently even in Cincinnati he found "brick satyres upon his religion whose best followers met in garrets to extol their Lord and King."[21] And his effort is patent to make the backwoodsman's eyes pop with wonder and flash with indignation when he allows that he has seen magnificent pulpits in the East, costing two or three thousand dollars apiece![22] Campbell's willingness to play the role of demagogue is nowhere more apparent than in his attacks on the hireling clergy. Kings and clergymen are much alike: both have got upon thrones—"The king upon a golden throne, or a gilded one—the priest upon a wooden one, sometimes gilded, and sometimes crimson-cushioned, too."[23] The ministers who have received a college education require educated congregations to understand them: indeed, "it is more difficult to understand the clergy than the Bible."[24] Such a clergyman is a hireling because "he learns the art and mystery of making a sermon, or a prayer, as a man learns the art of making a boot or a shoe. He intends to make his living, . . . and he sets himself up to the highest bidder."[25] It is all done for filthy lucre. "The modern clergy say they do not preach for money. Very well; let the people pay them none, and they will have as much of their preaching still. Besides, there will be no suspicion of their veracity."[26]

But only an unreconstructed aristocrat would equate democracy and demagoguery. Jackson and Campbell cannot be dismissed as hypocrites manipulating the masses merely for their own advantage; they believed in the people. Campbell's set piece in which he describes the frontiersman[27] reflects genuine admiration; and the responsible role into which he sought to bring the general membership of the church derived equally from the democratic spirit at its best and from his own understanding of the New Testament, with which he held it to be at one.[28]

4. *The sense of destiny.* Early nineteenth-century America believed profoundly and extravagantly in its destiny; this free land was not merely a haven of refuge for the oppressed who fled from autocratic regimes, it was a beacon to mankind holding up the light of freedom before the whole world and inspiring rebellion against tyranny everywhere. The ordinary American belligerently

affirmed his equality with any man anywhere in the world, whatever his assumed distinction, and maintained that his system of government was superior to all others. The old Calvinistic concept of election had become secularized, but was still powerful: this people and this land had been chosen to lead the world to a brighter day. The phrase "Manifest Destiny" became a powerful political slogan, though the presumed nobility of the end sought was sometimes used to justify questionable means of attaining it. The conviction of destiny amounted almost to religious fervor. So the historian George Bancroft wrote in 1858:

> The hour of the American Revolution was come. The people of the continent with irresistible energy obeyed one general impulse, as the earth in the spring listens to the command of nature, and without the appearance of effort bursts forth to life in perfect harmony. The change which Divine wisdom ordained, and which no human policy or force could hold back, proceeded as uniformly and majestically as the laws of being, and was as certain as the decrees of eternity.

Once again there is striking analogy, if not a causal connection, between the ethos of the American people generally in the political sphere and that of Disciples in the ecclesiastical realm. A sense of high destiny, of having achieved that for which mankind had long waited, of occupying a decisive role in the supremely fateful issue, of being just on the verge of momentous universal realization of the ideal, characterized the one as well as the other. Disciples' pride in being "a peculiar people," their sense of mission, their excitement that the gospel had been literally restored, their urgency about the "plea," all demonstrate a high sense of destiny.

With Alexander Campbell the conviction reached the intensity of a virtual messianic complex. The New Reformation was a movement of destiny, and he was its prophet. A criticism of Campbell by one of his contemporaries shows remarkable insight; wrote John R. Graves, attacking Campbell's New Testament in the *Tennessee Baptist* for June 10, 1854: "The ambition of your life has been to become an acknowledged Reformer—

a second Luther—to be the acknowledged head and leader of the whole Christian world and to receive the fragrant incense of its homage." Campbell lent substance to such charges in his merciless attacks upon religious leaders past and present, in his ill-becoming arguments with Stone over the name of the church and with Scott over the prior leadership of the Restoration, in his acceptance of such deferential titles as Bishop Campbell and Father Campbell, more particularly in his view that his movement marked the genuine Reformation which was to transfigure the church, and most intensely in his expectation of the Millennium when he and the Disciples should have fulfilled their mission. Schlesinger finds Campbell's language concerning the Millennium reminiscent of that of Albert Brisbane and other disciplec of Fourier,[29] and his judgment is doubtless right. More important for our own argument is that emerging in a context of belief in manifest destiny, the ethos of Disciples became characterized by a high pitch of Messianism, an overriding sense of mission, a millennial hope that was soon to find fulfillment not by the miraculous advent of the Son of Man coming upon clouds of glory but by the victory of the plea over sectarianism and infidelity. The belief in the importance of this imminent and glorious realization appears to have been a major influence in Campbell's establishment of his journals and his college, his acceptance of a missionary society, which he would earlier have denounced as unscriptural and ecclesiastical, and his unfulfilled desire for even a higher degree of "church organization."[30]

5. *The emergence of Disciples as a separate people.* While not itself an environmental factor from the outside, the dissolution of the Mahoning Baptist Association in 1830 and the consequent separation of Disciples from the Baptists was a historical event which exercised profound influence on theory and practice and demonstrated the historical relativity of positions hitherto regarded as dogmatically absolute. Faced with the responsibility for a movement of thousands of believers, Campbell could no longer afford to be a mere iconoclast. He set himself to the de-

velopment of institutions which he was even willing to call "church organization," and of a college where aspiring preachers might study the Bible as well as the classics. Some of his followers could not follow this shift; his ardent admirers and defenders resorted to various ingenious devices to explain it or to explain it away while his opponents flailed him unmercifully as inconsistent. Their charges hurt, and he sought to parry them with the query, "Must we assume the ground, Once in error, always in error!"[31]

Whether Campbell and his devotees remained convinced of his consistency or not—the question is still hotly debated—the program of the movement was profoundly changed. It had begun as an assault on existing ecclesiastical institutions; since 1830 it has been driven by an inner compulsion to build up an ecclesiastical institution, an effort which has been perennially weakened, distorted, or frustrated by the initial distrust of ecclesiastical institution.

6. *Other influences.* Other forces and influences of the period of founding ought to be discussed, but can merely be suggested.

The autocratic behavior of certain ecclesiastical courts in the experience of Stone and Thomas Campbell bred into Disciples an almost irrational antipathy against any sort of connectional authority in the church or any form of creed. Likewise the violent opposition of the established denominations to the new movement understandably drove it into a sectarian isolationism which vitiated the catholicity of its intent.

The relatively simple and undeveloped state of institutions, both political and ecclesiastical, on the frontier left considerable initiative to local groups and leaders without official standing. In such a situation, as I have suggested elsewhere,[32] the plea to dissolve all denominational organization and simply come together on the common understanding of the New Testament was temporarily a practicable strategy for Christian union, though an illusory one. Yet because it worked for a short time in a transient and now nonexistent situation at the time of their founding, Disciples have clung to that strategy almost without question till fairly recent times. Yet as surely as the frontier was the advancing stage of civilization, the social institutions of the West were bound to become more powerful and more complex. The plea of Disciples for Christians of all bodies to forsake their institutions and come to those of Disciples or to none at all is today irrelevant, irresponsible, and—one is compelled to say—dishonest, because it is utterly fanciful and improbable in such a culture as ours.

The missionary situation of early nineteenth-century America, with the bulk of the population unchurched yet standing in a Christian tradition and conditioned by prevailing presuppositions of biblical authority, affected Disciple dogma. There was available a large body of unbaptized adults so that Disciples too readily assumed their own situation at that time, and the strikingly parallel minority situation of the church in the Book of Acts, to be the constant and normal condition of the church; hence they developed as normative a doctrine of baptism which is relevant to a missionary setting but inadequate in societies where the bulk of the population has at least formal church connections and the majority of the candidates for baptism are the children of church members. The spectacular response of the unchurched frontiersmen to the preaching of the evangelists was taken as the validation of the position and the seal of divine approval.

The popularity of debates and the polemical style of early nineteenth-century American journalism imbued the ethos of Disciples with a streak of pugnacity which was long considered a mark of orthodoxy. Campbell had hammered out the position in a few dramatic and well-publicized debates; and every preacher in the next generation rode forth on his polemical charger. Campbell raised his editorial voice in the rhetorical invective which the men of the time took for eloquence and power; later Disciples continued the name-calling.

To generalize concerning the impact of these influences on

Disciples in the period of their founding, it must be emphasized that the effect of these environmental forces was not trivial or incidental, but crucial. To point out these particular characteristics of a time now long past is qualitatively quite different from saying that Campbell traveled by riverboat or carried a gold-headed cane. For the forces we have discussed were so immediate and so powerful that the first generation of Disciples accepted them without question; they formed the central doctrines of the movement, its institutions, its character, in response to influences which we now know to have been transitory and partial but which they regarded as normative. Thus the position which they reached so laboriously and regarded as dogmatically absolute is now seen to have been historically relative after all. The judgment must be pronounced on such central dogmas of Disciples as restoration, the abolition of the clergy, their particular "plea," the wholesale repudiation of creeds and of ecclesiastical organization, their specific program for Christian union, even their doctrine of baptism. The present distress of Disciples, even the appointment of the Panel of Scholars, is evidence that the changing forces of history with every passing decade have rendered the original formulations less and less tenable, less and less relevant to the issues before the contemporary church.

The Middle Period

Already in the middle period of their history, Disciples were exposed to new forces and influences which began to alter their life and thought. We may consider the period as beginning just after midcentury, in Campbell's declining years, and as terminating in the formal recognition (1906) of the division between Churches of Christ and Disciples.

1. *The death of Alexander Campbell.* The magnitude of the implications of this event has scarcely been suggested by the historians of Disciples or by the diagnosticians of their ills. I am proposing the thesis that with the removal of Campbell from

the scene the bankruptcy of the plea becomes evident, at least to us who view it in retrospect.

The original Disciples indignantly repudiated the allegation that they were Campbellites; they claimed to be New Testament Christians, and various leaders among them quite openly resented Campbell's eminence. If they were not Campbellites, the question may well be asked, What was their principle of coherence? Presumably loyalty to Christ and acceptance of the New Testament, but this was proposed as a platform for the unity of all Christians. Until Peter Ainslie began to lead Disciples in the exchange of ecumenical courtesies, however, they were not widely noted even for kindliness toward other Christians, to say nothing of a sense of oneness with them. They really belonged to "the movement," they were a "people." And they had a powerful sense of coherence. What provided it? Not a creed or confession of faith; they repudiated such. Not an ecclesiastical institution; they repudiated that too. Not a common tradition; they had none. They were held together by three things: (1) their common understanding of the plea, which remained fairly stable while the historical context within which it arose persisted, and thereafter soon began to break up; (2) their hatred of denominationalism and distrust of the denominations all around them, as well as of the particular denominational practices which Disciples had disavowed; and (3) the living leadership of Campbell. When he was removed, Disciples were left with neither a fixed position nor a dynamic principle of coherence. For a while the social context remained sufficiently similar to that of their origin for their plea to retain the appearance of plausibility, and they continued to grow in numbers, but the spectacular rate of increase in which they long gloried slowed down more and more. And even though they grew for a while, at Campbell's death they immediately began to fall apart. No one succeeded him, for his leadership was charismatic, not official, and the leaders who came after had diverse spirits.

Gradually that group which supported the convention and the

agencies related to it made these institutions their actual, though long unavowed, instrument of coherence, and today there is a strong trend toward vesting them with full ecclesiastical status. By contrast, no success has been achieved in the formulation of any body of common beliefs, and sentiment against a "creed" appears still to be more deep-seated in the prejudices of Disciples than the aversion to ecclesiastical organization. Meanwhile, of course, not all the heirs of Campbell have proved willing to rally round the "cooperative" institutions. Two other recognizable groups have emerged—Churches of Christ and "independents." Their principle of coherence appears to have been largely their common opposition to given practices or institutions; so neither of these groups is well defined or free from tendencies toward further subdivision. There is evidence that some "independents" may find a measure of coherence around particular institutions of their own, but the original repudiation of ecclesiastical structures renders this problematical.

One clear lesson emerges from this experience of Disciples. A religious community finds its coherence in one or more of the following instruments: (1) a common formulation of dogma, (2) a common ecclesiastical structure, (3) a common tradition, (4) a charismatic leader. Disciples claimed to have none of them but actually found coherence for a time in the leader. With his death, their brief tradition proved an inadequate bond; some of them began to develop ecclesiastical structure and in that task continue to be engaged.

2. *Sectionalism.* Though Disciples did not divide over slavery, the schism between them and Churches of Christ followed sectional lines to a large extent, and the leaders of the two parties symbolized the political and military animosity between North and South.[33]

3. *Constitutional theory.* There is striking similarity between the strict constructionism of John C. Calhoun toward the Constitution of the United States and that of David Lipscomb and his associates toward the New Testament. The question should

be investigated, though a causal relationship must not be claimed without sufficient evidence, for other schisms in the church have occurred over this essential issue. Yet it can be reasonably maintained that the minds which found Calhoun convincing on the Constitution and fought for the principle would find Lipscomb convincing on the New Testament.

4. *The unevangelized West.* The existence of a vast unchurched element in the population gave shape to the early common institutions of the brotherhood. They were missionary societies. Most of our state organizations still bear this archaic and inaccurate title; in The United Christian Missionary Society, the Division of Home Missions and Christian Education now sustains many portfolios affecting the life of the local congregation, for which Disciples of the middle period and earlier would never have consented to establish an agency. The vast field of the unclaimed West which lay ripe unto the harvest enabled Disciples to grow with dramatic rapidity. It was common for Disciples to interpret their quick expansion as evidence of heavenly favor and as a divine authentication of the plea. As long as the rural West lay open they had good reason to believe they were "taking the country."

5. *Urbanization.* In the growing cities which were gaining an increasing proportion of the population and coming to dominate the culture, however, the demands of larger, more sophisticated congregations led to the modification of original practices among the Disciples. A professional ministry was required and ultimately came in all wings of the movement, though no clear and convincing biblical basis for the "one-man system" was ever discovered. Fine church buildings were erected. Musical instruments were introduced despite the conscientious objection of those whose only previous knowledge of instruments associated them with saloons. The one communion cup yielded to individual glasses, and (under the influence of the rising temperance movement and the salesmanship of the inventor of pasteurized grape juice) wine gave way to the unfermented fruit of the vine.

It was not easy for Disciples who had flourished so luxuriantly on the rural frontier to adapt to the demands of the strange new world of cities that was emerging in their midst. The nostalgia for the old-time meeting at the crossroads schoolhouse, for the exhilaration of gathering a new rural congregation, for basket dinners and fried chicken, for a way of life that was passing, long hampered many Disciples from an effective witness in the worldly, impersonal cities. The fact that congregations adapted to cultural change at markedly different rates contributed to the separation between the "antis" (Churches of Christ) and the "digressives" (Disciples).

6. *Changing immigration.* The rigidity of Disciples in clinging to familiar procedures was demonstrated in their failure to respond in effective ministry to the new immigrants flooding into the country after midcentury. As long as the settlers from abroad were dominantly English-speaking Protestants in background, Disciples grew with the influx. But among the Irish Catholics on the East coast, the Germans and Scandinavians in the Midwest, the Orientals in the West, and the Southern and Eastern Europeans at the end of the century, Disciples did no significant work. Rather they joined in extolling the Anglo-Saxon blood and decrying the threat to the nation's religious and political heritage.[34] Their failure was in marked contrast to that of the Baptists, in many ways so similar to Disciples, who carried on a notable ministry to the new foreign language groups.

New intellectual movements. At the beginning of the twentieth century the familiar thought-forms which had characterized American Christendom three generations earlier had been badly shattered. Many earnest preachers were still trying to exude enough conviction to glue the traditional structures back together, but the more thoughtful and less fearful knew that they were living in a new day. W. T. Moore, for example, spoke of the "scientific demands of the age," to which he believed that the "rationality" of Disciples particularly equipped them to speak.[35] The "higher criticism" of the Bible raised issues for exciting journalistic debates between Herbert L. Willett and J. W. McGarvey and left older assumptions regarding biblical authority no longer self-evident. With increasing acceptance of the theory of evolution and the doctrine of progress, the root of the restoration ideal was cut. H. L. Willett declared,[36]

> Restoration of the conditions prevailing in the apostolic churches is both impossible and undesirable. . . . Moreover the movement of the church is forward, not backward. The real cry of the church should be "Forward to Christ," not "Back to Christ," for our Leader is ever before.

Drawing on Campbell's distinction between the covenants and his sermon on "The Progress of Revealed Light," some Disciples now found it helpful to speak of "progressive revelation."[37] The new concern for the "social gospel" seemed to an oncoming generation a more exciting, more relevant ideal than restoring the ancient order of things. Recognition that the growth of public education had given the people generally a higher level of culture and intellectual maturity[38] prompted calls for a more literate, better prepared ministry. As older brotherhood colleges moved, however, toward greater sophistication and openness to the newer intellectual formulations, the Bible College emerged to champion the traditional pattern of beliefs.

Other influences of the middle period ought to be discussed, such as new international involvements by the United States and the awakening interest in missions, or the effect of personal animosities on partisanship within the brotherhood. Enough has been presented, however, to indicate that the forces of history were beginning to make manifest the relative character of positions originally regarded as absolute and that new forces were imposing new characteristics on the movement.

Our Own Times

During the past half century, forces and influences characteristic of our own times have profoundly altered the life and thought of Disciples. For this period I am thinking primarily of the "cooperative" group, although the effect of these forces may also be observed upon the "independents" and the Churches of Christ.

The impact of the city. In the urban congregations which set the patterns of churchly life, the professional ministry has expanded to the multiple ministry, with specialized staff to deal with religious education, youth work, music, business administration, calling, counseling; the original conception of the congregation as an intimate company of believers under the spiritual tutelage of elders from their own ranks has effectively vanished from the minds of the people. Disciples possess in practice everything that pertains to a separated, professional ministry, a clergy, except a doctrine of the ministry and the respect for the office which such a doctrine entails. Ways of worship have been radically overhauled to accord with urban and suburban sophistication; immersion, instead of an occassion for glorying, seems to have become an occasion of embarrassment, with the act of baptism increasingly being administered privately or semiprivately. In the heterogeneous and sophisticated suburban communities, open membership has become widely practiced. The weekly or monthly payment of urban income has made the weekly pledge an essential element in churchmanship and the annual budget an item of central concern in the life of the minister and congregation. The increasingly massive and impersonal character of metropolitan life has left former conceptions of Christian unity largely irrelevant to the life of the congregation and the experience of the ordinary Christian.

Managerial skill and organizational concentration. The organizational revolution of the twentieth century has profoundly altered the life of the congregation. The minister has become the "pastoral director," among Disciples no less than in other communions, his role shaped more than he realizes by programs, manuals, and demands issuing from the agencies. The presumed New Testament pattern of elders and deacons lingers in public worship as a cultic anachronism from frontier days, but the church is administered through functional committees. The planting of new churches is no longer the undertaking of isolated evangelists but a carefully organized operation involving large investments of members and funds. Congregational polity is being modified in the area of ordination and even in the placement of ministers; the autonomy of free agencies has been radically qualified by the budgetary power granted to the Commission on Brotherhood Finance and the self-imposed discipline of common counsel through the Council of Agencies. The entire structure of denominational life is in for thorough review and likely revision; the haphazard accumulation of organizations inherited from the middle period just does not make sense in this era of organizational efficiency. Among the people there is less individualism, far less Messianism than in the past; the cooperative Disciple, for whom the plea has lost its relevance, is more other-directed than inner-directed in his church life. The day of dominant leadership in brotherhood affairs by colorful individuals is past. Decisions are made in committees, "listening conferences," and other formal or informal groups. The younger minister tends to be an "organization man" rather than a pioneer with qualities of originality and imaginative leadership.

The "holistic" trend. Modern development of means of instantaneous communication and the emergence of massive entities in business and government have profoundly affected the life and ethos of the people. Concomitant with the drawing together of nation-states in such bodies as UN, NATO, SEATO, and Common Market has been the emergence of the World Council of Churches, The National Council of the Churches of Christ in the United States of America, and other manifestations of the ecumenical movement. Disciples' understanding of themselves and of their reason for being has undergone a radical transformation, "from the restoration of New Testament Christianity to the ecumenical renewal of the church."[39] The amalgamation of major industrial and financial enterprises has been reflected in the merger of denominations, with increasing numbers of Disciples hoping to participate in such a union. The tendency in American political life to shift the base of responsibility from the local community to Washington finds its counterpart in the desire of many Disciples to give institutional expression to the life of the whole "church" and in the movement for brotherhood restructure. The decline of individualism, the widespread appeal to contemporary Americans of those churches which emphasize traditional confessions and liturgies, the "churching" of the majority of the population, and the institutionalizing of religion have rendered the "missionary" conception of baptism held by early Disciples much less relevant to our times. Most of the persons now baptized in our churches are not penitent converts or adult believers but quite young children of church members. Disciples too have become an "established church."

Internal influences. The separation between Churches of Christ and Disciples of Christ was a shattering blow to the ethos of the brotherhood. The restoration plea had proven itself not the magic wand of union but the occasion of division. Within the present century the growing rift between "cooperative" and "independent" Disciples has been rendered more ominous by the development of almost totally separate institutions for each group—journals, church school curricula, hymnals, summer camps and conferences for youth, conventions, colleges, seminaries, and yearbooks. This not-quite schism has further shaken original confidence in the plea. The rise of a professional ministry with seminary education under the influence of new movements in theology has further weakened the old formulations of "our position." The plea that sought to transcend the particularities of history seems to have vanished with the passing of the particular historical forces that produced it.

Conclusion

In the early nineteenth century, the idea of going back to the church of the New Testament and ignoring all intervening history was so self-evident, so compelling, that scores of efforts at such restoration were made in America. Under the influence of Stone, Campbell, and Scott a number of these coalesced; in their conviction that they were doing things just as the apostles had done, Disciples approached religious ecstasy, and the emotional attachment which many heirs of Campbell still cherish toward the concept blinds them to the fact that it has lost whatever intellectual validity it once appeared to possess.

Recent studies make clear that restorationism rests upon a false understanding of the New Testament; historical criticism has shattered the concept of the New Testament as a constitution and that of a rigid pattern prevailing throughout the apostolic church, while form-criticism has demonstrated the amazing extent to which that church reshaped its life in loyalty to its living Lord under changing historical conditions. Restorationism presupposes an inadequate view of revelation: revelation is not the verbal transmission of laws and regulations, but the encounter of God with man in which he makes himself known through events. Restorationism assumes an untenable view of history and an indefensible notion of being able to transcend the relativities of history. Pragmatically, the restoration plea has proved incapable of uniting the Christian world; more shockingly, it has demonstrated itself as a divisive influence even among those who proclaim it.

The present paper has suggested that the various presuppositions, now repudiated, on the basis of which restoration was postulated, were themselves historically conditioned. They were self-evident to the minds of the fathers precisely because they were dominant ideas in the popular world view of early nineteenth-century America. The paper has further indicated that the distinctive elements in the life and thought of Disciples were not as absolute as the fathers imagined, but were also historically conditioned. Their original structure of faith and practice was profoundly modified by the forces and influences of subsequent history, though the illusion of having restored the apostolic church persisted for a long time among all Disciples and still persists among many. Increasingly, however, it has become clear that while the position of the fathers was dogmatically absolute, it was historically relative.

Where does this leave us? Are we to conclude that the church has no abiding character of its own, that it is simply the creature of historical forces and influences and can never escape from the flux and partiality of historical relativity?

To the latter part of the question, we must answer Yes. The church of Christ on earth must ever find itself compromised by the relativities of history. For its calling is in history, in an arena of anguish, of constant change. And the church has nothing absolute in itself; it cannot make itself the ground of its own hope. This is the perennial temptation of the church—to absolutize itself and to place its trust upon some infallibility, some absolute, something in itself and other than God. Of all the Christian churches, denominations, sects, or movements that ever sought to be absolute, Disciples had one of the simplest and most plausible structures of faith and practice. But it, like all the others, proved to be relative.

The abiding character of the church is not in its form or structure, its sacramental practice or its formulation of dogma, for all these are historically conditioned and quite relative. Indeed, they must be if the church's ministry is to be relevant to the need of men in time. The hope of the church is not in herself, but in God, and the abiding element in her life is her witness to the gospel of his grace. He has set her in history, where he has made himself known, and her adaptation to changing historical conditions is part of her lot; indeed, by faith she may discern the hand of God moving in historical events. But as long as she remains in this world she can never get outside history, even though she must ever look beyond it. Precisely in that situation where God has set her she must proclaim the gospel of divine grace and by her obedient response to the demands of his own revealed nature bear witness in history to the goodness and mercy of God.

NOTES

1. Alanson Wilcox, *A History of the Disciples of Christ in Ohio,* (Cincinnati: Standard Publishing Company, 1918), p. 13.
2. *Ibid.,* pp. 42-45.
3. Moses E. Lard, *Lard's Quarterly,* I (1863), 22.
4. Alexander Campbell, *The Christian System* (St. Louis: Christian Publishing Company, n.d.), p. 10.
5. Oliver Tomkins (ed.) *The Third World Conference on Faith and Order* (London SCM Press Ltd., 1953), p. 183.
6. In Perry E. Gresham (ed.), *The Sage of Bethany: A Pioneer in Broadcloth* (St. Louis: The Bethany Press, 1960), pp. 25-44.
7. *Theory and Practice in Historical Study: Report of the Committee on Historiography,* Bulletin No. 54 (New York: Social Science Research Council, 1946), p. 112.
8. Langdon Gilkey, "The Imperative for Unity: a Restatement," *Ecumenical Studies Series,* IV (Sept. 1958), p. 11.
9. Ellwood P. Cubberley, *A Brief History of Education* (Boston: Houghton, Mifflin Company, c. 1922), pp. 291-294.
10. Robert Richardson, *Memoirs of Alexander Campbell* (Philadelphia: J. B. Lippincott and Co., 1870), Vol. II, p. 97, quoting from *The Christian Baptist.*
11. Quoted by H. H. Farmer, "The Bible and Preaching," *Encounter,* XIX (1958), 158, For the impossibility of a break with the past see A. L. Rowse, *The Use of History* (London: Hodder and Stoughton Limited, 1946), pp. 21-26.
12. George Bancroft, *History of the Formation of the Constitution of the United States of America* 2nd ed. 2 V. (New York: D. Appleton and Co., 1882).
13. *The Millennial Harbinger,* Series III, Vol. VII (1850), 308.
14. Alexander Campbell, "Christian Union—No. 1," *Christian Baptist,* II, 163.
15. See Schlesinger, "The Age of Alexander Campbell," in Gresham, *op. cit.,* pp. 25 ff.
16. Merle Curti, "Intellectuals and Other People," *American Historical Review,* LX (Jan. 1955), p. 267.
17. James H. Lanman, "Social Disorganization," *American Monthly Magazine,* II, 577-578, 582, Dec. 1836, quoted in Arthur Schlesinger, *The Age of Jackson* (Boston: Little, Brown & Co., 1948), p. 351.
18. Frederick Jackson Turner, *The Frontier in American History* (New York: Henry Holt and Company, c. 1920), p. 207.
19. R. H. Luthin, "Some Demagogues in American History," *American Historical Review,* VII (Oct., 1951), 25.
20. *Ibid.,* p. 26 Robert Richardson comments on Johnson's academic limitations and strongly suggests (though with subsequent qualification) that Campbell was the true author of the Sunday Mail Report, which appeared in 1829 under Johnson's name. *op. cit.,* I, 535-537; II, 334-335.
21. *The Millennial Harbinger,* 1831, 23.
22. "Turning Out the Apostles," *The Millennial Harbinger,* 1834, p. 17.

23. *The Christian Baptist,* Vol. I, 1823, p. 29.
24. *The Christian Baptist,* I, 10, 180.
25. "The Bishop's Office—No. 1," *The Christian Baptist,* III, 9, 361.
26. "The Clergy—No. V," *The Christian Baptist, 7* (Feb. 2, 1824), 121.
27. Alexander Campbell, *Popular Lectures and Addresses* (Philadelphia: James Challen and Son, 1863), p. 175.
28. D. Ray Lindley, *Apostle of Freedom* (St. Louis: The Bethany Press, 1957).
29. Cf. Schlesinger, "The Age of Campbell," Gresham, *op. cit.,* p. 42.
30. Cf. R. Frederick West, *Alexander Campbell and Natural Religion* (New Haven: Yale University Press, 1948), pp. 185-210; Harold L. Lunger, *The Political Ethics of Alexander Campbell* (St. Louis: The Bethany Press, 1954), pp. 115-120.
31. *The Millennial Harbinger,* 1845, 27.
32. Ronald E. Osborn, "Problems of Disciple Participation in the Ecumenical Movement," *The Scroll,* XLV, 3 (Winter, 1953), 23-24.
33. Cf. D. E. Harrell, "Brothers Go to War," *World Call* XLIV, 9 (Oct. 9, 1961), p. 26-28, a popular presentation of conclusions documented in his doctoral thesis at Vanderbilt on the social history of Disciples.
34. Cf. Ronald E. Osborn, *Ely Vaughn Zollars, Teacher of Preachers, Builder of Colleges* (St. Louis: Christian Board of Publication, 1947), p. 99.
35. See W. T. Moore, *The Plea of the Disciples* (Chicago: The Christian Century Co., 1906), pp. 54-59; 88-92.
36. Herbert L. Willett, *Our Plea for Union and the Present Crisis* (Chicago: The Christian Century Co., 1901), pp. 7ff.
37. Moore, *op. cit.,* p. 10.
38. *Ibid.,* p. 55.
39. Joseph M. Smith, unpublished paper, "Changes in Disciples' Understanding of their Christian World Mission," p. 27.

14

The Influence of Population Mobility

On the Present Life and Thought of Disciples of Christ

HUNTER BECKELHYMER

DISCIPLES of Christ are a New Testament people. To all of our early leaders, and many of our latter-day leaders and followers as well, this means that the New Testament alone is our rule in faith and practice. The attempt has been sincerely made to cut through centuries of accumulated tradition in pursuit of the church's pristine purity of doctrine and order. If it is held that centuries of Christian tradition must not be allowed to modify the ancient order of things, much less should contemporary secular circumstances be permitted to do so. To be sure, our forebears made considerable allowance, through their concepts of expediency and opinion, for adaptations of the church's methods in reaching the ear of the world in which it lived. By some the adaptations were made gladly, by some grudgingly. Church school literature, missionary societies, musical instruments, and in latter days even audio-visual equipment and the air waves, have with varying degrees of enthusiasm been pressed into the service of the restoration plea. But it was not the intention that these adaptations to the ways of the world should alter or modify in any way the basic purpose or message of our movement. The world in which we live could oblige us to adopt its finest techniques. But that changing world held no implications for the content of our theology, nor the intent of our efforts. To the degree that our basic ideas were changed at all, it has been the influence of latter-day New Testament study and theological currents that have changed them. Or so we like to assume.

Just as theology has its practical implications, however, so-called secular events have their theological import. It has always been so. The mission to the Gentile world began not with Paul's labored rationales, nor with the considered action of the council of Jerusalem. It had its beginnings in the scattering of the disciples during the persecution that broke out following the martyrdom of Stephen in Jerusalem.[1] If the New Testament church of New Testament times was thus shaped, in part, by population mobility, it is not too light a thing that we should consider the implications of population mobility for the "New Testament church" in our day.

Areas of Population Increase

First, let us look at some over-all population trends during the past twenty years. During the decade of 1940-50 the population of the continental United States increased 15 percent. During the same period the resident membership of Disciples of Christ churches increased only 4.6 percent. During the following nine years, from 1950 to 1959, the population of the country increased another 14.7 percent. Meanwhile the increase in Disciples of Christ members was 9.5 percent. Although our churches have been increasing in membership, and have doubled their rate of increase in the past decade over the one just previous to it, our rate of growth has been less than that of the country as a whole. Consequently the percentage of our membership in the total population has decreased.[2] Meanwhile the number of people who claim religious affiliation of some kind has in the past two decades increased more rapidly than the population in general, and in 1958 stood at an all-time high of 63 percent of the total population.

The increase in population, of course, is not equally distributed through all parts of the country and all types of communities. Nor are Disciples of Christ churches evenly distributed through all parts of the country and all types of communities. A study of the population gains and movements relative to the location of our churches becomes, of course, infinitely complex. The most thorough study of this kind which has been made is that made by Dale Medearis, covering the decade of 1940-50, and entitled *Population and Disciples of Christ*. It showed, among other things, a continuation of the movement of people from rural to urban areas. However, as our own observation of blossoming suburbs tells us, the main growth is taking place at the rural edges of the larger cities. Indeed, in the decade of 1940-50, these "rural parts of counties in standard metropolitan areas" experienced a higher percentage of growth than any other type of community—41 percent. In these same areas, however, the gain in Disciples membership during the decade was only seven tenths of one percent.[3] Rather surprisingly, the type of community in which our churches made their largest increase percentagewise during the decade was the large cities themselves. In cities of 50,000 and over, our membership increased 25.8 percent while the population of these cities was increasing 18.1 percent. Large cities were the only type of community in which our membership growth exceeded that of population growth.[4]

Incidentally, it is no longer correct to refer to us as a rural people. A higher percentage of our membership (74 percent) is in cities and towns than the percentage of the total population therein (62.6 percent). It is in towns from 1,000 to 50,000 that the percentage of our membership is significantly higher than the percentage of the total population in those places—47.5 percent against 37.1 percent. We are a town people in 1950.[5]

It is with the general long-term movement of the population

from rural to urban—and particularly from urban to suburban —that we need most to be concerned. According to Conrad Taeuber, assistant director of the United States Bureau of Census, this is the shape of things to come. The 1950 census recognized 168 standard metropolitan areas—that is, counties or groups of counties surrounding cities of 50,000 or over. In 1950, 56 percent of the population lived in these areas. In 1956, 59 percent of the population lived in these areas. However, between 1950 and 1956, only one fifth of the population increase in these areas occurred in the central cities themselves. The remainder, or four fifths, of this increase occurred in the incorporated and unincorporated areas outside of these central cities. By rough calculation, the people in the suburbs increased by 3,840,000 in the six-year period from 1950 to 1956. "This trend seems firmly established and likely to continue for some time."[6]

Mobility and Church Membership

We turn now to a more specific examination of the effect of population mobility upon the church relationship of the people who do the moving. According to a sample survey made by the U.S. Bureau of Census, 31,800,000 Americans changed places of residence in the one-year period from April, 1956, through March, 1957. This is 19.4 percent of the population of our country, or one person in every five. About two thirds of these moved to a different house in the same county. Of the remaining one-third, about half crossed county lines, and half state lines as well.[7] In volume of moving, this is equal to the entire population of America moving to different residences in a five-year period. Actually, of course, many of the movers move every year or so, while some people live a lifetime in one house. But by any standards, this still represents a very fluid populace, and a real problem for local parishes, as any pastor can testify.

In preparation for the Oberlin Conference in 1957 on "The Nature of the Unity We Seek," Professor J. Leslie Dunstan of Andover Newton Theological School, prepared "A Report on a

Study of the Mobility of Church Members." Its purpose was to discover "the effect the moving of people had upon their denominational connections." Professor Dunstan distributed more than 15,000 questionnaires, mostly through councils of churches. Of these 727 were returned, 530 of them filled out carefully enough to be usable in the tabulations. To my knowledge, no more thorough studies of this kind covering the churches of the nation as a whole have been made.

The responding churches represented fifteen denominations, including our own. Disciples were represented in the tabulations by 23 churches with a total present resident membership of nearly 15,000.[8] The largest representation was Methodist with 112 churches, and the smallest was Augustana Lutheran with 3. The fact that only 8 Southern Baptist churches replied further underscores the warning that we must not press our generalizations too far, although it is perhaps safer to generalize about Southern Baptists and Lutherans than it is about some other communions.

The information gathered from the 530 churches by Professor Dunstan included the following: (1) the number of members currently on the church roll, (2) the number of members received in the past ten years, and (3) the number of these members received during the past ten years who had come from other denominations, and the denominations from which they had come. The study did not reveal how many of these new members where "floating members" coming in and going out of a relatively stable membership during the period. But, on the other hand, neither did the study reveal how many of the present members had come from other denominations prior to the ten-year period under study. While these limitations of the study must of necessity qualify the conclusions we draw, these two unknowns would tend to cancel each other out.

Professor Dunstan's tabulations reflected differences in degree of stability among the different sections of the country, as we would expect. And they also showed different degrees of stability in different types of communities in which the churches were located. For instance, in the northeastern part of the country, the churches had received, in ten years, new members equal in number to 55.6 percent of their present resident membership. In the West, the reporting churches had received, in ten years, new members equaling 87.5 percent of their present resident membership. The national average was 63.7 percent.[9]

Among the eight categories of communities in which the reporting churches were placed, the percentage of new members to present membership was lowest in the open country (40.9 percent), small town (51.8 percent), and central business, or "downtown" churches (56.2 percent). By contrast, the churches which had received the highest number of new members relative to their present membership were in the inner city (60.8 percent), the long-established suburb (67.5 percent), and highest of all, of course, the new suburb (88.5 percent). The over-all average, as stated above was 63.7 percent.

The percentage received from other denominations is broken down not by region or type of church, but by denomination. The denominations receiving the lowest percentage of new members from other communions were understandably the Southern Baptists with 7.9 percent and the Missouri Synod Lutherans with 12.4 percent. Those with the highest percentages of new members coming from other communions were the Congregationalists (38.8), and the Presbyterians U.S.A. (40.3 percent). These figures may take on added significance in light of another study to be reported. Disciples of Christ were relatively high in the number of new members in proportion to resident membership (84.4 percent), and about average in the percentage of new members received from communions other than our own (32.6 percent).[10] Professor Dunstan's interpretation of the total study is that "The figures show that for the reporting churches there were, among the members received during the past ten years, somewhere between 30 percent and 50 percent who came from other denominations."[11]

One set of figures emerged from the Dunstan study that will be of particular interest to Disciples of Christ. From the records of the particular 530 churches reporting in this study, there were 5,944 Disciples who changed their membership from one congregation to another. Of these, 4,112, or 69.2 percent, found their way into another Disciples congregation. This percentage of denominational loyalty is significantly higher than that of any of the other 14 denominations, not excepting Southern Baptist, which was second in this respect with 63.4 percent of 5,160 transferring members remaining Southern Baptist, and Missouri Synod Lutheran which was fourth with 58.5 percent. Of all 97,015 Christians who transferred, 55.2 percent found their way into another congregation of the same communion that they left. As would be expected, when Disciples did not transfer to Disciples Churches, they went mostly to Congregational, Presbyterian, American Baptist, and Methodist Churches, in that order. Our new non-Disciple members came to us preponderantly from American Baptist, Methodist, Presbyterian, and Congregational Churches—the same four in almost inverted order.[12]

On Changing Denominations

When church members, because of moving to a different neighborhood or community, transfer their membership to another congregation, what governs their choice? Denominational loyalty is one factor, but certainly not the only one. The availability of a congregation of their own communion in the new community is certainly a large factor. In this respect the smaller communions, or those that are largely regional, are at a definite disadvantage in retaining their members who move. Convenience is a large factor. City pastors well know that a main thoroughfare to be crossed is a formidable barrier for children who are sent to Sunday church school. Marginal church folk send or let their children go to the nearest church in the neighborhood whatever the denomination. Other factors which play a part are the personal appeal of the incumbent ministers, newly formed friendships, attractiveness and adequacy of church plant, and other local variables which across the country would tend to average out, and not work to the advantage of any one communion against the others. Beyond these factors is surely a general and undefined feeling of "at homeness" in the theological and liturgical climate of the new church home, which many find across denominational lines.

One factor, however, which we unfortunately must consider is that whole denominations, and not just given congregations within them, tend to take on a class standing. Our population is mobile geographically, and mobile across denominational lines. It is also to some degree mobile across class lines, and acutely aware of these lines. This subject has been examined with considerable perception by Vance Packard in his book *The Status Seekers*. In it he devotes a chapter to the class images which many denominations carry, and dares to rank the major denominations according to their class standing. At the top, of course, is the Episcopal Church. A sociological analysis was made of the leading wedding announcements in the New York *Times* involving socially prominent families of the area. Of those held in Protestant churches, three fourths were in Episcopal Churches. Two thirds of the Philadelphians who are in both the *Social Register* and *Who's Who* are Episcopalians. Corporate executives are ten times as likely to list Episcopal as their religious preference as are Americans at large. "Other denominations strongly favored by the two top social classes in America," says Mr. Packard, "are Presbyterian, Congregational, and Unitarian. Corporate executives for example favor Presbyterian Churches second only to Episcopal. They are six times as likely to be Presbyterian as are Americans at large." Perhaps the upward mobility of young Americans socially, accounts in part for the fact that the Congregationalists and Presbyterians receive a higher proportion of their new members from other denominations than do any other American communions.

Next down the social scale, Mr. Packard lists the Methodists, then the Lutherans. Below the Lutherans are the Baptists. At the very bottom of the social scale there are few churchgoers. They suspect, Mr. Packard believes, that they are not wanted by either churches or ministers. According to Liston Pope, the new Pentecostal and Holiness sects represent on one hand a protest couched in religious form against social exclusiveness, and on the other hand a compensatory method, also in religious form, for regaining status, and for redefining class lines in religious terms.[13] That Mr. Packard's evaluations are not wholly subjective is attested by the fact that he based his rankings on a study made by the Federal Council of Churches in 1948 which listed the percentages of membership in the different denominations made up from the different income brackets. Just where Disciples fall along "The Long Road from Pentecostal to Episcopal," Mr. Packard does not divulge, although it may be in the Federal Council study. A shrewd guess would be somewhere between the Methodists and Baptists. Of particular interest is Mr. Packard's conclusion: "In earlier days, people who moved to a new community typically chose the church that came closest to harmonizing with their own doctrinal viewpoint. And these doctrinal viewpoints were often passionately felt and held. Today, the doctrinal meaning of joining a particular church is far less important in the decision than the social or business meaning."[14] Selah.

Issues to Be Faced

Several major issues arise urgently for our consideration from the information here presented. Among them are these.

First, what are we trying to do in establishing new churches? Is our purpose to have Disciple churches available to catch our Disciple members who move? Is our purpose to increase the Disciple percentage of the Protestant community, or at least maintain it, by going where the people are going? Or do we seek to do one denomination's share of providing churches where they are urgently needed? Our denominational leaders, state and national, are keenly aware of the movement of people to the newer suburbs of the big cities; and a sizeable effort is under way, belatedly, to establish new churches. Comity arrangements, whether formal or informal, are observed. We do not feel the urgency of entering an area ministered to by a Methodist and a Congregational church, although we might feel that there is room for us in an area served only by an Episcopal and a Holiness church. By the same token, Methodists and Congregationalists would not be apt to come in to compete with us, although the Southern Baptists and Lutherans would. Have we not here a gentleman's understanding, perhaps expediently motivated by lack of funds, that we and certain other communions will reciprocally minister to each other's erstwhile members in our respective bailiwicks? If this be true, our practice is considerably ahead of our theology at this point. What may be emerging is a healthy division of responsibility for the Protestant witness in new neighborhoods, as it exists in the foreign mission field.

If one of our congregations essays to serve the cooperative Protestant constituency in a given neighborhood, and other communions tacitly so recognize us, does not this have profound implications for our thought and practice? Should not our efforts be toward the softening of the lines of denominational particularity, rather than seeking to recover and reassert them? Is there not a point at which courtesy becomes more truly Christian than correctness, and our responsibility to our religious neighbors an obligation more divine than our responsibility to our forebears? When any church *de facto,* or by explicit or implicit agreement—is the sole representative of cooperative Protestantism in a given community, it seems to me that a moral obligation is upon it to offer communion to all Christians, and to honor in transfer the membership standing of churchmen from other communions. Like the New Testament church and its Gentile mission, we tend to solve this issue in a Christian way at the practical level before we have faced it at the theological level. It is now time that we do the latter. We need a theology of comity, a clear philosophy of what our purpose really is in planting new churches in new neighborhoods. Although a denomination may feel warmly its own traditions and historical habits, it does not really need a distinctive theology or cultus to justify its continued existence and expansion as a denomination. If it be a redemptive and reasonably efficient unit in the total Christian enterprise, it has sufficient reason for existence and continuation. Perhaps Christian unity shall come not by all Christians becoming converted to one denomination, nor yet by the merging of denominations, but by their becoming nearly indistinguishable in Christian service, basic teaching, and charity.

According to the Dunstan study, from one third to one half of the present membership in American Protestant Churches came from some other denomination than the one they are now in. We can logically expect that percentage to increase. Who would suppose that this mobility across denominational lines represents genuine conversions in viewpoint, conviction, or theology? In some instances it does, to be sure. In most instances, however, it surely represents convenience, congeniality, taste, or —dare we hope?—simply the fact that the member considers himself to be a Christian, or wants to be one, and does not really care in which communion he becomes one. Twentieth-century American life is homogenizing the denominations at the congregational level. We may live to observe the day when the Church of Christ on earth is essentially, intentionally, and unconstitutionally one. The hand of God may be working through the events of our modern day to make our denominational lines not nonexistent, but largely meaningless.

Second, we must not be so sanguine about the tendency of denominations, or congregations, to acquire a class status or meaning. Better far theological disputes and cultic exclusiveness than invisible class or race barriers to fellowship. The former differences are imperfections in Christian faith; the latter are perversions of it. The former are at least relevant to growth in Christian understanding; the latter are foreign to it. It is not gain for the kingdom that in a day when population mobility is taking the rigidity and sting out of denominational differences, class differences should become more fixed upon the churches. It is loss when a denomination exchanges a doctrinal viewpoint for a class viewpoint. How a congregation can serve a one-class neighborhood without becoming a one-class church is an issue we must face. There always have been and can well be, in Christ, liberal and conservative, immersed and unimmersed. But the discriminations symbolized by the terms "Jew and Greek," "barbarian and Scythian," "slave and free man" have no place.

Just as the scattering of the disciples into Gentile territory after the martyrdom of Stephen was used of God to widen the Christian fellowship and deepen its thought, so God may be using the movement of population in our day to his own ends which it is our duty to detect and enunciate.

NOTES

1. Acts 8 ff.
2. Figures computed from figures of U.S. Census Bureau, and Disciples of Christ yearbooks.
3. Dale Medearis, *Population and Disciples of Christ.* United Christian Missionary Society, Indianapolis: Fig. 6, p. 15.
4. *Ibid.*, Table B, p. 13.
5. *Ibid.*, Table A, p. 11.
6. Conrad Taeuber, "Population Changes to 1975," *Annals of the American Academy of Political and Social Science,* Sept. 1957.
7. *World Almanac*, 1959.
8. J. Leslie Dunstan, "A Report on a Study of the Mobility of Church Members" unpublished. Table 2.
9. *Ibid.*, Table 3.
10. *Ibid.*, Table 2.
11. *Ibid.*, p. 4.
12. *Ibid.*, Table 6.
13. Vance Packard, "The Long Road from Pentecostal to Episcopal," in *The Status Seekers* (New York: David McKay Co., Inc. 1959), *passim.*
14. *Ibid.*, p. 196.

A CONCLUDING ESSAY

15

"One Holy Catholic and Apostolic Church"

The Continuing Witness of Disciples of Christ

RONALD E. OSBORN

DISCIPLES of Christ since midcentury have found themselves engaged in large-scale restudy of their tradition and witness. Under the auspices of various groups the work goes on. Of necessity, a great deal of it has required analysis and reappraisal of the fathers' position, and the process has often seemed negative. While it is necessary to discern and to abandon what is no longer true or significant, Disciples must also give themselves to constructive statement. Restudy must go beyond demolition.

It is appropriate, therefore, to conclude this volume on the *Reformation of Tradition* with an effort to discriminate the continuing witness of Disciples. What elements in the message of the fathers, after all outmoded or no longer relevant impedimenta have been stripped away, are still significant in the church of today?

A convenient framework for discussion of this question is provided by the ancient Christian confession: "We believe . . . in one Holy Catholic and Apostolic Church." To the best of my recollection, the categories of the so-called "Nicene" Creed have not been used as a framework for discussing the doctrine of the church on the part of Disciples, except by the late

Frederick D. Kershner, whose presidential address at the International Convention in Denver (1938) was built upon these topics.[1] The four marks of the church—unity, holiness, catholicity, apostolicity—are important categories of ecclesiology and are much in the forefront of current ecumenical concern.[2] It may be instructive to examine briefly under each of these headings the traditional Disciple position, the continuing witness, and its present significance. Because of our historic emphasis, the order of consideration will vary from that set forth in the ancient confession.

I. The One Church

We begin with unity. "We believe in one church."

1. *Unity as given.* From the outset Disciples have emphasized the insight so often repeated in ecumenical circles today concerning the givenness of unity among all Christians. The great affirmations coming out of Edinburgh, Amsterdam, Evanston, and New Delhi have fallen with familiar accent on Disciple ears. The givenness of unity among all Christians is explicit in Proposition 1. of Thomas Campbell's *Declaration and Address:*

> The Church of Christ upon earth is essentially, intentionally, and constitutionally one; consisting of all those in every place that profess their faith in Christ and obedience to him in all things according to the scriptures, and that manifest the same by their tempers and conduct, and of none else; as none else can be truly and properly called Christian.

The plea for unity as voiced by Disciples has thus been oriented toward the divine intention for the church. Even when proclaimed with an attitude which appears to others sectarian—"I am a Member of the Church of Christ . . . Because Christ is the Founder of Only One Church"[3]—the insight as to the given unity is clear. Disciples need offer no apology concerning their characteristic understanding of unity as divinely instituted for the church in its very nature; at this point we speak in concert with the biblical witness, with the church of the centuries, and with the most responsible ecumenical thinking of our day.

2. *Unity as imperative.* It has become theologically fashionable to speak with Rudolf Bultmann when he says, "though Christian existence can, on the one hand, be described by the indicatives . . . nevertheless, so long as it moves within this world, it stands under the imperative."[4] The unity God gives to the church is eschatological, inherent in its nature yet not fully realized in history, promised for the end of the age yet obligatory upon Christians in their present behavior towards one another.

From the days of Barton W. Stone who declared, "Christian union is my polar star"[5] and of Thomas Campbell's *Address* with its plea, "We entreat, we beseech you . . . , dear brethren . . . to concur in this blessed and dutiful attempt," Disciples have considered themselves under a mandate to labor for the oneness of believers. Their early vigor in evangelism, their unwillingness to let the most violent controversy in American political history become the occasion of division among themselves, their uneasy conscience and sense of deep frustration over their own schismatic tendencies, the eagerness with which they greeted the rise of the ecumenical movement and their desire to make a major contribution to it—all these central elements in their own history have evidenced their conviction that unity is an imperative laid upon Christians. The fervor with which such men as J. H. Garrison, Peter Ainslie, C. C. Morrison, and many others, in the face of deep misunderstanding by their own brethren, labored to awaken Christendom from its sectarian complacency sprang from the essence of their heritage as Disciples. The earnestness with which nearly every assembly of the International Convention of Christian Churches deals with resolutions concerning every aspect of Christian unity reflects a breadth of sensitivity to the divine imperative. Disciples now rejoice to realize that Christians of all communions have acknowledged the imperative to unity and are striving to manifest more fully the oneness that God intends for his church. While none of us may claim to have been fully obedient to the divine demand, Disciples rightfully cherish the passion of their fathers to labor at the task of unity.

3. *Unity as personal.* To the degree that unity among Christians is an expression of a relationship which God intends for them, personal attitudes become an important means of obedience to the divine imperative. So Barton W. Stone pleaded, "Let every Christian begin the work of union in himself,"[6] and Thomas Campbell stated the matter forcefully in Proposition 9:

> That all that are enabled, through grace, to make such a profession, and to manifest the reality of it in their tempers and conduct, should consider each other as the precious saints of God, should love each other as brethren, children of the same family and Father, temples of the same Spirit, members of the same body, subjects of the same grace, objects of the same Divine love, bought with the same price, and joint-heirs of the same inheritance.

The beauty of such a full fellowship, when at least proximately realized in the life of a congregation, constituted one of the major joys of our fathers in their Christian faith, as it has done for other Christian people.

Doubtless Disciples have not always taken as much initiative as they should to cultivate such attitudes toward members of other churches in the same community. We share the sin of sectarianism and parochialism with the rest of Christendom. Yet many who have taken their Disciple tradition seriously have felt bound by conscience to do all within their power to draw Christians of various communions into engagement with one another. For decades in evangelism, in religious education, in social action, in the military chaplaincy, in ministerial associations, in ecumenical organization at every geographical level, individual Disciples have been impelled by their heritage to become agents of reconciliation among Christians of varying names and practices. Such a ministry is open to laymen and ministers alike, in Middletown as well as in New Delhi.

Perhaps the largest contribution of Disciples to the ecumenical movement has been through personalities who had the gift of conciliatory initiative in personal relationships. Such a ministry will always be needed. A brilliant German theologian who spent some weeks lecturing among American Disciples expressed privately his gratification at this type of personal quality which he discerned among our people, ministers who impressed him as authentic men of God with no outward show of clerical garb, ecclesiastical title, episcopal rank, or theological pretension. If in the present stage of ecumenical development, particularly in the highly publicized gatherings of the World Council of Churches and the National Council, attention centers on bishops and theologians, the importance of earnest ministers of reconciliation in every community must never be forgotten. Disciples may rejoice in the fact that their tradition commits them to a personal obligation in the matter of Christian unity, to seeking out in love the scattered children of God.

4. *Unity as institutional.* At this point the original witness of Disciples has required revision. For our fathers regarded the ecclesiastical institutions of their day as divisive, as limiting the liberty which is in Christ, and as unscriptural. This line of reasoning lay back of the dissolution of the Springfield Presbytery and of the Mahoning Baptist Association, the fervent emphasis on congregational polity, the suspicion of missionary societies and other agencies, the vocal opposition to councils of churches, and the vehement assertion, now begun to fade but still a matter of conviction with many, that we are not a denomination. The fathers sought a type of Christian unity that would result from the elimination of all ecclesiastical institutions except the congregation.

In spite of themselves, Disciples found themselves convinced of the necessity of institutions. They developed state associations of churches or missionary societies, state conventions, national agencies, and national (international) conventions; finally they accepted denominational status by membership in councils of churches. Some Disciples have become convinced that our destiny toward unity is to be fulfilled by merger with some other communion; considerable enthusiasm developed in turn over negotiations with the American Baptists, involvement in the Conference on Church Union ("Greenwich Plan"), and conversations with the United Church of Christ. The original distrust of institution persisted among the (noninstrumental) Churches of Christ, the "independent" group of Christian Churches, and even among those Disciples who were painfully developing institutions. For a hundred years a valiant effort was made to keep the institutions nonecclesiastical and a fabulous maze of interrelated but autonomous agencies resulted. The movement to "restructure the brotherhood" marks an implicit acceptance of ecclesiastical institution as participating authentically in the nature of the church, the body of Christ.

The situation is ironical. For in practice, institutions prove themselves essential to a religious communion, whether it wants them or not; a generally accepted agency, a denominational organization, a council of churches intensifies the reality of unity by giving it a form of expression which it would otherwise lack. The irony resides in the fact that no religious institution as an organization in history embraces the universal church of Christ. Every such institution is partial and, in effect if not in intent, divisive; at the same time the institution participates in the oneness which Christ gives to his church. The partiality may be humbly accepted as one of the necessities of existence in human history and the tendency toward divisiveness held in check by a refusal to absolutize the institution, by a determination to keep it submissive to the demands of the larger unity which is in Christ.

Disciples have proved themselves able at this point to modify the witness of the fathers and to accept ecclesiastical institution (agency, denomination, council of churches) as an essential though partial means of expressing unity among Christians. I am convinced that we have made a correct and wholesome decision on this issue. Yet even here we must give heed to our heritage. While seeking more adequate institutions for Christian witness, service, and fellowship, we must ever remind ourselves that no such institution—the restructured brotherhood, a United Church of Christ including Disciples, or any other ecclesiastical construct we can imagine—is the whole and perfect church of Christ on earth. Disciples are not therefore necessarily recreant to their plea for unity simply because they have not succeeded in a denominational merger; the questions to be asked in any conversations looking toward such a union are whether the two communions concerned have significant reasons for remaining apart or sufficient reasons for coming together. In which way may they give more authentic witness to the gospel?

We Disciples must constantly alert ourselves, and all larger institutions in which we share, against the tendency of organization to require conformity. It is our calling, I believe, to seek for institutions which better express the oneness of God's people but which, at the same time, do not demand the free Christian man to forfeit his integrity.

5. *Unity as sacramental.* While our fathers (and most of their children until the present generation) disliked the term *sacrament* as unscriptural and as carrying connotations they did not accept, they set baptism and communion in a place of primary importance in the church's life.

The communion of the Lord's supper became for Disciples the crucial and distinctive act in the worship of the church. It was interpreted with reference to unity—in the emphasis that was put on reconciliation among estranged brethren before coming to the table, in the reluctance with which Disciples abandoned the "one loaf" and the "one cup" in deference to more sophisticated standards of sanitation, and especially in the practice of open communion. While this practice was not characteristic of Disciples in the generation immediately after their separation from the Baptists (1830), it has been so for a long time now and relates Disciples to Thomas Campbell's irenic gesture in 1807 in refusing to "fence the table." Disciples commonly interpret their practice of open communion as an expression of their witness for Christian unity. At ecumenical conferences from Lausanne (1927) on, Disciples have taken every opportunity to remind their fellow Christians that the holy table belongs to no church but to the Lord, and that all his followers are invited to the feast of reconciliation.

The act of believer's baptism became a witness to the reality of the one church, for all that heard and believed were baptized into the one body. While the doctrine of baptism was developed primarily with reference to faith and repentance and to the remission of sins, its function as a churchly ordinance binding together all who had been baptized into Christ was never underplayed. The "one baptism" was cherished by Disciples as one of the seven great unities set forth in Ephesians 4. For a long time they cherished the belief that all Christians would ultimately come to accept the immersion of penitent believers as the only scriptural or proper baptism, and as long as they did so they preached their understanding of the practice as a contribution to the unity of the church.

The ambiguity of their witness on baptism in its relationship to their witness on unity has long troubled Disciples. It troubled Barton W. Stone. For half a century it has troubled an increasing number of our people, and the practice of open membership has grown apace. Most of its practitioners have defended it as a means of expressing Christian unity, though it has certainly become an occasion of disruption among Disciples themselves.

Disciples are in the process of gradually deciding whether the achievement of larger unity must await the conversion of other Christians to our understanding of baptism, or whether the practice of infant baptism and of believer's baptism may exist together within one united church. The Section on Baptism at the North American Conference on Faith and Order (Oberlin, 1957) suggested that the two views of baptism, when each is understood in its fullness, are remarkably similar in their witness.[7] But the Oberlin statement is basically theoretical. If Disciples continue their conversations with the United Church, perhaps they may discover whether or not the statement can be given practical implementation; indeed, these discussions may well serve to clear the air on this issue, with the result that Disciples will either take their witness into a united church or come to a new conviction that its importance requires their continued separate existence.

Disciples must admit that their views of the sacraments are not universally held throughout Christendom. But they nevertheless conceive of unity in sacramental terms. They may be grateful for their historic understanding of baptism and the Lord's supper as witnessing to the oneness of the church, even while seeking to find ways of making that witness more effective.

6. *Unity as local.* The pragmatic temper of the early Disciples impelled them not toward grandiose schemes for the unification of Christendom, but toward removing the scandal of division in their local communities. This was the genius of Stone and Thomas Campbell. It was the plea of the early evangelists who invited Christians of various communions to drop their party names, creedal distinctions, and separate ecclesiastical loyalties and to come together into one Church of Christ, under his name alone, bound only by the clear requirements ("positive ordinances") set forth in the New Testament. Their hope—and in some communities, their realization—was to bring together in unity the divided people of God while granting wide liberty in opinion and in matters considered nonessential. The fact that an identifiable company of people—Disciples, "Campbellites," or what you will—sponsored this approach gave it a color of partisanship which proved its undoing. Alexander Campbell's Messianic belief "that a *nucleus* had been formed, . . . around which may one day congregate all the children of God"[8] sounded an imperializing tone which did not endear him to other re-

ligious leaders. It is difficult, if not impossible, for anyone who offers an approach to unity to escape the charge that he offers it on the basis of everyone's coming to his point of view, and Campbell did not escape it. The important point is that, at its best, the Disciple plea sought the removal of all barriers among the Christians in any particular place.

It now appears that the World Council's Commission on Faith and Order has committed itself to an understanding of unity quite similar *in principle* to that espoused by the early Disciples. The much-quoted St. Andrews statement, subsequently accepted by the Central Committee (and the Third Assembly) reads as follows:[9]

> The Commission on Faith and Order understands that the unity which is both God's will and His gift to His church is one which brings all in each place who confess Christ Jesus as Lord into a fully committed fellowship with one another through one baptism into Him, holding the one apostolic faith, preaching the one Gospel and breaking the one bread, and having a corporate life reaching out in witness and service to all; and which at the same time unites them with the whole Christian fellowship in all places and in all, ages in such wise that ministry and members are acknowledged by all, and that all can act and speak together as occasion requires for the tasks to which God calls the Church.

Disciples have sought for a long time to manifest the genius of the conception of unity here set forth. An acknowledgment of the oneness which prevails among all Christians and unites them in the one church is the central contention of the *Declaration and Address.* A generation later Disciples were not always certain that they could recognize members of some denominations as authentic Christians, but the way toward such recognition seemed clear if all would simply yield to the New Testament standard. Our fathers were not inclined to accept the legitimacy of denominational churches *as churches,* a recognition which the World Council of Churches, by definition, has been more ready to grant. Even so, different communions still place different interpretations on some of the phrases in the St.

Andrews statement—"holding the one apostolic faith" or "ministry and members . . . acknowledged by all." Nevertheless this is language Disciples understand concerning a goal we seek arising from a conversation in which we are prepared to participate.

Summary. In the matter of unity Disciples possess a heritage which is relevant to the central concerns of Christendom today. We have found it necessary to modify the fathers' thoroughgoing repudiation of ecclesiastical institutions and are examining anew our doctrine and practice of baptism in the light of its implications for the oneness of the church. But we may give thanks to God that in the fullness of its meaning we have received an understanding of and a dedication to the unity of all Christians which has prepared us to enter gratefully into the ecumenical developments of our time and to witness to what we have seen and heard.

II. The Apostolic Church

Unity alone is not sufficient to characterize the true church; it has other marks which define its nature and its relationship to Jesus Christ. "We believe in one apostolic church." Apostolicity indicates authenticity, an essential conformity of message and mission with that of the apostles, the faithful witnesses of the life and teachings, death and resurrection of our Lord.

1. *The Restoration of Primitive Christianity.* Apostolicity was an explicit ideal of Disciples from the outset. The proposal to "take up things just as the Apostles left them" was the heart of Thomas Campbell's *Declaration and Address.*[10] The ideal was "in our church constitution and managements, to exhibit a complete conformity to the Apostolic church" and "willingly conform to the original pattern laid down in the New Testament." Nothing was to be "received as a matter of faith or practice, which is not expressly taught and enjoined in the word of God, either in express terms or approved precedent." The goal was to "restore unity, peace, and purity, to the whole church of God."[11]

Disciples were thus committed to the ideal of apostolicity, but the fatal definition which Thomas Campbell gave it was that of restorationism. While his intentions were catholic, in the interest of freedom and unity, his ideology proved in the long run to be sectarian because of a defective view of the Bible which he shared with many in his day and which he left as a legacy to trouble Disciples. It is most clearly stated in Proposition 4 (a proposition which we must now declare to be mistaken):

> The New Testament is as perfect a constitution for the worship, discipline, and government of the New Testament Church, and as perfect a rule for the particular duties of its members, as the Old Testament was for the worship, discipline, and government of the Old Testament Church, and the particular duties of its members.

Instead of the liberation which Thomas Campbell sought in this proposition, Disciples found in the restoration principle a source of legalism, frustration, and endless controversy. The trouble arose from a series of false assumptions which can only be outlined here:

1. The false assumption that the New Testament is a constitution for the church.

   A comparison of 1 Corinthians (or any other book in the New Testament) with Leviticus, for example, will quickly reveal that the New Testament is not a constitution, nor does it contain one, in the sense of specific prescriptions for the order, worship, faith, and life of the church. As a compilation of occasional literature, the New Testament is silent on many such matters.

2. The false assumption that the practice of one church as recorded in the New Testament was universal throughout the early church.

   The presuppositions of the fathers imposed a uniformity on their understanding of the "New Testament Church" which was not there at the beginning. It is now generally recognized by biblical scholars that patterns of church government, for example, varied considerably in differing geographical regions within apostolic times.

3. The false assumption that the practice of a given church was static and unchanging.

   The "constitutional delusion" of the fathers caused them to overlook the fact that the New Testament reveals to us the life of the early Christian community across three generations, that the period from the earliest books to the latest covers two generations, and that noticeable developments in doctrine and practice occurred during that period.

4. The false assumption that the New Testament gave shape to the church.

   The church was formed by the gospel as proclaimed by the apostles; the New Testament records scattered and unsystematic samplings of their preaching and their directives to the churches. But fidelity to the gospel rather than to deductions about ancient church organization should give shape to the church.

5. The false assumption that the history of the church after the apostolic age represented necessary corruption and decline, and that the nature of the church could be more truly understood by leaping over the centuries rather than going back through them.

   The doctrine of progress (not now being espoused) had not yet come into vogue. Our fathers shared the view of an original Golden Age from which mankind had fallen away. Hence they did not take history seriously.

6. The dubious—I am prepared to say, false—assumption that once the books of the New Testament had been completed the Holy Spirit ceased to guide the church except by these writings.

   The church could no longer follow the first-century practice of facing a problem prayerfully and taking counsel in the light of its best understanding of the gospel. (Consider, *e.g.*, the decision to admit Gentiles to the church.) From now on it was limited to the written word.

Because of these false assumptions and other difficulties not indicated here, the restoration principle soon began to confound those who had so eagerly seized upon it as a means of achieving the oneness of Christians. The subsequent divisions within the movement are due not so much to the bad spirit of a people whose professions of unity must be regarded as hypocritical as they are to the ambiguity, confusion, and contradiction arising from the ill-starred attempt to make a constitution out of the New Testament.

Various efforts have been made to salvage the restoration principle. One was to speak where the scriptures speak, to keep silent where they are silent. But are the silences prohibitive or permissive? The schism of 1906 occurred over that unresolved question. Liberal Disciples sought to "restore the spirit" of the New Testament. But such terminology gives color of validity to the idea of restoration which it seeks to repudiate and only adds to the confusion.

The researches of twentieth-century biblical scholars and historians have undercut the foundations of the restoration assumption.[12] Many of the papers constituting this volume and the two succeeding volumes in this series explicitly repudiate restorationism,[13] as do numerous other studies recently written by Disciple scholars.[14] As an interpretation of apostolicity, restorationism is no longer tenable.

2. *The original faith and order.* In both the Campbells, father and son, a liberal temper existed in tension—or more likely in contradiction—with a legalistic temper. Thus both of them could state the plea in words which justify the literalist or in other words which sound prophetic in ecumenical circles.[15] The latter type of utterance is Alexander Campbell's reference to

contending "for the original faith and order, in opposition to all the corruptions of fifteen centuries."[16] Here is a concept of apostolicity emphasizing purity and freedom, but also authenticity. Thomas Campbell likewise wrote in this vein when he maintained that "nothing ought to be inculcated upon Christians as articles of faith; nor required of them as terms of communion; but what is expressly taught and enjoined upon them, in the word of God."[17]

The concept of the apostolic faith and order has much to commend it. For it suggests at once an emphasis on that which is essential to the life of the church as over against that which is peripheral or transitory. The Campbells sought to distinguish between essentials and nonessentials, as the Protestant Reformers before them had done in the *adiaphora* controversy. But to limit the field of essential and nonessential to faith and order suggests the possibility of useful discrimination.

The apostolic faith was that utter trust in God resulting from the understanding of his saving deeds wrought through Jesus of Nazareth, whom the apostles gladly confessed as Son of God, Savior, and Lord. Such faith indicates primarily a matter of relationship, but it is a special type of relationship with a unique Reality—namely the God and Father of our Lord Jesus Christ. Hence any discussion of apostolic faith must take into account the essential content of the gospel of God, the whole-souled acceptance of which makes possible that relationship of trust in him which is biblical faith. At their best, Disciples contended for apostolic faith in this sense,[18] as over against the highly intellectualized dogmatic formulations which under the influence of Greek philosophy and of eighteenth-century rationalism the church had come to regard as the sole authentic expressions of the faith. Disciples may still regard as sound the emphasis on apostolic faith.

Order refers to those forms of governance and procedure which are at any time considered essential in the life of the church, and embraces such concerns as ministry, sacraments, liturgy, and confessions of faith. The original order of the church (meaning that established by the end of the apostolic period) must by definition have contained all that was *essential* to its life.

Disciples would do well to join with others in seeking to assess the true role of order in the apostolic church. A re-examination of New Testament teaching at this point might help us to see that while some form of order is necessary, no particular *form* is to be construed as *essential* in the sense that it *constitutes* the saving relationship or the essence of the church, or construed as *indispensable* in the sense that without the particular form salvation or the existence of the church is impossible. The witness of the New Testament from John the Baptist to Jesus to Paul is, in effect, that "God is able from these stones to raise up children to Abraham" (Matt. 3:9). Disciples have already made this point in ecumenical discussion,[19] and, for our own part, our original insistence on the absolute character of "positive ordinances" requires to be tempered.

At the same time the New Testament takes seriously the utility of forms, the necessity of some kind of order, and the gracious ministry of ordinances.

Forms are necessary to the life of any institution. Those which the church employs in any era of its history should be the most meaningful forms available to it for witnessing to that faith which is central to its life. The church is therefore under obligation to bring a sympathetic and intelligent understanding to the forms of the apostolic church, both to determine what in them was historically conditioned and therefore transitory (footwashing, for example) and also to discern what bore witness to the gospel and how it did so. Considering the power of tradition and the normative quality implicit in the concept of apostolicity, there is a strong if not necessary presumption in favor of relating the forms of the contemporary church's life to the earliest forms. What is necessary is that the forms should be authentically and not capriciously related to the saving event to which they witness.

Order is needed for the life of the church; we must be careful neither to insist on elements which the apostolic church did not require nor to overlook the concerns to which it gave attention through its developing patterns of church order.

Rites (of the nature of sacraments or ordinances) are required, both for the public life of the institution and particularly for the Christian nurture of the believer. Man is a body-soul complex, and a purely spiritual conception of religion will not satisfy him; nor is it true to the gospel. Baptism and the Lord's supper are provided as gracious ministrations of the mercy of God. Luther was held steady in time of trial by the reminder, *Baptizatus sum,* and the assurance which Walter Scott offered to those who followed the "five steps of salvation" was of the same gracious nature.

While the church is always in danger of absolutizing one or another element in its order, Disciples and all others need to reflect anew on the apostolic use of order yet freedom within it, on the apostles' trust constantly in God rather than in the form. With that understanding clear, since some forms are necessary, Disciples are in a strong position to take their lead from the original order of the apostolic church.

A brief summary of particulars may be helpful.

(1) Careful study of the church's ministry in the apostolic age reveals the ministry of reconciliation borne by the whole people of God, the royal priesthood, and a specialized ministry consisting of men recognized by the church as qualified and set apart for its service. Such a study also reveals that uniformity of orders did not characterize the New Testament ministry, but that the type and duty of officers varied with the needs.

(2) Again, the New Testament attitude toward the sacraments is one of gratitude for these means of grace, not of binding legalism concerning the manner of administration. The traditional Disciple practice of baptism as

the immersion of a penitent believer provides a context within which the biblical references to the act may be read and understood in fullest fidelity to apostolic custom,[20] and Disciples need offer no apologies on this score. What we do need to re-examine is our attitude, which has sometimes tended to make baptism a work of salvation rather than a seal of faith and means of grace, and our repudiation of fellow Christians whose baptism has not been according to our own understanding.

(3) As to communion, Disciples have rightly understood that the worship of the church is essentially kerygmatic, properly characterized by both word and sacrament, each bearing witness to and mediating the gospel of divine grace. While Disciples have made the eucharist an unfailing part of the church's gathering for worship on the Lord's day, their reasons for this right emphasis have not always been sufficiently profund, nor has their liturgical expression of the communion always been worthy. Yet we may be grateful for the opportunity that is ours to enter into our inheritance and to share the gifts that God has given to us.

(4) The confessions found in the New Testament are joyful outpourings of whole-souled devotion to Jesus Christ as the Revealer of God, not hair-splitting definitions of dogma. This is not to pretend that the New Testament is undogmatic or lacks concern over incipient Gnosticism, Docetism, and other latent heresies. But the confessions which belong to the essential order of the church are affirmations of Christ's lordship rather than exercises in metaphysic.

To contend for the original faith and order may not be stylish in all theological circles, but it is theologically and biblically sound. This is far different from that "repristination" which would limit the church to antiquated procedures or formulations. At the same time it guards against declaring essential for the church's life doctrines or orders unknown to the apostles. Disciples may confidently affirm this conception of apostolicity.

3. *Biblical theology.* The principle of speaking where the scriptures speak eventuated in two distinctive emphases, sometimes overlapping, sometimes contradictory. One was restorationism, seeking in the New Testament, a "blueprint" for the contemporary church, insisting upon a "Thus saith the Lord" for every expression in religion; this error Disciples are repudiating. The other emphasis, however, is wholesome and continually fructifying for the life of the church and of the believer: it is a serious effort to discern the teachings of the Bible, in their full range of development and to ponder gratefully their witness to the grace of God. It is the enterprise now known as biblical theology. In this enterprise Disciples have been engaged from the beginning.

Barton W. Stone and Thomas Campbell began the emphasis. The latter has conventionally been regarded by Disciples as an apostle of unity, but his latest biographer discerningly designates him "Man of the Book."[21] Alexander Campbell and Walter Scott, through their voluminous writing, influenced the brotherhood toward that serious preoccupation with biblical doctrine which characterized it in its entirety until the revolution in Christian thought brought on by higher criticism, which still characterizes the conservative and traditional elements among Disciples, and which is manifesting itself anew, at a more sophisticated level, among those Disciples influenced by current theological developments on an ecumenical scale.

Alexander Campbell and his associates developed a methodology for theological work which characterized Disciple essays in biblical doctrine.[22] They popularized, for example, the slogan, "Bible things by Bible words," deprecating as strange language not found in the New Testament "scholastic jargon, and . . . the names of the dogmas which have convulsed Christendom:"[23]

'The Holy Trinity', 'Three persons of one substance, power and eternity,' 'co-essential, co-substantial, co-equal,' 'The Son eternally begotten of the Father,' 'An eternal Son,' 'Humanity and divinity of Christ,' 'The Holy Ghost eternally proceeding from the Father and the Son,' 'God's eternal decrees,' 'Conditional election and reprobation,' 'God out of Christ,' 'Free will,' 'Liberty and necessity,' 'Original sin,' 'Total depravity,' . . . 'Visible and invisible church,' . . . &c. &c. &c.

Later Disciples have consented to use terms not found in the Bible for convenience in discussion, but their heritage has warned them not to magnify such a term or the postbiblical concept it represents into an essential of the faith.

Campbell likewise popularized a series of rules for the proper interpretation of scripture,[24] these being in essence the generally accepted principles of sound exegesis worked out by Erasmus and the Renaissance humanists.[25] On the basis of these, liberal-minded Disciples of a later generation were able to argue—not too cogently—that Campbell had anticipated higher criticism.[26] Important in Campbell's thought from the beginning was the distinction between the Covenants, Old and New; this had the unintended effect of making the Old Testament an all but lost book among many Disciples, but it did confine the pattern-hunters to the Christian dispensation. One of the most significant of Campbell's principles was the insistence on considering together all the biblical passages which bear upon a particular question and seeing them in relationship to one another.[27] The intention, for the most part realized, was to avoid erecting a peculiar structure of doctrine on one or two isolated texts.

The result of all these emphases was to provide a quality of amplitude and of genuine theological sturdiness to Disciple discussions of doctrine (especially on Campbell's part) which might not have been expected in a people who so ardently repudiated creeds, human opinions, and the theological enterprise generally. All through the nineteenth century, even though they disavowed the unscriptural term "Trinity," and despite the strong trend toward Unitarianism in general Christian thought, Disciples maintained a high Christology; it was not till liberalism and the intellectual forces which produced liberalism severed the biblical roots of Disciple thought that any significant lowering of their Christology occurred. Fair samples of the older type of Disciple work in biblical theology, varying in significance and profundity with the author's responsiveness to the intellectual currents of his own time, are Campbell's *Christian System,* Walter Scott's *The Messiahship,* Robert Richardson's *The Holy Spirit,* Robert Milligan's *The Scheme of Redemption,* J. W. McGarvey's *Commentary on Acts,* E. V. Zollars' *The Great Salvation,* T. W. Phillips' *The Church of Christ, by a Layman,* and A. McLean's *Where The Book Speaks.* While one finds a certain unintended sectarian spirit running through these books and certain dated presuppositions which alter some of the conclusions, they made available to Disciples in language not hidden from the average man, a reasonable biblical theology which shaped the life of the brotherhood.

It ill becomes a generation which was not itself subjected for the first time to the intellectual forces which beat upon traditional Christianity at the close of the nineteenth century to berate liberal theology as naïve, culture-conditioned, or loose to the Christian witness. Liberalism represented a struggle for the intellectual integrity of the Christian faith, and the forthright honesty of the liberal champions, if not all their conclusions, constitutes a heritage not to be despised. Disciple liberals generally followed the lines of biblical interpretation laid down by their own Herbert L. Willett (*The Bible Through the Centuries*) and William Clayton Bower (*The Living Bible*) and by Harry Emerson Fosdick (*A Guide to Understanding the Bible*). They did not provide the brotherhood, however, with a restatement of biblical doctrine or of ecclesiology, except for Glenn McRae's *The Message and Program of the Christian Religion.* During this period Disciple intellectuals emphasized the heritage of freedom, the concern for unity, and the dangers of legalism. Gradually the brotherhood began edging toward a theological wasteland; against this drift the outcries of the brethren "loyal to the plea" were ineffective because of a fundamentalist orientation which had never really faced the new issues. It must also be said that most of the decisions made by the brotherhood in the period when liberal presuppositions were dominant were right decisions, especially those of an ecumenical nature. Disciple pragmatism and the understanding of the Christian spirit which was "in the bones" of the brotherhood prompted constructive action, even if no sufficient theological rationale was provided. The tragedy of the era was the breakdown of effective discourse between "cooperatives" and "independents," and their gradual institutional separation which resulted.

The new emphasis which entered American theology in the 1930's made slow headway among Disciples, partly because nearly all their intellectuals had adopted liberalism. Disciples were relatively slow to respond to the new interest in biblical theology and to recognize its possibilities for a new relevance in their own witness. Gradually, however, they came to realize that this was not a new fundamentalism or a new legalism; it is an effort to give serious attention to the prophetic and apostolic witness as the Bible makes it known. Within the new framework of thought, some Disciples have begun to write works of significance to the brotherhood and to ecumenical discussion generally. Among these may be mentioned William Robinson, *The Biblical Doctrine of the Church;* Stephen J. England, *The Apostolic Church;* and William R. Baird, *Paul's Message and Mission.*[28]

It still remains for other Disciple scholars to draw upon our own tradition and contemporary scholarship to produce new manuals for the brotherhood on general biblical doctrine and on churchly practice. It may be, if this task is performed with sufficient sense of responsibility, that new possibility remains of closing the breach between "co-operatives" and some "independents." Beyond this task is our obligation to contribute in a much larger way than we have done to ecumenical discussion and to biblical and theological scholarship generally. For the biblical witness to the gospel must be seriously pondered and then expressed in terms meaningful to men in our time.

By their inheritance of biblical theology, now being renewed in terms of contemporary thought, Disciples have an authentic claim to apostolicity.

4. *The call to mission.* A constant peril to the church is the tendency to forget that apostolicity moves at a level of redemptive depth far beneath a concern for precision in faith and order or correctness in doctrine; the authentic witness of the apostles is essentially mission. It is the church heralding the gospel to the world.

The longtime Disciple preoccupation with evangelism is essentially apostolic. Indeed, the fervor which characterizes the writing of many of the pioneers discloses an awesome sense of the numinous in the belief that they were preaching the apostolic gospel and administering apostolic baptism in the apostolic way and were witnessing the growth of an apostolic church. This conviction brought dignity and grace to many a frontier church meeting in brush arbor or barn, and the crude but reverent administration of river baptism humbled many who came to scoff. The Disciple emphasis on the first Christian Pentecost, on Peter's sermon, and on the Book of Acts generally, imbued the brotherhood with a spirit of evangelism which characterized it as long as there were hearers to whom Walter Scott's formulation spoke. By the end of the nineteenth century evangelism had become to many Disciples a process rather than a motivation, and as the teaching of the five-finger exercise proved less effective, the old fire has not characterized the use of the newer methods.

It is worth noting that the characteristic organizations developed by Disciples during their first century were missionary societies. While the suspicion of ecclesiasticism lingered, they still found themselves drawn together in concern for the redemptive task, at home and abroad. A sense of mission has continued to characterize Disciple organizations to the present. Indeed, the whole program-planning enterprise, which is so distinctive of our communion today, represents, at least implicitly, a concern for mission. Granted that it often deteriorates into a concern with methods and manuals; the conviction that the church must have a program represents a lingering sense of the call to witness and holds promise for a fuller realization of apostolicity.

One other aspect of mission requires mention. It is effective identification with his hearer on the part of the witness so that the gospel is spoken in terms of compelling relevance. This gracious trait characterized the ministry of our Lord, as it did that of the apostle Paul ("I have become all things to all men, that I might by all means save some"—1 Cor. 9:22). To a remarkable degree it characterized the witness of our fathers in Midwestern America till the end of the nineteenth century; and it reached not primarily crude backwoodsmen in coonskin caps but thoughtful men and women who were leaders in cultural and political life. Disciples still count public figures who are identified with our movement in a nominal way; in the nineteenth century such persons as James A. Garfield, Jeremiah S. Black, Burke Aaron Hinsdale, T. W. Phillips, Ovid Butler, Mrs. Zerelda Wallace, Governor Ira J. Chase, Z. T. Sweeney, and others of their type were Disciple to the core, and often by choice rather than inheritance. The Disciple formulation spoke so clearly to the mind of that time. Disciples may recover their former effectiveness in evangelism when they learn to address the gospel as convincingly and helpfully to the needs and understanding of contemporary man.

Summary. In the realm of apostolicity, Disciples find in their heritage a mistaken emphasis on restoration which should be abandoned, a wholesome concern for the original faith and order of the church and for biblical theology, and a call to mission. The valid elements in this phase of our tradition are to be pondered, cherished, and given expression in the work of redemption.

III. The Holy Church

"We confess one holy . . . church." Holiness implies a distinctive ethical quality in the lives of believers, but its primary meaning asserts the church's relationship to God. The church is his. Its people are his. He has claimed us for his own.

How significantly does the historic plea of Disciples witness to the holiness of the church?

1. *A confessing church.* From the time that they came to understand baptism as the immersion of a penitent believer, Disciples have held to the doctrine of a gathered church in contrast to the *Volkskirche* embracing the entire population of a so-called Christian nation. With Disciples this concept is a doctrinal conviction, not simply an inference from the American environment with its religious liberty and its multiplicity of denominations. The steps into the church were set forth as Hearing, Faith, Repentance, Confession, Baptism. According to their thinking the church is to be composed only of those who by their own faith have accepted God's gift of salvation and have by their own oath committed themselves to Jesus Christ as Lord. The church is not an institution coterminous with society or embracing the population in general. It is the body of Christ.

Such a conception of the church has been advocated by many. It characterizes the plea of the Baptists for a regenerate church membership. It marked the conviction of the first generation of American Puritans, which was compromised only after violent struggle in the Half-way Covenant, a concession adopted out of political necessity. Revivalism implicitly conceives of the true church in this way. Luther thought of the church as ideally composed of persons whose lives had been transformed by the experience of justification; unwilling to surrender the gracious inclusiveness of the *Volkskirche,* he held the two conceptions in unresolved tension.

Believing that the holiness of the church demanded a people separated from the world by their individual act of allegiance to

Christ as Lord, Disciples nevertheless made no claim to perfection. For just this reason, Alexander Campbell maintained, believers should accept the humble designation of *disciples,* learners, rather than the term *Christians,* which others might consider pretentious. But only such persons who submitted themselves as humble learners at the feet of Christ should constitute the membership of the church.

Disciples have doubtless failed to take with sufficient seriousness the role of confirmation as the completion of baptism in those churches which administer this sacrament to infants. In the light of their full doctrine of baptism, we are scarcely in the position to contend, as we have sometimes seemed to do, that we alone regard the holiness of the church with full seriousness (especially if we acknowledge that in many cases among us the baptism of eleven-year-olds is almost as automatic, following instruction, of course, as is confirmation in their communions). Nevertheless our practice of baptism of believers only maintains an important witness concerning the nature of the church as a gathered community rather than a culture-religion. It is a plea for holiness.

2. *A righteous church.* Campbell considered the three great chapters of the Christian institution to be faith, worship, and morality. The life of holiness expected of all disciples represented an earnest effort to follow the ethical teachings of the New Testament, to walk in newness of life.

To the concern for personal morality of the highest order, the biblical *form* of baptism, total immersion in water, has been seen by Disciples as bearing an important witness. They have regularly linked the interpretation of baptism to Romans 6 and Colossians 2-3. One of the most eloquent statements of our traditional understanding at this point—and a fine example of the relevance and power of biblical theology—is that by William Robinson:[29]

We come now to the ancient impressive symbolism of the rite—that of *immersion of the whole body in water.* Water itself is symbolic of purification, but in this case it was not the purification of the filth (dirt) which might attach to the flesh, as in the case of an ordinary bath, but 'the answer of a good conscience towards God.' It was moral cleansing—the end of one kind of life and the beginning of another, lived in the power of God through the resurrection of Jesus Christ. It was such a new kind of moral life that it could only be lived by supernatural power. It was the whole body which was immersed. Think of the implications of that! The lower limbs and feet could never again be engaged on errands of hurt to any human creature, on running to and fro with intent to do mischief; the sexual organs could never again be devoted to lustful and harmful purposes, in fornication and adultery—they also had been baptized; the hands could never again administer hurt to any of God's creatures; the mouth could never again lend itself to false speech, whether lascivious, covetous, or malicious; the eyes could never again look upon evil with pleasure; the ears could never again listen to slander and false evidence and take pleasure in it; and the brain could never again devise schemes of craftiness and terror. It was total immersion and it meant total surrender to the will of God and the way of Christ, the resisting of every temptation to fall to a lower standard in ways of life, whatever the respectable standards of our environment might be. Christians were a different race of people with entirely different standards of life, and they were in possession of a new power which would enable them to manifest their new standards and to work as a leaven within the world transforming it. Such was the meaning of their baptism and the faith into which it admitted them.

Disciples have ever acknowledged that the holiness of the church lays upon its members an imperative to lives of righteousness.

3. *A purified church.* Campbell's designation for his movement was "The New Reformation." The intent was to cleanse the church of all corruption, whether inflicted by immorality, or the pride and traditions of men. The device of restorationism which became the means of achieving the "unity, peace, and purity" of the church—and which we now see to have been faulty—was applied at first with unmitigated thoroughness. "The rubbish of the centuries" must be cleared away, and the tendency was to declare illegitimate any expression which was

not specifically commanded in the New Testament. Thus the restoration ideal gathered to itself a typically sectarian ethos, and many Disciples prided themselves on being "a peculiar people." Whereas other sectarians took pride in a unique doctrine or manner of dress, the heirs of the Campbells were smug in their form of baptism or the refusal to use a musical instrument in worship. Certainly a great deal of the passion with which the restoration plea was proclaimed derived from this sectarian ethos of peculiarity.

Yet however misdirected the sectarian emphasis may be in its application, and however limited its spirit in the understanding of grace, the sectarian bears a needed witness to the holiness of the church. Disciples who have repudiated the restorationist dogma in favor of some more acceptable conception of apostolicity may be grateful for the zeal of the fathers toward the purifying of the church. Particularly did they see the recovery of the church's lost unity as a contribution to its holiness. Thomas Campbell's eloquent excoriation of the sinfulness of division lodged itself in the Disciple blood.[30]

> Division among Christians is a horrid evil, fraught with many evils. It is antichristian, as it destroys the visble unity of the body of Christ; as if he were divided against himself, excluding and excommunicating a part of himself. It is antiscriptural, as being strictly prohibited by his sovereign authority; a direct violation of his express command. It is antinatural, as it excites Christians to contemn, to hate, and oppose one another, who are bound by the highest and most endearing obligations to love each other as brethren, even as Christ has loved them. In a word, it is productive of confusion, and of every evil work.

With the earnestness arising out of such a conviction, Disciples have given themselves to a ministry of reconcilation among Christians on behalf of the church of Christ which they confess to be one and holy.

4. *The church of God.* While the tendency to regard holiness as indicating a mastery of sin and thus as demanding the highest ethical concern is not out of harmony with biblical thought, it

easily declines into an emphasis on human effort and achievement which minimizes or negates the gospel of grace. Biblical holiness is the nature of God himself which he imparts as a new quality of life to those he has chosen for his own. The church is holy, therefore, not because its members are good, but because it is called of God. Disciples have made much of two texts which emphasize this evangelical concept of holiness:

> . . . Christ loved the church and gave himself up for her, that he might sanctify her . . . by the washing of water with the word, that the church might be presented before him in splendor, without spot or wrinkle or any such thing, that she might be holy and without blemish (Eph. 5:25-27),

and

> You are a chosen race, a royal priesthood, a holy nation, God's own people, that you may declare the wonderful deeds of him who called you out of darkness into his marvelous light. Once you were no people but now you are God's people; once you had not received mercy but now you have received mercy. (1 Peter 2:9-10.)

The entire life of the church is grateful response to what God has done. Disciples saw the whole people of God as drawn intimately into the most sacred ministrations of the church; they were all called to worship and to witness. Thus local members of the congregation who engaged in secular work during the week—Disciples rejected as unscriptural the terms *laity* and *clergy*—were entrusted with the ministry of the Lord's supper as elders (bishops) and deacons; elders also bore responsibility for the ministry of the word. The church was present in the holy priesthood of its corporate membership rather than in the office of a separated ministry. Thus on the frontier scattered congregations of the faithful kept the feast of communion and listened to the Word "in decency and in order," even though there was no one present whom outsiders would recognize as a clergyman. This common practice of the earlier days has sometimes been misconstrued by Disciples themselves and by others as a downgrading of the office of the ministry. But this was not the intention nor the necessary effect. The intention was to reaffirm the scriptural concept of the holiness of the whole people of God, of the common calling to ministry (both in liturgy and in service), of the corporate responsibility for the most sacred concerns of the church's life. Disciples have long since developed a specialized ministry with a high standard of educational preparation; in doing so they have sometimes lost sight of their earlier conviction concerning the common ministry. As long, however, as the orders of elders and deacons persist within each congregation, the possibility remains of reaffirming this high concept of the royal priesthood. It is significant that foremost thinkers in the field of world mission are discussing some type of local lay ministry—essentially what Disciples knew in their most rapidly growing period—as the only means of coping with the problem of leadership in the "younger churches."[31]

The central meaning of the doctrine of holiness is that the church belongs to God. This Disciples sought to show in using the names Church of God, Church of Christ, Christian Church, and in seeking to recover for all the disciples or brethren the New Testament title of *saints.* All believers are "called to be saints," all are the people of God.

5. *The church and the Holy Spirit.* The crucial failure of the Disciple fathers in seeking to understand the biblical concept of holiness derived from their inadequate doctrine of the Holy Spirit. Current biblical scholarship emphasizes the remarkable degree to which the early church was the community of the Spirit, and ecumenical theologians are giving attention to the proper role of the Spirit in the life of the contemporary church. Except for Robert Richardson, however, and a minority witness stemming from his influence, Disciples effectively ruled the Holy Spirit out of present history by restricting his operation to the influence of the word as found in the Bible. The reasons for the fathers' limitations at this point are obvious: namely, the excesses of revivalism which were attributed by frontier evangelists to the Holy Spirit, and a doctrine of conversion, then commonly accepted, which demanded interior evidence of the Spirit's ac-

tion as a prelude to salvation. While the doctrine doubtless intended to witness to the idea of prevenient grace, the Disciple protest against it and the proffer of salvation to all who would rationally believe, repent, and be baptized actually constituted a ministry of grace to many who were constitutionally unable to undergo the "experience" considered necessary for salvation.

Most Disciples retain a healthy skepticism toward any claims to guidance or power from the Holy Spirit, and the more specific the claims the greater the skepticism. At the same time some of the more thoughtful among us are manifesting an uneasiness toward an understanding of the church of Christ which leaves it only with an ancient book to guide and empower its life. Apparently no contemporary Disciple has published extensively concerning the Holy Spirit, but the feeling of inadequacy in our inherited doctrine at this point doubtless represents a movement toward a fuller manifestation of holiness in the life of the church.

Summary: In seeking to realize the holiness of the church, Disciples have failed to give adequate acknowledgment to the ministry of the Holy Spirit within the community of redemption. Nevertheless our witness has emphasized important aspects of holiness: responsible confession, righteousnes, the cleansing of the church, its peculiar status as the possession of God. No one who contends for the holiness of the church has grounds for pride in his own achievements. But Disciples may confidently look to their heritage for an authentic witness to significant aspects of this major doctrine.

IV. The Church Catholic

"We believe in one catholic . . . church." Unfortunately most Protestants shudder at the thought, confusing the grace here attested with the proper name of the Roman church which they have been taught to repudiate. The revulsion is so serious that major Christian bodies have misguidedly amended the Nicene confession to read "one holy Christian and apostolic church," and the modern worldwide movement for the recovery of the church's unity has settled, within the past quarter-century, for the not-truly-equivalent term *ecumenical.* Yet the principle of catholicity is essential to any conception of the church which does justice to the biblical doctrine of the church and to the gospel of God's grace. Fundamentally catholicity implies that quality of the church's life which transcends all local and particular distinctions, personal or cultural, and which may be recognized by any Christian anywhere as authentic. The term witnesses to the universality, the inclusiveness, the validity, the common inheritance of the church. Likewise it testifies to all that makes for the completion or perfection of the church. It is an expression to which the whole people of God are gradually and gratefully returning.

1. *The claim to catholicity.* One of the losses suffered in the separation of the churches is the partisan use of comprehensive terms. Such adjectives as evangelical, spiritual, sacramental, pentecostal, orthodox, and even Christian, which the whole church needs for the fullness of its life are often appropriated by sections of the church to their own exclusive use and consequently are frequently repudiated as antithetical to the true faith by those against whom they are directed. So it is with the word *catholic.* At its first assembly, the World Council of Churches allowed itself, with some hesitation, to characterize "our deepest difference" as that between the "Catholic" and the "Protestant" conceptions of the church.[32] Disciples among others have protested this unwarranted usage, which seems to deny catholicity to certain sections of the church and to imply a particular definition of catholicity.[33]

Any claim to catholicity must be carefully examined to determine whether the claim is really justified, especially with reference to the question, "Is the usage called 'catholic' in this case recognized by all as authentic or is it being demanded of all?" The matter of orders is a case in point. A bloc of churches in the

World Council continually contends for a "catholic ministry," meaning a ministry in apostolic succession, with the historic episcopate. Such a ministry may be called catholic in the sense that it may claim general though not universal (witness the reservations of the "Holiness" churches) recognition; it is not catholic if that term is construed to mean a general acknowledgment of the necessity of this particular ministry. Moreover, the proponents of the "catholic ministry" must acknowledge that apostolic succession and historic episcopate are no necessary guarantee of oneness; consider the multiplicity of bishops—especially in the great sees of the ancient East—who are not in communion with one another. The Disciple claim to having a catholic baptism is similarly ambiguous.

As early as 1906, W. T. Moore commended the Disciple plea on the grounds of catholicity.[34]

> The Disciple movement unquestionably furnishes a *common* ground, or a ground that is thoroughly catholic in every respect. A careful examination of the principles of the movement . . . will reveal the fact that there is nothing in these principles that may not be accepted by every evangelical denomination in Christendom. . . . In order to have a common ground, or a position that is entirely catholic, it is necessary that everything should be thrown overboard that is not essential in the making of Christians, and in keeping the unity of the spirit in the bond of peace.

Moore then proceeded to "indicate a few points where the catholicity of Disciples may be clearly made evident." He listed (1) the appeal to the scriptures "as furnishing an infallible rule of faith and practice," (2) the position with respect to Christ—accepting the "Scriptural Creed" (the Petrine Confession) but rejecting all speculative views as tests of Christian fellowship, (3) "the common ground that the Holy Spirit" operates "through the truth," (4) "common ground upon which all Christians may unite in evangelizing the world"—the recognition that the gospel "must be preached to every creature," (5) a doctrine and practice of baptism "which is practically universally admitted to be both Scriptural and valid," (6) the acceptance of any scripture name and the exclusion of all names "that are divisive in their character," and (7) their teaching on church government and the subordinate place of the church in the "remedial system," with primary consideration being given to Christ.

A few years later, Peter Ainslie developed the same principle with a more compelling turn of phrase when he characterized Disciples as witnessing to (1) a catholic name, (2) a catholic confession, (3) a catholic conception of the ordinances, (4) a catholic book, (5) a catholic polity of church government, and (6) a catholic brotherhood.[35] In 1924 H. C. Armstrong repeated this list in essentially the same form.[36] F. D. Kershner has suggested that to it there might be added (7) a catholic spirit, and (8) a catholic day of worship.[37] Armstrong manifested the former in characterizing the Disciples as follows:[38]

> The Disciples hold by the historic faith of the Church Universal, and believing in all those great doctrines of truth which have made up the body of general Christian belief they lay special emphasis on the principles of Christian unity, fellowship and brotherhood, spiritual liberty and democracy, and the abolition of all creeds and denominations, because these divide Christians.

In subsequent years, this witness to the catholicity of the Disciple plea seems to have declined, possibly because it lent itself to a sort of contentious pride in our correctness, possibly because the churches most preoccupied with catholicity keep other concerns at the center of the deepening ecumenical discussion. Yet Disciples who long for us to make a significant ecumenical witness will do well to maintain the emphasis on the catholicity of intent which is our heritage, as well as on the catholicity of achievement.

2. *The demand of catholicity.* If we ponder carefully the implications of catholicity, we soon realize that what is crucial in the life of the church is what is universal, that the emphasis must fall on the general rather than the particular. Catholicity implies a generous inclusiveness, and the holy catholic church embraces

believers out of many cultures and nations and languages, all of which condition their understanding and expression of the Christian faith. While such peculiarities are interesting and colorful they are relatively unimportant in comparison with the common elements in the faith. The same is true of the particular emphases of the various denominations.

All this is to say that while every denomination as a particular and limited historical expression of the church will be unique, its uniqueness is theologically the least important thing about it. What is important is its catholicity, and the more catholic it becomes, the less it will be unlike other denominations, as they also become more catholic, in the central concerns of churchly life. The concept of unity here suggested is not that of the least common denominator, but rather a growing together toward perfection.

Many Disciples are confused at this point. Remembering the satisfaction of the sectarian ethos which derived from restorationism and the almost messianic sense of mission which characterized the earlier days of our movement, they are troubled over our seeming loss of uniqueness. The view is often expressed that unless a communion has something unique to offer, it has no reason to exist. This is fallacious ecclesiological thinking. A denomination exists separately *because* it is unique; it does not seek uniqueness *in order to* exist separately. The constant imperative upon every fragment of the church of Christ is to press for a fuller expression of catholicity. The more fully catholic a denomination becomes, the more natural is its union with some other; the purpose of its existence is catholicity, not uniqueness.

The Disciple fathers discerned the essence of this truth, though they mistakenly believed that it was possible to get out of the denominational system entirely, so they denied that they belonged to any sect, party, or denomination; they belonged simply to the one church of Christ. This wholly commendable commitment to catholicity long blinded Disciples to the historic fact that whether they wished it or not, they were a denomination. But now that we know ourselves to be a denomination, our chief loyalty must be to the one holy catholic and apostolic church. This spirit was expressed by Dean Kershner in the address already mentioned[39]—and Disciples should lament the fact that this note is no longer heard among us as much as once it was.

> . . . We wish to say that we at least do not belong to, nor have we the remotest interest in, a "denomination which sprang from the Eighteenth Century Enlightenment in England" or which owes its origin to John Locke or Alexander Campbell or any other human teacher. We belong to the one holy, catholic, and apostolic church of Christ founded by our Lord and made known to the world through the New Testament Scriptures.
>
> There is no carping or invidious criticism intended in this statement. Doubtless there is a sense in which what we frequently style our movement began in the nineteenth century. . . . But we must . . . remember that Mr. Campbell and his associates did not at any time claim to be the founders of a church but only to be reformers seeking to restore the true and universal Church of Christ.
>
> Like others, we have found since Campbell's days that the denominational consciousness is very easily fanned into a flame. What we are pleading for tonight is that we shall have a passion for the church universal which will bring to it all the wealth of sacrifice and devotion which we have too often bestowed only upon our separate particularities.

Instead, then, of frustratedly asking ourselves, "What have we left that is unique to offer the religious world?" the question we put to ourselves ought to be, "What elements in our life continue to negate the catholicity of the church, and how may we overcome them?"

Catholicity demands reform. It also demands a sense of spiritual identification with the whole people of God. In the Apostles' Creed two phrases follow in significant sequence: "I believe in . . . the holy Catholic Church, the Communion of Saints." Thus the principle of catholicity is linked with the participation of one Christian in the spiritual struggle and witness of all Christians—in the world today, and in the long history of the church which has gone before.

During the past two generations and especially at present, Disciples are, to their own great spiritual enrichment, acceding to the demands of catholicity. They cherish the history of the whole church and honor the great Christian names of every century and of all communions. Their deepening interest in liturgy is leading to an appropriation of the spirituality and the rites of the Great Church. Their scholars and theological students are rightly occupied, not with their own peculiarities, but with the central problems confronting the entire Christian world, especially those engaging ecumenical attention. All these are marks of growing catholicity.

3. *Catholicity as freedom in Christ.* In addition to universality the term *catholicity* implies the gracious inclusiveness of the church under the lordship of Christ. Consequently the emphasis which Disciples and other so-called left-wing Protestants have placed on freedom in Christ must be understood as an important aspect of catholicity. The story has often been told of Barton W. Stone's examination for ordination. He was asked, "Do you receive and adopt the Confession of Faith?" Some of its declarations troubled him, and he answered as others had been permitted to answer; "I do, as far as I see it consistent with the word of God."[40] The appeal to the Bible represents catholicity; it commands much wider acceptance than any creed.

Similarly the Basis of the World Council of Churches, as recently amended, is more inclusive, hence more truly catholic, than the more detailed, more precise confessions of faith which emphasize metaphysical precision. The Basis read:

> The World Council of Churches is a fellowship of Churches which confess the Lord Jesus Christ as God and Savior according to the Scriptures and therefore seek to fulfill together their common calling to the glory of the one God, Father, Son, and Holy Spirit.

The role of creeds and confessions of faith with respect to freedom and catholicity is the subject of much confusion. Many Disciples misunderstand the attitude of the fathers toward creeds. While Benjamin Franklin and other preachers of the second generation repudiated them absolutely and fixed within the minds of Disciples a phobia which has only begun to abate, the position of the fathers must be stated more precisely. The objection was not to formulations of the faith but to the use of speculative statements as instruments of exclusion. In Proposition 7 Thomas Campbell acknowledged a legitimate use of creeds: "Doctrinal exhibitions of the great system of divine truths, and defensive testimonies in opposition to prevailing errors, [may] be highly expedient; and the more full and explicit they be, for those purposes, the better." The point was that since "these must be in a great measure the effect of human reasoning, and of course must contain many inferential truths, they ought not to be made terms of christian communion."

Alexander Campbell himself acknowledged—in the very chapter in which he was protesting the use of language not found in the Bible—that "I find all *confessions* of FAITH, properly so called, like the *four* Gospels, tell the same story so far as matters of fact or faith are concerned."[41] His attitude toward the Apostles' Creed was quite positive, inasmuch as he considered it a witness to historical events rather than to speculative inferences; we might say that it is kerygmatic rather than speculative. (Royal Humbert's note on Campbell's willingness to accept the Apostles' Creed and the ambiguity of his rejection of the later formulations is an important correction to much Disciple confusion regarding the thinking of the fathers.[42])

After a long period marked by complete repudiation of any document even slightly suggesting a creed, some Disciples have begun to recognize certain legitimate and even necessary uses for statements of faith.

(1) The use of common confessions in worship has been growing ever since Willett and Morrison published *Hymns of the United Church* (1919) with its "aids to worship," though for the most part these have been limited to compilations of scriptural passages. Some Disciples are using the Apostles' Creed on occasion; one notable congregation alternates in the use of nearly

a dozen affirmations, some in biblical, some in modern phraseology, as a regular part of the order of worship.

(2) Brief summaries and explanations of Christian doctrine have proved essential for Christian teaching, especially the catechizing of candidates for baptism. Isaac Errett's little essay on *Our Position* (1872) was assailed as a creed, but conservative and liberal Disciples have continued to multiply such compendiums ever since, and publishing houses have promoted the sale of such study books or workbooks. It must be admitted that too often more attention has been given to the catechetical process than to doctrinal content; in any case, the practice of Disciples has become an admission of the need for "doctrinal exhibitions of the great system of divine truths."

(3) A further function of a corporate affirmation of faith is to proclaim the mind of the church at large on crucial elements of Christian witness. Within a free society a church which glories in extending to all its members the freedom that is in Christ may probably never hope for absolute unanimity in understanding any point of Christian doctrine or even in phrasing an understanding that may have been reached. But the common mind of the church on issues of moment concerning the faith ought to find utterance as a guide to the body at large and as a guard against the doctrinal idiosyncrasies of individual ministers and members. There is large room here for the expression of consensus without moving into the realm of exclusion, to say nothing of persecution. The "messages to the churches" from various ecumenical conferences have something of this character; some of them—like the Edinburgh (1937) Affirmation of Union—manifest such authenticity as expressions of the common faith that they have come into wide use in worship.

(4) Any confession of Christian faith sufficiently catholic as to gain wide acceptance during any period of the church's history merits the grateful consideration of subsequent generations. In the nature of the case, a specific creed is addressed to specific

issues confronting the church in a specific era. With the passage of centuries, the particular issues may no longer appear so relevant; even the categories of thought may be irrelevant to a subsequent world view; it has been held, for example, that the Nicene formulation is meaningless in terms of the categories of contemporary philosophy. Yet the church will always find needed instruction concerning the center of its faith by carefully considering the creeds of earlier generations and the issues which gave rise to them. Most Disciples could gladly subscribe to the provision in the Constitution of the United Church of Christ:[43]

> The United Church of Christ acknowledges as its sole Head, Jesus Christ, the Son of God and the Saviour of men. It acknowledges as brethren in Christ all who share in this confession. It looks to the Word of God in the Scriptures, and to the presence and power of the Holy Spirit, to prosper its creative and redemptive work in the world. It claims as its own the faith of the historic Church expressed in the ancient creeds and reclaimed in the basic insights of the Protestant Reformers. It affirms the responsibility of the Church in each generation to make this faith its own in reality of worship, in honesty of thought and expression, and in purity of heart before God.

In the same spirit, many Disciples have already gladly responded to the witness of the new Statement of Faith adopted by the United Church.

Disciples are coming to see, therefore, that the freedom in Christ which is one aspect of catholicity does not forbid the legitimate use of statements of faith. Indeed, some Disciples are beginning to rejoice in their newly discovered freedom to use corporate affirmations which witness to the gospel which the church bears.

If some Disciples must still rethink their inherited prejudice against creeds, many Christians in churches which do have creeds must also re-examine their thinking. For some continue to speak of creeds as though they were precise and authoritative utterances enjoying a literal and unvarying acceptance which they do not in fact possess. Disciples have become accustomed to the shock and condescension with which our lack of official creedal formulation is often greeted. I once underwent vicarious chastisement on behalf of the brotherhood because of our creedlessness at the hands of a strongly neo-orthodox theologian of considerable influence in Faith and Order, who insisted that creeds are necessary to assure the faith against doctrinal corruption. Knowing the violence with which he rejected liberalism, to say nothing of modernism, I derived some malicious pleasure in reminding him that Disciples, without benefit of creed, had come through the era of liberalism with no greater weakening of their christology than that experienced by his own church and other churches which make even more of creeds.

Actually none of the historic creeds is as catholic as its proponents would like to imagine, if by its catholicity they mean that it is in its entirety a meaningful or even acceptable statement for everyone who professes it. The simplicity of the Basis for the World Council of Churches is a tacit admission of this fact. No one in the churches historically committed to the ancient creeds should delude himself with the notion that they have fixed the limits of the theological enterprise for the areas of dogma on which they have spoken. My own belief, if I understand the men aright, is that most of the leading names in theology today—including Paul Tillich, Rudolf Bultmann, Donald Baillie, Nels Ferré, Daniel Day Williams, and many more—would need to be excommunicated by any church which really insisted on the letter of the Nicene Creed. It is also my humble judgment that the Nicene Creed witnesses to a truth in the gospel which at least some of these theologians do not take with sufficient seriousness. Nevertheless it is a more authentic expression of catholicity to allow freedom in Christ to such able, honest, and earnest believers than it would be to silence them. This kind of freedom is essential to true catholicity.

W. E. Garrison has eloquently argued the case for liberty in his significant book, *The Quest and Character of a United Church.*[44] Though this work has not yet commanded the attention or the assent which it deserves (and though it seems to this writer to develop insufficient meaning to Christian unity beyond the ideal of freedom—a negative rather than a positive definition), it may well prove to be the most important contribution of Disciples to ecumenical thinking. The genius of Disciple anticreedalism, anticlericalism, antiecclesiasticism is not iconoclasm; it is that concern for Christian freedom which is an essential dimension of catholicity.

4. *The ground of catholicity—the lordship of Christ.* Ultimately everything in the life of the church derives from Jesus Christ the Lord. He is the Logos, the revelation of God to the church, the community of believers. He is the teacher of the church. He is her Savior, who loved her and gave himself up for her. He is her risen Lord, who brought life and immortality to light through the gospel. He is the author and finisher of her faith. He is the chief cornerstone in the temple, without which the entire ecclesiastical structure collapses. He is the head of the body, the church. From him the whole body, joined and knit together by every joint with which it is supplied, when each part is working properly, makes bodily growth and upbuilds itself in love. He is the source of the church's life, her salvation, her righteousness. In him as he made himself known to the apostles and through them to the church, she finds her oneness, her holiness, and her catholicity. In short, from the standpoint of the church's faith, he is Alpha and Omega, the beginning and the end of all things.

While no communion should venture to suggest that it has any peculiar title of possession upon our common Lord (see 1 Cor. 1:10-13), Disciples may gladly give thanks that from the beginning of our history the emphasis has been on the centrality of Christ in every aspect of the church's life. Barton Stone sought to honor him by taking the simple name *Christian.* Walter Scott regarded the Petrine Confession as the Golden Oracle, emblazoned its words over the door to his school, and titled his major book on our position *The Messiahship.* Alexander Campbell was remembered by Isaac Errett for his "dear old theme of the Personal Dignity and Official Power and Glory of the Son of God." The briefest and most telling slogan of Disciples was "No Creed but Christ." The evangelism, the piety, the ethics, the ecclesiology, the hymnody, the preaching of Disciples were characteristically preoccupied with the message concerning Jesus Christ, or with the plea for the restoration of the New Testament church, which to them meant giving full acknowledgment to his lordship. Whatever the shifting moods of theology, the figure of Jesus Christ has been at the center of our devotion, as indicated in Hunter Beckelhymer's study: "Representative Preaching about Jesus: Two Generations of Disciples of Christ."[45]

Nor was the Christocentric emphasis of Disciples at its best the "Jesusolatry" condemned by H. Richard Niebuhr. We have much more commonly referred to Jesus Christ as Son of God, Savior, or Lord than as God; in practice prayer has been addressed to God the Father rather than to the Son, and some Disciples (of the old biblicist tradition as well as of the liberal school) have maintained that prayer is not properly directed to the Son at all. The preaching about Jesus has been for the most part devoid of sentimentality, as one would expect if one knows the rational temper of Disciples; at the same time the deepest religious emotion tends to center about the confession of faith (in the words of Matt. 16:16) and the breaking of bread.

So typical of Disciple thought is the emphasis on the centrality of Christ that when the Panel of Scholars launched its work, it agreed with virtually immediate unanimity, which was never subsequently questioned, that the point of beginning should be christology. A large proportion of the papers written for the Panel deal explicitly with some phase of that theme or move out from it.

While Disciples see the whole life of the Christian and of the church as deriving from the relationship to Jesus Christ as Lord, their thinking about Christian unity has stressed the point. The catholic name is *his* name; the catholic confession centers in *him* and is both intellective and existential (or volitional) in character. The church is *his* body. The great expression of motivation for unity in the experience of most Disciples is *his* high priestly prayer "that they may all be one," and the intent of unity as Disciples see it is the fulfilment of the evangelistic mission—"that the world may believe" in Jesus Christ. Disciples do not ask men to join the church, but to confess Jesus Christ as Lord and to commit their lives in obedience to him: membership in his church automatically follows. The classical themes of Disciple preaching have been the Good Confession, the Transfiguration, the Last Supper, the Resurrection, the Great Commission, Pentecost, the conversions recounted in Acts, and the Pre-eminence of Christ. The Disciple image of denominational preaching (often, we readily admit, an outlandish caricature) called to mind pulpits preoccupied with speculative, peripheral, and divisive themes. In the interest of the church's wholeness Disciples sounded the cry, "Back to Christ!" We have seen him as ground and guarantor of the church's catholicity.

Emerging from an era of parochialism into the growing ecumenical mood of the twentieth century, Disciples have rejoiced to confess with others the lordship of Christ. The first satisfactions we found in the ecumenical movement, especially before it became so heavily preoccupied with theology, arose from the conviction that separated Christians were being drawn together by their allegiance to him and by their common commitment to his cause. The declaration of the Jerusalem Conference of the International Missionary Council in 1930 ("Our message is Jesus Christ . . ."), and the Edinburgh (1937) Affirmation of Union ("We are one in faith in our Lord Jesus Christ . . .") were often and earnestly repeated by Disciples. We rejoiced in the fact of Amsterdam and Evanston, though it must be confessed that most Disciples were bewildered at the tidal wave of continental theology. We were gratified to see Faith and Order direct major attention to the theme of Jesus Christ and his

Church, though again there has been reservation lest the work become too speculative. We responded heartily to the theme of New Delhi, "Jesus Christ the Light of the World."

The entire ecumenical movement has come to focus in the person of Jesus Christ and particularly in the concept of his lordship. Increasingly the realization is growing of the overwhelming significance of that lordship—over the church, over the life of the believer, over the institutions of society, over the whole of human culture, over the entire cosmos. (Incidentally, Professor Joseph Sittler's sermon on the cosmic claims of Christ was delivered, at least in incipient form, to a meeting of Disciples sponsored by the Council on Christian Unity, at Kansas City, prior to the New Delhi Assembly. Disciples received it warmly, but with no notion that it was something "new," as the press reports from New Delhi seemed to suggest. This is what Christ's lordship has always meant: it is only new to the world when the world first really hears the church saying it.)

The claims of Christ and his redemptive influence extend throughout the created universe. And the church, which is his body, must therefore manifest that catholicity which, wherever she is found, attests to his saving grace, his renewal of life and spirit, the demands of his lordship, his sustaining presence, and his final triumph. Wherever he is thus mediated to needy men through the ministry of word and sacrament, there is the holy catholic church.

Summary. While catholicity is a term subject to various meanings and emphases, Disciples have sought to manifest a catholic spirit, to exhibit in their churchly life the essential marks of catholicity, to witness to the freedom that is in Christ, to center their message and life in him who is the ground of the church's catholicity, indeed of its very existence. This is not what catholicity, means to some Christians, but it is a pattern of emphases without which any notion of catholicity would be utterly inadequate.

V. The Witness We Bear

The intent of this paper has been neither to glorify Disciples nor to evade difficult issues. If God has not left himself without witness among any people, he surely has not done so within any part of his church. Whatever the particular Christian tradition, it would bear authentic testimony, at least in part, to the one holy catholic and apostolic church of Jesus Christ our Lord. The fact that this is so—that Disciples of Christ, like other Christian communions, may rightfully claim that their tradition authentically communicates the oneness, holiness, catholicity, and apostolicity of the Great Church—does not mean that no major problems remain to be solved or that the fullness of Christian unity will be easily achieved. It does mean that we may thank God for our heritage, both our special legacy as Disciples and the great tradition from the whole historic people of God. It means that we must ever seek through the reverent reading of the scriptures, through the careful study of church history, through the fullest ecumenical sharing we are able to develop, to understand ever more fully the true nature of the church and the meaning of Christ's lordship over it. It means that we are called to proclaim in confidence and in earnestness to a perishing world the good news of God which upheld our fathers in the faith and which now sustains us.

"What have you that you did not receive? If then you received it, why do you boast as if it were not a gift?"—1 Corinthians 4:7

"And what you have heard . . . before many witnesses entrust to faithful men who will be able to teach others also."—2 Timothy 2:2

NOTES

1. *International Convention, Disciples of Christ, Denver, Colorado, October 16-21, 1938,* Christian Board of Publication, St. Louis, 1938, pp. 21-37. Dean Kershner also gave major attention to the Nicene marks of the church in his classes on Christian doctrine in the School of Religion, Butler University.

2. See John A. F. Gregg, "One, Holy, Catholic, Apostolic Church," in *The Universal Church in God's Design,* The Amsterdam Assembly Series, Vol. I, Harper & Brothers, New York, n.d., pp. 59-66; Conrad Bergendoff, *The One Holy Catholic Apostolic Church* (The Hoover Lectures, 1953), Augustana Book Concern, Rock Island, 1954; Lesslie Newbigin, *The Household of God,* Friendship Press, New York, 1954.

3. Leroy Brownlow, *Why I am a Member of the Church of Christ,* published by author, Fort Worth, 2d. ed., 1945, pp. 1, 5, 22-27.

4. Rudolf Bultmann, *Theology of the New Testament*, tr. Kendrick Grobel, Charles Scribner's Sons, New York, 1954, I, 101, 332 ff.

5. *The Christian Palladium,* VIII (1840), 286; Quoted by William Garrett West, Barton Warren Stone, *Early American Advocate of Christian Unity,* Disciples of Christ Historical Society, Nashville, 1954, p. 224.

6. *The Christian Messenger,* XI (1841), 334; quoted by West, *op. cit.*, p. 129.

7. Paul S. Minear (ed.), *The Nature of the Unity We Seek: Official Report of the North American Conference on Faith and Order* (St. Louis: The Bethany Press, 1958), pp. 194-199, Section 3, "Baptism into Christ."

8. *The Christian System,* p. 113.

9. World Council of Churches, *Minutes and Reports of the Thirteenth Meeting of the Central Committee* (Geneva: World Council of Churches, 1960), p. 113.

10. *Declaration and Address,* p. 16.

11. *Ibid.*, p. 3.

12. See, for example, B. H. Streeter, *The Primitive Church;* John Knox, *The Early Church and the Coming Great Church;* Rudolf Bultmann, *Theology of the New Testament;* Carl Becker, *The Heavenly City of the Eighteenth Century Philosophers;* John Baillie, *The Belief in Progress;* A. T. DeGroot, *The Restoration Principle.*

13. See, *e.g.,* papers by D. Ray Lindley, Ralph G. Wilburn, W. B. Blakemore, Dwight E. Stevenson, and the present writer.

14. See the "Preparatory Studies" for 10 area consultations on Christian unity in *Ecumenical Studies Series,* IV (1958), No. 1; also the issue of *Encounter on Apostolicity, Tradition, and Restoration,* XX (1959), No. 3.

15. See D. Ray Lindley, *Apostle of Freedom,* The Bethany Press, St. Louis, 1957.

16. A. Campbell, *op. cit.*, p. 10.

17. *Declaration and Address,* p. 16.

18. John S. Sweeney, *Sweeney's Sermons,* Gospel Advocate Publishing Co., Nashville, Tenn., 1897, "The Simplicity That Is In Christ," pp. 63-80.

19. Osborn, Short, and Tobias, "A Response to Oberlin," *Ecumenical Studies Series,* IV (1959), No. 3, pp. 27-29.

20. Bultmann, *op. cit.,* I, 39 ff., 133-144, 299, 311-14.

21. Lester G. McAllister, *Thomas Campbell: Man of the Book* (St. Louis: The Bethany Press), 1954.

22. See Cecil K. Thomas, *Alexander Campbell and His New Version* (St. Louis: The Bethany Press), 1958.

23. A. Campbell, *op. cit.,* pp. 132-136.

24. *Ibid.*, pp. 16-19.

25. See Frederic Seebohm, *The Oxford Reformers,* E. P. Dutton and Co., New York, 1914, pp. 204-5.

26. Benjamin Lyon Smith, *Alexander Campbell* (St. Louis: The Bethany Press), 1930, pp. 216-217.

27. Thomas, *op. cit.*, pp. 146-147.

28. See also the special issue on Biblical Theology, *Ecumenical Studies Series,* V. (1960), No. 1, containing papers prepared by members of the Commission on Biblical Theology, Council on Christian Unity.

29. William Robinson, *Completing the Reformation: the Doctrine of the Priesthood of All Believers,* The College of the Bible, Lexington, 1955, pp. 55-56.

30. *Declaration and Address,* Proposition 10.

31. See John V. Taylor, *The Growth of the Church in Buganda,* SCM Press, Ltd., London, 1958, pp. 137-141, for a discussion of the problem in one field.

32. See W. A. Visser 't Hooft (ed.), *The First Assembly of the World Council of Churches* (New York: Harper & Brothers), 1949, pp. 51-52.

33. W. E. Garrison, *A Response to Amsterdam,* Association for the Promotion of Christian Unity, Indianapolis, n.d., pp. 6-7. See also R. Newton Flew and Rupert E. Davies (eds.), *The Catholicity of Protestantism,* Lutterworth Press, London, 1950.

34. W. T. Moore, *The Plea of the Disciples of Christ,* The Christian Century Company, Chicago, 1906, pp. 65-68.

35. Peter Ainslie, "The Disciples of Christ," *The Christian Union Quarterly,* VIII, 4 (April, 1919), 32-36.

36. H. C. Armstrong, *The Disciples of Christ: Who They Are and Why They Are,* Association for the Promotion of Christian Unity, Baltimore,

37. F. D. Kershner, in *International Convention, 1938,* p. 31.

1924, pp. 50-51.

38. Armstrong, *op. cit.,* p. 9.

39. Kershner, *op. cit.,* p. 36.

40. Elder John Rogers, *The Biography of Elder Barton Warren Stone* (Cincinnati: J. A. and V. P. James, 1847), p. 29.

41. A. Campbell, *op. cit.,* p. 132.

42. Royal Humbert, *A Compend of Alexander Campbell's Theology,* The Bethany Press, St. Louis, 1961, p. 266, n. 3.

43. The Constitution of the United Church of Christ, as approved by the Adjourned Meeting of the Second General Synod of the United Church of Christ, July 6-8, 1960, Cleveland, Ohio, for submission to the synods and the churches.

44. Winfred E. Garrison, *The Quest and Character of a United Church* (New York: Abingdon Press, 1957).

45. Hunter Beckelhymer, "Representative Preaching about Jesus." *Vide supra,* pp. 78-97.

INDEX

Abbott, Byrdine Akers, 30, 91
Adams, Hampton, 30
Agencies, 195, 197-198, 263-264, 280, 285, 309-310, 327-328
Ainslie, Peter, 24, 30, 94-95, 209, 238, 279, 307, 338
Ames, Edward Scribner, 24, 30, 165, 167-169, 170, 172, 173, 179, 243, 252
Anderson, Henry T., 81, 82, 86
Anticlericalism, 184-185, 200-210, 271, 273
Apostolicity, 226, 229-230, 245, 315-328
Arianism, 62-68, 76, 81
Armstrong, C. J., 125
Armstrong, H. C., 338
Association of Disciples for Theological Discussion, 253, 262, 264
Athanasius, 136
Atonement, 68-74, 76, 83-85
Authority, 85-87, 90, 91-92, 127, 184-198, 219, 235-236, 240, 241, 245, 248, 250, 271

Baillie, Donald M., 68-69
Baird, William R., 15, 326
Bancroft, George, 274
Baptism, 25, 26, 40-41, 47-48, 120-121, 132, 136-137, 139, 140, 150-156, 218-219, 239, 277, 312-313, 321-322, 329-331
Baptism of Holy Spirit, 120
Barth, Karl, 107-108
Baxter, William, 83
Beckelhymer, Paul Hunter, 15, 347
"Representative Preaching about Jesus," 78-97
"The Influence of Population Mobility," 291-302
Bethany College, 206, 207, 259-260, 275, 276
Bible, 34, 35-37, 39, 43, 45, 46, 48, 55-57, 63, 72, 77, 81-82, 95, 114, 120-132, 165-167, 173-175, 188-189, 192, 206, 218, 219-224, 226-228, 240, 243-245, 251, 258, 323-327, 341
Blakemore, W. B., 15, 17, 77, 168-169
"Foreword," 11-13;
"Reasonable, Empirical, Pragmatic," 161-183
"The Sociology of Disciple Intellectual Life," 257-264
Blythe, James, 62-63
Board of Higher Education of Disciples of Christ, 8, 9
Bower, William Clayton, 24, 172, 325
Brunner, Emil, 52, 53
Bultmann, Rudolf, 307
Burgess, O. A., 83-84
Burke, Edmund, 269
Burnet, David Staats, 79, 81, 83
Burnham, Frederick W., 90, 92
Bushnell, Horace, 179

Calhoun, Robert L., 77
Calvinism, 62, 63, 72, 141-144, 146-149, 164, 259, 274
Campbell, Alexander, 29, 33, 40, 44, 45-49, 62, 73, 106-107, 112-117, 118, 131, 136, 140, 142-146, 149-151, 162, 165, 168-169, 170-172, 178-180, 184-198, 199-207, 216, 217-218, 224, 226, 227, 228, 237, 239, 242, 248, 251, 258, 259, 266, 269-280, 283, 313-314, 318-319, 323-325, 330, 331, 342, 346-347
Campbell, George A., 94, 209
Campbell Institute, 260-261
Campbell, John Poage, 62, 70-71
Campbell, Thomas, 27, 42-46, 61, 112, 136, 174-175, 177, 178, 188, 199, 201, 203, 216, 225, 230, 235, 236, 241, 260, 270, 276, 306, 307, 308, 311-312, 313, 315-316, 318-319, 323, 332, 342
Cane Ridge, Kentucky, 61, 117, 150
Catholicity, 232-233, 245-247, 335-349
Challen, James, 83
Christian Baptist, 195, 200-201, 269
Christian-Evangelist, The, 124, 125, 260
Christian Standard, 124-125, 175, 260, 270
Christian System, 171, 173, 174, 325
Christology, 28, 61-77, 78-97, 98-110, 180-183, 242-243, 324-325, 345, 347
Church, 40, 59, 118, 140-141, 184-198, 288-289, 300-302, 305, 352
Churches of Christ, 280, 284, 286, 310, 318
Clague, James A., 15
Clark, Elmer T., 204-205
Clark, Neville, 116
Cleland, Thomas, 62, 68, 70-71
Clement of Alexandria, 103
College of the Bible, The (Lexington, Ky.), 208
Combs, George Hamilton, 93-94, 209
Communion, 41, 136, 137, 139, 180-181, 311-312, 322
Confession, Good, 105, 145, 182, 322
Congregation, 191-198, 203, 308
Constitution, 269-270, 280-281, 316
Convention, 197-198, 327

Index

Conversion, 40-41, 44, 92-93, 113, 115-130, 145-157, 334-335
Cooperation, 193-198
Council on Christian Unity, 261, 349
Crabtree, William E., 80, 95-96
Creed, 25, 26, 28, 35, 37, 39, 40, 43, 50, 51, 52, 54-56, 76, 79-82, 98, 105, 107-110, 191-192, 219, 233, 235, 236, 240, 246-247, 265, 280, 322, 341-346, 347
Criticism, biblical, 93, 94, 123, 175, 220-222, 258, 282, 283, 323-324
Cyprian, 139, 141

Davis, M. M., 120
Davison, F. E., 210-211
Debates, 277
Declaration and Address, 42-45, 61, 167, 177, 306, 307, 308, 314, 315-316, 332
Democracy, 194, 270-273
Denomination, 25, 26
Destiny, 273-275
DeWolf, L. H., 103
Dispensations, 40, 87, 118, 142, 324
Dowling, Frank, 90
Dunstan, J. Leslie, 295-297, 302

Ecclesiasticism, 25, 26
Ecumenical Movement, 25, 26, 27, 77, 209-210, 224-226, 242-243, 246, 285-286, 306, 308-309, 313-315, 318, 326, 336, 348-349
See also Faith and Order, World Council of Churches
Education, higher, 206-209, 283
Empiricism, 161-183
England, Stephen J., 15, 30, 221, 326;
"The Holy Spirit in the Thought and Life of the Disciples," 111-134
Epps, J., 202
Errett, Isaac, 57-58, 121-122, 165, 174-175, 202, 206-207, 231, 260, 343, 347
Expediency, 173-175, 248-249

Faith, 33-39, 42-60, 79, 87, 95, 102-107, 112-113, 116, 123, 130, 145, 149, 170, 178-183, 319
Faith and Order, 267, 314-315, 318-323, 345, 348-349;
Lausanne (1927), 312
Edinburgh (1937), 343, 348
Lund (1952), 267
Oberlin (1957), 295, 312-313
Fall, 142-144
Ford, Harold W., 30
Fortune, A. W., 30
Franklin, Benjamin (Disciple), 121
Freedom, 138, 184-198, 311, 341-346; see also Liberty
Frontier, 227, 266, 271-278, 282, 333

Gardner, Frank N., 15;
"The Revelation of God in Jesus Christ," 98-110
"Man and Salvation," 135-158
Garfield, James Abram, 93, 328
Garrison, J. H., 30, 50, 92, 123, 260, 307
Garrison, Winfred Ernest, 24, 30, 45, 161, 170, 172, 173, 200, 201, 203-204, 252, 267, 345-346
Gates, Errett, 24, 30
Gilkey, Langdon, 229, 264, 268
God, 44, 45, 52, 76, 98-100, 107-109, 244, 332-334
Golden Age, 221, 268
Gospel, 41, 83, 244, 319
Graham, Robert, 83
Graves, John R., 274-275

Haley, J. J., 89-90
Haley, T. P., 84, 88, 209
Hayden, A. S., 84
Hinds, Virgil V., 16
Hodge, William, 146, 218
Holiness, 329-335
Holy Spirit, 39, 87, 111-134, 146, 152-153, 190, 218-219, 237, 317-318, 334-335
Hook, Sidney, 267
Hopkinsville, Kentucky, 62
Hopson, W. H., 85-86
Humbert, Royal, 342
Hunley, J. B., 125
Hyatt, J. Philip, 16

"Independent" Christian Churches, 280, 284, 286, 310, 326
Infallibility, 226-227, 236
Ignatius of Antioch, 104, 137-138
Interpretation (of Scripture), 34
Irenaeus, 139

Jackson, Andrew, 271-273
Jefferson, Thomas, 202
Jenkins, Burris, 80, 179, 209, 212
Jennings, W. W., 267
Jeremiah, 29-30
Jesus Christ, 28, 37-39, 40, 44, 45, 46, 47, 49, 50, 51-53, 73, 78-97, 98-110, 126-127, 173, 179-183, 190, 221-222, 234-236, 346-349
Johnson, Richard Mentor, 272
Jones, Edgar DeWitt, 24, 90-91
Justin Martyr, 103, 138

Kellems, Jesse, 194
Kershner, Frederick D., 170, 306, 338, 340, 350
King, Joseph, 86
Kingsbury, Leslie, 170

INDEX

Knepper, George, 124
Knox, John, 190

Laity, 59, 333
Lamb of God, 83-84
Lard, Moses, 120-121, 231-232, 265-266
Legalism, 49-50, 121, 139-156, 219, 316, 318
Lemmon, Clarence E., 16;
"An Evaluation of Our Ministry," 199-214
Lexington, Kentucky, 73
Liberalism, 24-25, 30, 103, 123-124, 132, 161, 169-170, 172-173, 175-176, 260-261, 318, 324-325, 326, 345
Liberty, 34, 35, 43, 47-49, 59, 233-236, 239-241
Lindley, D. Ray, 16, 203;
"The Structure of the Church," 184-198
Lipscomb, David, 280-281
Locke, John, 114, 122, 156, 170, 203, 216, 222, 223, 228, 268-269
Lockhart, Clinton, 167
Longan, George W., 83
Loos, Charles Louis, 79, 81
Lord's Supper;
see Communion
Lunger, Harold, 250
Lunger, Irvin, 125
Luther, Martin, 51, 57, 103, 179, 235-238, 321, 329
Luthin, R. H., 271-272

Mahoning Baptist Association, 309
Man, 135-158
Marshall, Frank H., 121
Mathews, Shailer, 172
Maurice, F. D., 180-181
McAllister, Lester G., 42, 323
McCash, Isaac Newton, 91-92
McGarvey, John W., 120, 167, 226, 283, 325
McGready, James, 68
McLean, Archibald, 325
McLellan, Hugh, 92-93
McRae, Glenn, 24, 325
Mead, Sidney E., 165
Medearis, Dale, 293
Millennial Harbinger, 33, 194-195, 260
Miller, Raphael H., 209
Milligan, Robert, 30, 162-163, 165-168, 172, 173, 260, 325
Ministry, 12-13, 25, 26, 42, 56-57, 184-185, 192, 199-214, 281, 284-285, 321, 333-334, 337;
see also Anti-clericalism
Miracles, 120
Mission, 327-328
Montgomery, Riley B., 207-209
Moore, William T., 78, 79, 194, 206, 207, 208, 238, 239, 282, 337, 338
Morrison, Charles Clayton, 24, 30, 186, 188, 189, 232, 244-245, 246, 307, 342
Munnell, Thomas, 85
Murch, James De Forest, 30, 125
Mysticism, 162-163, 168-169

Neo-orthodoxy, 25, 30, 156, 165, 177-258, 326, 345
New Lisbon, Ohio, 49

Opinion, 34, 35-38, 42-49, 52, 55, 56, 59, 74, 106, 152, 233-234, 240
Ordination, 210, 211
Organization, 184-198, 220-221
Osborn, Ronald E., 16, 17;
"Crisis and Reformation," 23-30
"Dogmatically Absolute, Historically Relative," 265-290
"One Holy Catholic and Apostolic Church," 305-352
Owen, Robert, 142, 164, 171-172

Packard, Vance, 298-299
Paine, Thomas, 72, 202
Panel of Scholars, 7-9, 11-13, 15-17, 28, 30, 178, 257, 262, 264, 278, 347
Pattillo, Henry, 65
Pendleton, William K., 87, 260
Pension Fund of Christian Churches, 210, 213
Pentecost, 40, 125-126
Peters, Eugene H., 16
Phillips, T. W., 30, 121, 161, 325, 328
Pinkerton, L. L., 79, 81, 96
Piper, Otto, 128
Plattenberg, George, 230
Plea of Disciples, 23-25, 28, 50, 215-253, 275, 277, 279, 286, 305-352
Polity, 42, 47, 54, 59, 184-198
Pope, Liston, 299
Powell, E. L., 209, 212
Pragmatism, 173-183
Prayer, 129-130, 347
Preaching, 68, 78-97, 114, 146-147, 164, 178, 347, 348
Priesthood, 84-85, 184-185
Primitivism, 269
Procter, Alexander, 88-89, 209

Rationalism, 162, 164-165, 169, 171-172, 228-229
Reason, 63, 102-104, 132, 161-183, 186

Reformation, 29-30, 33, 34, 35, 40, 51, 217, 232-233, 242, 275, 331-332
Relativism, 223-224, 265-290
Restoration, 25, 26, 34, 41, 55, 59, 127, 187, 191, 192, 207, 215-253, 265-281, 283, 286, 287-289, 315-327, 331-332, 339
Restructure, 26, 241-251, 285, 286, 310, 311
Revelation, 98-110, 161-162, 166, 171-173, 181-183, 186, 237-238, 283
Rice, Nathan L., 115-116, 187, 192
Richardson, Robert, 33-42, 44, 45, 50, 114, 118, 122-123, 178-180, 200-201, 216, 260, 325, 334
Robinson, John, 161
Robinson, William, 234, 326, 330-331
Rogers, John, 226
Rousseau, Jean-Jacques, 268
Routt, Glenn C., 16

Salvation, 135-158
Sanctification, 41
Schlesinger, Arthur M., Jr., 267, 270, 275
Schlesinger, Arthur Meier, Sr., 266-267
Scott, Walter, 49-50, 115, 118-119, 125, 126, 140, 150, 178, 216, 218, 231, 260, 321, 323, 325, 327, 346
Sectarianism, 230-233, 306, 332, 339-341
Sectionalism, 280
Shackelford, John, 84
Shaw, Henry K., 267
Short, Howard E., 15, 16, 30
Sin, 142, 155
Smith, Harry D., 80
Smith, "Raccoon John," 114, 238
Smith, William Martin, 210
Snoddy, Elmer E., 146
Springfield Presbytery, 61, 245, 309
State Secretary, 211-212
Stevenson, Dwight E., 17, 178-182; "Faith versus Theology in the Thought of the Disciple Fathers," 33-60
Stone, Barton Warren, 27, 61-77, 105-107, 117-118, 122, 125, 130-131, 136, 146-154, 176-177, 201, 203-204, 218-219, 235, 243, 276, 307, 308, 313, 323, 341, 346
Stringfellow, E. H., 125
Sweeney, Z. T., 93, 328

Tertullian, 103, 139-140
Theology, 7, 8, 11, 25, 26, 33, 35, 43, 44, 45, 46, 47, 49, 50 52, 53-54, 57-58, 59, 76, 79-82, 87, 161-183, 206, 233-234, 247-251, 257-264, 299-302, 323-327
Tradition, 27, 28-30
Trinity, 74, 87, 111, 116, 118, 123, 125, 127, 131, 133, 188
Turner, Frederick Jackson, 266-267, 271

Union, Christian (see also Unity, Christian), 34, 39-42, 49, 171, 187
Unitarianism, 39, 62, 71, 73-74, 81, 118, 133, 165, 181, 188, 324, 331
United Christian Missionary Society, The, 8, 9, 211, 262, 281
United Church of Christ, 310, 311, 313, 344
Unity, Christian (see also Union, Christian), 25, 26, 46, 54, 60, 61, 72, 74-77, 81, 109-110, 176-177, 188-191, 216-217, 224-226, 233, 234-241, 246-247, 306-316, 318, 335-349

Walk, David, 86-87
Walker, Granville, 168-169, 171
Ware, C. C., 146
Warren, W. R., 210
Watts, Isaac, 64-68, 69, 76
Wedel, Theodore O., 190
Welshimer, P. H., 30, 89, 124, 165, 168
West, Earl Irvin, 30
West, R. Frederick, 171, 267
Westminster Confession of Faith, 63, 146
West, William G., 17, 77; "The Nature and Work of Christ in the Thought of Barton W. Stone," 61-77
Wickizer, Willard M., 17; "A Statement Concerning the Panel of Scholars," 7-9
Wieman, Henry Nelson, 108, 249
Wilburn, Ralph G., 17, 172; "A Critique of the Restoration Principle," 215-253
Wilcox, Alanson, 265
Willett, Herbert L., 24, 30, 89, 283, 325, 342
Woolrich, E., 125
World Convention of Churches of Christ; Study Committee, 30, 126-128, 261
World Council of Churches, 314, 336-337, 341, 345, 348-349
Worship, 132, 342-343

Zollars, E. V., 30, 79-80, 325